MANAGEMENT OF INTERNATIONAL ADVERTISING
A Marketing Approach

DEAN M. PEEBLES
Goodyear International Corporation

JOHN K. RYANS, JR.
Kent State University

ALLYN AND BACON, INC.
Boston   London   Sydney   Toronto

Library of Congress Cataloging in Publication Data

Peebles, Dean M., 1923–
  Management of international advertising:
  A marketing approach.

  Includes index.
  1. Advertising. 2. Export marketing.
I. Ryans, John K., Jr. II. Title.
HF5827.P43 1984   659.1   83–6031
ISBN 0–205–07988–1

Printed in the United States of America.
10 9 8 7 6 5 4 3 2 1   88 87 86 85 84   83

Contents

Preface

Worldwide marketing involves too many variables to reduce the direction of any single function to a policy of rigid rules—yet success comes from consistently doing the right thing most of the time. In each international company someone must sit in judgment over a universe of different national markets to assure that kind of consistency.

For most people new to the plural market planning responsibility, the temptation to surround the operation with procedural rules and framework structures familiar to those persons' past single market experience is irresistible and a natural reaction for survival—and security. Frustration will set in when the pieces do not fit the frame, and the result is usually the manager's overreaction to the differences discovered between different markets. Market "differences," which will later be viewed as merely workable variables, seem to cloud the picture so badly that one cannot see that there are actually far more similarities—that only the context is different.

Successful experiences produce the confidence needed to perform the multinational marketing function with sufficient flexibility to meet each new situation on its own terms, while at the same time keeping solutions within the framework of a targeted corporate policy.

This book's aim is to aid persons with multinational advertising responsibility to gain the needed confidence in the shortest possible time.

Marketing represents the most visible side of the corporation as it operates in multiple markets. And advertising in particular often offers your public—that is, your buyers (or prospective customer), government officials, other influentials, and the masses—their first—and perhaps their only—perspective on your company. In fact, we might use the term "world's window" to dramatically provide a not-too-subtle reminder that your publics "see" your company from the outside in, and in many cases this means they see your company according to the image projected through your advertising. Properly recognized, this can be an important plus for the multinational company. Unfortunately, we have observed that too often a multinational company proceeds with its total marketing effort as though it has but one world image: that found in the parent company's home market.

We approach the subject of international advertising management with a sober respect for just how fragile a corporate image can be when transplanted into many different national environments, left unattended, or manipulated by careless hands. Each tentacle of the multinational touches a different people of different cultural and life-style experiences—*and* most certainly with different levels of recognition and/or respect for its company or brand name.

A multinational management may choose to develop different images compatible to each culture, or to duplicate a successful home market image. Any desired corporate image is not an automatic happening. Specification, direction, and monitoring of progress toward such goals need to be high-priority headquarters subjects of interest. It is the foundation on which future growth depends. Remember, we are dealing here with a marketing function common to almost all international companies; however, most international companies are not similar to each other.

It is our purpose to raise the appropriate multimarket concerns, to offer proven promotional guidelines and approaches, and to suggest the potential problems and solutions. Success stories and recommendations are offered throughout. Finally, we have attempted to recognize possible differences in points of view and differences related to company size and product for most topics. We have simply seen too many of the often "suggested solutions" lead to failure and have dismissed them. Yet, it was unavoidable that on many issues we were not very objective. However, should any reader care to debate our conclusions and remind us of omissions, doing so can only serve to broaden future efforts.

——— ACKNOWLEDGMENTS ———

This book offers our *views* on the management of international advertising. Some may be controversial, while others have rather broad industry acceptance. In either case, they represent our positions and recommendations. We accept full reponsibility for the material presented here.

However, we could not have included such a variety of actual examples and illustrations without the excellent cooperation of many leaders in the field of international advertising. When we initially decided to write this book, we felt it was essential to include the best possible cases we could find to illustrate the various topics and issues. We feel we have achieved this objective with the assistance of the following individuals: Scott W. Anderson, Steiger Tractor Inc.; Robert Barrus, VM/B International; Wolf D. Dittmair, Digital Equipment Corporation; Dennis Hanano, Gates Rubber Company; Uwe Hofer, Troost-Campbell-Ewald GmbH; Clyde D. Marlatt, Jr., Coca-Cola Company; Frank G. Mitchell, Cessna Aircraft Company; Terry Quinn, ITT Europe, Inc.; James Shull, Hydril Company; David Simler, Digital Equipment Corporation; Patrick C. Smith, MSA International; Clark Springman, Symons Manufacturing Company; Maarteen Van Veen, Texas Instruments France; and W. S. Young, Johns-Manville.

Others have helped us, either by writing original material for the book (or allowing us to reprint our own recent articles) or by serving as initial readers or reviewers. The writers include Sylvan M. Barnet, Jr., International Advertising Association; Anna Marie Sarmento, Marplan Inc.; Bob Donath, *Industrial Marketing*; and Robert Roth, *International Advertiser*. Among the reviewers are Stephen W. Miller, Saint Louis University; Ivan R. Vernon, Cleveland State University; Frank N. Pierce, University of Florida; James Lynch, Sul Ross State College; Marilyn Liebrenz, George Washington University; James Larson, University of Texas at Austin; Lester A. Delano, Marschalk Campbell-Ewald Worldwide; Neal Gilliatt, Interpublic Group of Companies; and Willard C. Mackey, McCann-Erickson Worldwide.

In addition, early drafts of the book were used in our International Advertising Management Seminars at the World Trade Institute (New York), and we found the comments and suggestions of the seminar attendees to be most helpful.

Finally, we would like to acknowledge the special assistance of Don Clark, Creative Director, Goodyear International Company, and Janet Gifford and Amy Parkinson, Kent State University, for help in various production stages of the manuscript.

To our readers:

We dedicate this book:

To all those interested in world marketing at any level who feel as exhilarated by the challenges of and search for innovations in international market communications as do the authors.

To all those with long and varied experiences in this field, who have never lost their enthusiasm for discovering new intricacies in solutions to multinational advertising effectiveness.

And to all those new to careers (or who hope to have careers) in international advertising, who may be here encouraged in expanding their interest in those things which interest us.

1

The Management
of Change

The only constant in international business is *Change*. While the elements of change can seldom come under one's control, there are options . . . to simply become the result of change *or* to manage the effects of change to achieve one's objectives.

Many of today's leading world marketing executives gained their firsthand operating experience during the 1960s and early 1970s. These were the lush expansion years . . . the years of seemingly unlimited marketing opportunity, unlimited and low-priced energy sources, unlimited and available financing . . . an era of unprecedented potential. An aggressive corporation could expand as far and as fast as time would permit and its management's imagination could take it.

This management generation inherited its guidance from predecessors who gained their expertise in the immediate post–World War II period—an era reflected by severe shortages in basic staples, heavy demands for products needed to normalize life, and an eager desire to again taste luxury. Perhaps the best word to characterize such marketing was "speed" . . . "get there fastest with the fullest wagon."

None of the experiences during the past three decades should necessarily be considered useless or wasted on today's international marketers, however. The senior marketer who can make the greatest contribution is likely to be one with a wealth of experience . . . who has *so successfully* managed the evolution of change that he is hardly aware that change is taking place.

Today's international business scenario is far different from the "full wagon" or even the "lush days." Today and the foreseeable future seem

1

best characterized by the terms "flattening world markets" and "intense competition."

The U.S. marketplace has already been described by the headline, "The '80s: An Era of Marketing Warfare," and suggestions for tactics/strategies have been taken from Prussian General Carl von Clausewitz (1778–1831). As the president of one agency has suggested, "it's time for marketers to adopt military principles to their strategic planning."[1]

Is this pessimistic assessment true, and might the same thing be said about world markets? The answer to these questions is *yes*. The battle is just beginning, and the importance of *defensive* and *offensive* strategies is now being recognized. And at the heart of these struggles will be *international advertising* . . . perhaps the marketer's most significant and controllable weapon.

——— Today, Tomorrow, and Competition ———

To better understand the need for a book such as this one, it is essential to have a feel for the world business and social environment of today and the future . . . the '80s and '90s, at least. Certainly, we see world markets flattening out for most products. There exist fewer and fewer opportunities for expansion based purely on "unfilled want." For many industries there exists overproduction capacity in major parts of the world and the supply side is giving way to a demand orientation. It is the "marketers" who will survive in the overproduction capacity industries—others will become self-destructive by continuing to reduce prices to accommodate their own production volumes. In fact, terms like "marketing" are now becoming an active part of the vocabulary in countries such as Chile and Ecuador.

But the picture is still sorting itself out. Signals . . . often conflicting . . . include:

- a regeneration of nationalism and protectionism that has caused many countries to rethink their rate of industrialization
- a spiraling worldwide inflation . . . often energy triggered . . . that has dramatically raised the MNC's costs (many MNCs find further expansion expensive and too often with a return on investment that is less than marginally attractive)
- the continued offers of direct investment incentives by developing and developed countries alike . . . which often appear to conflict with national objectives and are clouded by *mandatory fadeout provisions*
- the rapid move to worldwide oligopolistic industries, i.e., industries characterized by few, but extremely powerful, corporations (the

---

[1] "The '80s: An Era of Marketing Warfare," *Madison Avenue* (May 1980), p. 35.

battleground may be a small l.d.c., but the combatants are suppliers from the United States, Germany, Japan, and possibly France)

- the equally rapid increase in the number of conglomerates . . . so that the nature of a firm's competition changes quickly (a poorly financed competitor suddenly becomes a subsidiary of one of the Seven Sisters)
- the unprecedented developments in technology that have made many markets generations behind and that have produced supply-side achievements so great that new products become quickly obsolete (product competition has become fierce)
- the growth in the communications field, e.g., satellite and cable TV, which makes news (and corporate messages) instantaneous worldwide (no longer can the corporation count on an announcement in France or Hong Kong to be limited to that market)

But what is perhaps even more difficult to describe adequately is the search for the "new product or industry." Once a potential new product category has been determined, such as has been seen recently in the United States in the business/home computer (less than main-frame) industry, competitors of all types and sizes begin to emerge. And an Apple suddenly finds itself confronted by an Exxon, an IBM, a Xerox, and more. This is competition at its finest, but it places a different sort of burden on the international marketer and, for us, on the international advertiser.

Advertising must play a new and more significant role in this era of change. Rapid and widespread communications requires . . . in fact *demands* that a major MNC's message have a degree of coordination . . . not bifurcation. The apparent evolution of the "Eurobrand" is a case in point. The Eurobrand has been described as being "single product for a single market embracing 12 or more countries."[2] The Eurobrand would be conceived entirely from a central point; the emphasis from original concept to final testing is on the search for intermarket similarities, not differences. The implications (and challenges) of this type of thinking on advertising alone is most significant and reflects the change the international advertising manager must be prepared to face.

—— A MOST IMPORTANT CUSTOMER/BUYER —— CHANGE FOR THE '80s

Everyone is familiar with the basic advertising concept of having a thorough knowledge of product—examining all benefits and all supporting product features, then comparing this analysis with parallel facts about the competitors'

[2]Eugene Bacot, "Eurobrand: A New Approach to Marketing," *Advertising Age/Europe*, Vol. 3, Issue 9 (October 1981), p. 9.

products. As a result, "vive la difference" becomes a theme. Advertising people have learned that to survive is to learn how to "find the difference" and to correctly communicate it to your target market.

——— Test the Change ———

Today, however, does your buying behavior research/experience still indicate as great an interest in specific product benefits as it did a few years ago? Are you now noticing that your buying decision scores are higher for *brand preferences?* Can you detect that confidence in brand name is becoming an increasing factor in customer price/quality measurement? In other words, we submit that more and more categories of products (consumer and industrial) are being perceived as "commodity products"—generally about the same between brands—and that confidence and quality are being related more frequently to the maker's name. The growth of corporate and image advertising in Europe in particular might be cited as just one evidence of the major firm's recognition of this change in buyer behavior.

Perhaps we should emphasize that we do not see this "commodity status" as demeaning or downgrading products or as evidence that they are all alike. Rather, it relates to many factors, ranging from the rapid technology changes in some industries that make it difficult for buyers to know the "state of the art" to the fact that many individuals, businesses, and governments are purchasing less frequently. Buyers are more concerned about making the best decision.

Looking at this phenomenon from a different perspective, customers, in any language, today are less motivated by such general claims as "technical breakthrough," "out of the space age," and "made with computer science." This is especially true of consumer products, because the "average" consumer feels inadequate to understand the intricacies of household appliance electronics or the modern miracles of soap chemistry. Consumers expect that most products today are, or should be, the result of modern technical sciences.

While we observed that total market growth is flattening out and, in many cases, leaving overproduction capacity, the 1980s can also be viewed as a "shakeout" period for producers that have not kept their products up to date with the latest technology in their industry. We subscribe that marketers in the 1980s should not be offended at finding their products in a commodity status—brand-name-dominated—they should consider themselves fortunate to have products technically good enough to survive as acceptable commodities. Many will not.

Yes, of all the evolutionary changes occurring in international business in recent years, none has been so sharply focused on the function of producer/consumer communications than is the shift to *brand image dominance.* The 1980s is the decade for MNC concentration on managed change of consumer communications—*advertising.*

—— Evolution, Not Revolution ——

The management of marketing change seen evolving during the 1980s, however, is not viewed as a revolutionary event that demands that everything known is to be forgotten . . . or that a "we need a whole new set of tools" syndrome is setting in. Advertising has evolved into the 1980s with all the sophistication necessary to match computer age management with robot assembly-line production. Modern advertising techniques are adequate to handle all foreseeable changes. And many marketers do not even find themselves in a catch-up situation . . . although many do! All that is needed is some shift in attitude and some corporate policy adjustment in recognition that "things just aren't like they used to be."

No one needs to tell corporate executives about today's volatility in the world finance market or offer added cautions regarding short-term borrowing. They are equally aware of the need for more critical cash flow restraints and more conservative inventory levels. Also, no one needs to tell them where in the world recession is gripping a market; they see sales falling without loss in market share. Why, then, should anyone expect marketing as usual and advertising in the same old way? The things that happen in a market happen to the people who live there. The consumers, whether private or industrial, are forced to take a new look at how they spend their money.

—— Transition Period ——

The next decade, therefore, represents a transition period for MNC marketers, as they adapt to more *intense competition, industry consolidations,* and flattening markets (worldwide). And this represents much more than the recognition that "doing business as usual" will not be a realistic alternative. Questions must be asked about communications principles and practices that have served well in the past, and the international advertising manager must be flexible in dealing with the answers.

We recognized, for example, in preparing this book that it is impossible to accurately predict the full impact that satellite television will have on international advertising. In particular, it is difficult to determine when its full impact will occur . . . but we know it is likely to be a factor sometime during the '80s. For those corporations that might find commercial satellite television, particularly in Europe, to be a viable medium, the need to have a fully coordinated single message—one appropriate to all markets—is obvious. And how significant will cable television be in Europe? Clearly, the MNC will need to be flexible regarding these new media . . . thoughtfully determining their full potential and not being caught in a "bandwagon hysteria" to adopt them.

Similarly, those MNCs that hold firmly to the belief that *culture* is the single overriding concern in every national market will need to rethink their position in the future. As we shall see shortly, there are many advantages to be gained from reducing the local/national advertising autonomy to which so many firms presently subscribe. Just how important is it to recognize local cultural differences when marketing many products? This is another question the international advertising manager must answer; the manager cannot simply rely on past principles that tended to emphasize the blunders that MNCs have made when trying a centralized approach in the past. Everyone has heard that "Body by Fisher" translated into "Corpse by Fisher" in *Germany* and has cited this and similar examples as the justification for local advertising control. The emphasis has tended to be for the international advertising manager to have to prove that a more centralized approach to multiple markets is possible . . . rather than to have to prove that cultural adaptation in each individual market is necessary. While this distinction may seem subtle to many of our readers, it is a *significant* distinction.

Cultural differences can be a barrier in certain countries for certain types of campaigns, particularly those which are not designed originally as multinational campaigns and that are executed without providing sufficient latitude for flexible transliteration. Of course, some marketing people have conducted research that suggest a significant magnitude of cultural differences exists . . . especially for special product categories. Such findings have provided local advertising agencies with support for their claims that local national advertising must be created and developed locally.

In the meantime, social psychologists, doing purely cultural evaluation studies unrelated to any commercial consideration, are giving us something new to think about. Perhaps it is not the way different peoples react to the same stimuli that make up what has been referred to as "cultural differences." Evidence is beginning to emerge to indicate that the differences are actually the stimuli themselves. In other words, different peoples in different parts of the world encounter different kinds of stimuli because of traditions and evolutionary modes of living. It seems that most people react similarly to similar stimuli, if the stimuli are recognizable in a reference of their life experience.

This kind of thinking returns the advertising strategist to the basic human psychological wants: food, drink, comfort, sex, love, safety, superiority, approval, long life . . . and so on. Thus, the basic obstacle to consolidated image advertising may not be cultural differences per se, but rather the flexibility for the transliteration of a consolidated image campaign into a communications stimulus that is in the reference experience of each cultural group.

Are your buyers really that different in Germany and Austria or Belgium and the Netherlands? Undoubtedly, the answer does differ according to product or to the customary end use of the same product. The answer may be quite different if you are talking about an industrial product, say precision equipment or specialty concrete products, or a consumer item. Further, the answer may well be different if you are talking about the cultural differences between Nigeria and Norway. Many will argue that neither the industrial nor consumer goods producer could ignore the vast differences in culture that may be found between a developed and a developing country. But do we recommend a single advertising approach or campaign for *all markets* . . . one that does treat all buyers alike?

——— CULTURAL DIFFERENCES VS. ———
ENVIRONMENTAL DIFFERENCES

The authors have observed that when discussions on international advertising move to considering "cultural differences," frequently the points raised are *environmental* rather than *cultural* differences . . . referring to the *advertising environment.*

In the planning of multinational (or pan-regional) campaigns, we frequently use the rationale that cultural differences are real; they need to be recognized, understood, and accommodated for. However, in the main they are workable variables. Flexibility of campaign design and skillful transliteration of a strategy will successfully adapt most well-conceived campaigns for most countries of the world. Advertising environmental differences can represent more formidable obstacles, and these topics are discussed within the appropriate chapters throughout the book.

Cultural Differences	*Advertising Environmental Differences*
1. Religious	1. Media
2. Political	a. existence
3. Social habits	b. effectiveness
a. marriage	c. cost efficiency
b. death	d. quality
c. eating	2. Laws governing
d. alcohol	a. products advertised
e. tobacco	b. products by media
f. sex	c. product description
4. Racial attitudes	d. methods of presenting products
5. Nationalism	3. Consumer protection agencies
6. Trade customs	4. Trade regulations
7. Bureaucracy	

One cannot take a television campaign to countries that have no commercial television, or attempt advertising cigarettes on several of the media. Product comparisons or lightly clad female models may be against the law (as well as being anticultural). And consumer protection agencies can effect boycotts against products that ignore their rules. Therefore, an advertising campaign that is in good taste and that recognizes the laws and limitations of an advertising environment *should be easily adjustable to accommodate most cultural differences.* What we are asking is that the advertising manager examine closely the "cultural can'ts" and determine if they are real or if they just require a bit of accommodation and a degree of "management."

――― CENTRAL CONTROL OF ADVERTISING ―――

What Does Coordination Mean?   Management of change and central control of advertising are not labels intended to exclude a local management from the acts of managing a local market. And, in fact, total central control can have results as equally devastating as total local autonomy. However, a theme throughout this book is for increased centralized management of the advertising function. Why? . . . Well, we do have two objectives we hope to achieve through such a theme. First, we see the need for the MNC to take a concerted corporate action that will result in a consolidated corporate "world brand image." The time is rapidly passing when an MNC can hope to maintain a different image in each market. Second, and more broadly, we want MNCs to carefully consider (or reconsider) their position regarding the "local market advertising sovereignty" issue. This consideration may result in a continuation of such a policy, some modification of it, or even a switch to more central direction of the advertising programs. Regardless of the decision, we feel that now is an appropriate time for the MNC to raise questions about the merits of such a policy for its product advertising and to consider the benefits of greater centralized controls.

In discussing the first objective with individuals at various levels of management in different international firms who are presently unwilling to commit to any type of central coordination, we hear the following:
From headquarters:

1. "We have never stressed that advertising consider any uniformity between markets."
2. "Maybe a uniform advertising image would not produce the best advertising for each market."

From local subsidiary management:

3. "We have never had any guidance on uniform image from the home office."
4. "We don't want (New York) telling us how to run our business in (Sweden)."

While most international firms do have some form of marketing/advertising coordination, many of them like to play down definition or description of such policies as only being "consultancies"—"or just making sure everything is going right." They want to avoid commitment to any form of central control because they view the labeling as home office domination that releases a local market management from targeted sales/profit goals.

Yet, as we suggested earlier, it becomes increasingly important to recognize that (1) communications changes are making it more and more difficult to isolate markets and (2) corporate brand image is replacing product attributes as the buyer's decision criterion. These changes strongly call for the firm to shift from a market-to-market to a worldwide brand image approach.

Second, we feel that it is time to take a careful look at the question of centralized advertising. As we have noted, many firms do employ some degree of centralization, whether it is merely in the initial budget allocation or it encompasses virtually all of their nondomestic advertising efforts. It is not our purpose to become advocates for totally centralized coordination or for standardization of all the firm's campaigns. At the same time, we hope to raise some questions about stereotypes, such as the one that suggests that every national market is different regardless of whether you are talking about a consumer or an industrial product. And we hope to fairly present the benefits (and difficulties) that centralization produces.

Many MNCs do practice certain forms and different degrees of international centralization—and, they generally profess, to advantages. Home office management see their involvement as a protection of their total overseas investment and as a means of directing the future growth and profiles they project for their company. Many local, overseas managements see the headquarters advertising services as saving money and providing top-quality advertising campaigns; but probably the biggest vote of appreciation is that it saves them much time and avoids much home office criticism. One overseas manager said, "Advertising used to take up too much of my time. I was always justifying my advertising to the home office, defending the judgment of local advertising people and never being quite sure I was right. Now, I feel confident my advertising is professional, with proven ideas and there are no longer conflicts in judgment."

But all is not roses. We also hear complaints that home office advertising is wrong—that it shows no understanding of a market situation or that it is too general and ineffective—a waste of money . . . and it certainly can be. Providing an effective worldwide (or Pan-European) advertising campaign is not easy and cannot be done without much investigation and local market input. Advertising, being a highly subjective, value judgment subject, is also vulnerable to personality characteristics. Positive thinkers make an effort to cooperate in the success of any form of home office advertising service. Negative thinkers automatically perceive any such service as wrong because it is not their idea.

Nothing Is Absolute. In marketing principles, advertising in particular, nothing is *always* or *never.* We use the terms "control" and "coordination" to describe any form of home office influence on local market activities. If we are thinking only in terms of a uniform use of the corporate logotype or product brand names to protect legal registration, we still are considering a form of headquarters control that requires a system of management coordination.

This book discusses many types of international advertising management systems, involving different degrees of different methods of central management control. It recognizes the multiple problems that can arise whenever a headquarters attempts to assert greater control over advertising. It will point out advantages to a multinational corporation's long-term international market development in taking a more active part in how the firm is presented to its many publics.

It is our intention to bring to our readers new dimensions and different perspectives in (re)considering the importance of:

- consolidated corporate image
- profitable return on advertising investment
- evaluating multinational advertising quality
- pooling of creative resources
- how to cause advertising agencies to organize themselves to best serve the multinational advertiser
- how to best effect economies of scale
- coping with "cultural differences"
- advertisers' obligation to every host country

Not Reinventing the Wheel.   Everything in this book, of course, is being done to some degree by many international advertisers. This is not speculative theory. We have already stressed the future importance of worldwide brand image advertising. This is new only to those who have never considered the principle. In the early 1960s Esso introduced the famous campaign "Put a Tiger in Your Tank" (see article in the appendix to Chapter 12). This campaign played to almost every nationality and culture in the world and was enormously effective in creating the image that Esso gasoline puts power in your car. At the time this campaign appeared, some advertising people thought it a phenomenon—not for everyone. Others took it as proof that such an approach was possible across cultures—and they have used it successfully.

Role of Headquarters Management.   Why does an MNC headquarters need a staff of experts . . . production, distribution, finance, marketing, *advertising,* and so on, if it is not to advance new ideas and to handle problems? If it were only to keep score, accounting procedures alone would suffice. *Problems*— things not going right—and *progress* through long-term direction and innovative thinking make up the rationale for the existence of an international headquarters operation.

For more than three decades of modern international marketing experience there have been memorable business cycles—even crisis years, if you will. Yet, perhaps *no one* in active international marketing management today is really equipped with operational experience that he or she can call upon to direct them through the world markets of the 1980s and into the 1990s. Some marketers, not many, might be willing to face world markets today with a *maintenance-of-position* philosophy. Most marketers will insist on growth — brand by brand and market by market. With restraints on expansion through increasing demand, the emphasis changes to growth through shift in brand demand — or brand growth only at the expense of competitors' share of market. As consumers increasingly relate quality/price/value to brand names, corporate marketing strengths will increasingly depend on the management's ability to consolidate the corporate image — and such an effort will require some form of headquarters coordination. The form may vary, but the importance of taking control is the essential element.

—— INCREASING IMPORTANCE OF ——
INTERNATIONAL ADVERTISING

Direction at Headquarters Level. While advertising people are not usually modest, they do normally confine their universe to the subject of advertising. And, they are occasionally humble. A founder of one important international advertising agency and a recognized philosopher/sage of the business was often quoted as having said, "It is possible to be born a writer or born an artist, but God so hated advertising men that he never made a whole one." Senior executives of international corporations should ask themselves these questions in regard to their managing directors or subsidiary presidents throughout the world: "Do *all* of our managing directors throughout the world have sufficient knowledge about advertising to effectively make large advertising investment decisions each year? . . . Do they have qualified local advisors, with *sufficient understanding and desire to perpetuate our long-range worldwide corporate plans?* . . . Did God ever made a whole managing director?"

Without some form of guiding direction from headquarters, the value from advertising investment input can range from excellent to impotent to counterproductive, as corporations shift and change local market managements. The true value from advertising investment comes from consistently doing the right thing for a long time.

Aside from the visual appearance of the advertising campaign itself, let us look at other elements that require the *management of change* in this critically challenging world market period when an MNC could be moving in as many different advertising directions as there are overseas subsidiary companies.

Advertising vs. Sales Budget Appropriations. If a local market is held responsible for "bottom-line performance" only — or is controlled only by total expense spending — there is little or no control over how much money is allocated for advertising. It could be too little or too much according to successful corporate experience for certain products in different industries . . . or it could be dependent on the different priority analyses of changing managements.

As you will see in Chapter 2, there are many considerations for budget appropriating. It will suffice to say here that too often a sales budget will receive a disproportionate amount when the only function of sales is to sell into the lines of distribution . . . where the advertising is the only contact with the ultimate consumer in order to empty out those channels.

Functional Corporate/Brand Image.   We have discussed a fragmented image for a brand between the different national markets; but, left unattended, a brand image can become fragmented to a point of utter diffusion within a single market.

This occurs when the local management changes its campaigning too frequently, operates too many disassociated small campaigns for too many different products . . . or when local markets just use occasional advertisements—no campaign at all.

Objective Measurement of Advertising Performance.   Self-evaluation is a hard habit to form. Small overseas subsidiary companies are not apt to regularly evaluate their own advertising performance unless they are being held accountable for advertising performance. Therefore, we have come full circle. Unless an MNC headquarters is aware of the *objectives*, and the proposed *advertising strategy* and *execution* for *each subsidiary market*, headquarters will not know what *performance* to hold the local market *accountable* for. If the local market does not objectively evaluate its own performance, we are apt to have a situation where advertising is directed locally by "gut feel" and "flown by the seat of the pants."

Finally, there are the ever present *increasing-cost concerns.* Virtually every international advertiser could effect certain cost savings through a greater centralization of its overseas advertising activities. The amount of duplication of production costs alone—filming, taping, artwork, and the like—is staggering in many firms. And the argument that the MNC would be trading quality for cost reduction if it used some standardization of creative efforts is fallacious . . . no one is suggesting that the firm would sacrifice quality. Rather, the question is whether the firm is maximizing its advertising dollar or lira in terms of buyer impressions.

—— Summary ——

In summary, world marketing 1980s style will require much closer attention to detail by the MNC's headquarters. Advertising in particular is taking on far more critical importance in the atmosphere of static demand and the competitive challenges for brand share shift. When future growth depends on product innovation and brand image, brand image is at least one area not to be abdicated away from headquarters control.

Further, the advantage of centralization of much of the advertising decision making, especially that portion that could benefit from intermarket coordination, must not be ignored. Numerous illustrations of the experiences of

MNCs, such as Henkel, Digital Equipment Corporation, Cessna, and Goodyear, are found in the following chapters. Their use of centralization . . . in some form or other . . . demonstrates the potential of such an approach.

——— 10 KEY POINTS ———

1. The need for advertising coordination is becoming more critical in an era of rapid and widespread communications; the MNC can no longer afford to be giving mixed . . . often conflicting . . . signals to its customers.

2. The predicted growth of the *Eurobrand* represents another step toward viewing multimarkets as *one*; a concentration on the search for buyer similarities rather than differences.

3. Confidence in *brand name* is becoming an increasing factor in customer price/quality measurement, while product benefits are receiving less attention.

4. MNC marketers can expect to have to adapt to more *intense competition, industry consolidations*, and *flattening markets* (worldwide) in the '80s.

5. Culture is no longer the single overriding consideration in market-to-market *advertising decisions.*

6. International advertising managers are increasingly focusing on the potential of employing a centralized advertising approach to multiple markets.

7. We suggest that flexibility of campaign design and skillful transliteration will successfully adapt well-conceived campaigns for most countries.

8. The *advertising environment* rather than *culture differences* appear to be more significant to today's international advertising manager. And the former is more manageable.

9. MNCs can no longer avoid the need for the international advertising manager to effectively *manage* its worldwide advertising system; cost concerns alone call for a rethinking of this home office manager's role.

10. The argument that under home office management the MNC would be trading quality for cost reduction if it used some standardization of creative efforts is fallacious . . . we are not suggesting that the firm would or should sacrifice quality. We wish to ensure that the firm is *maximizing its advertising dollar or lira in terms of buyer impression.*

2

Using Objectives as a Management Tool

— INTRODUCTION —

This chapter concentrates on performing a function that is much more difficult than establishing objectives for an advertising campaign. The discussion concentrates on directing others to establish objectives for different advertising campaigns, which must all solve different problems in different parts of the world.

Advertising objectives in this context are designed to perform many more internal management functions than are usually associated with advertising objectives.

To the headquarters of a multinational advertiser, the system of establishing advertising objectives can serve as the basic vehicle for worldwide intercompany communications on the subject of advertising. To a basic extent, the *offer* and *acceptance* of advertising objectives with a single overseas multinational subsidiary company becomes a *contract* with headquarters. The *consideration* in the contract is *advertising budget authori-*

zation, and the fulfillment of the contract is the *accountability of results* as originally agreed to. All communications during the contract (budget year) can relate to the terms agreed to in the objectives.

A system of multinational advertising objectives should not be viewed as a burden on subsidiary companies. Properly organized and administered, subsidiary companies should look upon such a system as their most effective means of communicating their position and intentions to headquarters. Headquarters should consider themselves equally committed to the agreement—performance promised and investment agreed to. However, performance and investment can be adjusted during a budget year if:

- the performance of the advertising is not recording predicted goals— the goals and the budget can be reduced (the opposite can also occur)

- objectives are accepted but not the budget requirement—the subsidiary company will need to "bargain" for lesser goals to fit the budget
- after a reasonable period, there has been no performance commensurate with investment in the opinions of either party, either party may elect to cancel the agreement, write new strategy, create a new campaign, establish new goals (objectives), and negotiate a new budget agreement

Using objectives as a management tool will be discussed within the context of the following:

- perspective on management position
- worldwide vs. local objectives

- benchmarks: a necessity
- objectives provide the linkage
- role of objectives
- steps in managing through objectives
- potential measurable objectives appropriate for international advertisers
- the target is still sales
- measurable awareness levels
- corporate image
- home-office-initiated campaigns
- retail advertising as an exception
- get all promised goals in writing

When headquarters does not approve advertising budgets until after they approve advertising objectives (and strategies), lines of communications can be kept open and clear to the most remote parts of the world all during the critical annual program-planning period.

From M.B.O. to Theory Z, every new management approach or "theory" seems to have one common characteristic; its stress on establishing objectives.

Nothing is more *essential* to effective international advertising management than the establishment of clearly defined, measurable objectives. And these objectives must be presented in a form that permits them to be readily *communicated* to everyone involved in the corporation's overseas marketing and promotional efforts, including subsidiary and advertising agency personnel.

Why are *objectives* so critical to effective international advertising/communications management? Basically, the firm's advertising and communications objectives provide the primary year-round link between the home office and the field and, additionally, serve as the annual performance measure (benchmark reading). In other words, these stated objectives become the means by which the international advertising manager can ensure that advertising plays its designated role in achieving the corporation's broader marketing goals.

——— Some Background ———

Before proceeding further, it seems appropriate to put the question of international advertising in a perspective in which it might be viewed by a multinational corporate executive, as compared with a corporate executive for a single national market. Frankly, the basic difference is the psychological barrier that often inhibits the internationalist's personal analysis of day-to-day operational activity. Unlike the monomarket executive, the internationalist does not live in the environment where his own advertising occurs. Most of his "feel" for local market activity comes from periodic sales and profit reports. The advertising expenditure has no real personality, and its impact cannot be viewed "behaviorally" with the feel that comes only from years of executive experience.

Rather, international advertising expenditures are treated as a "recurring operational expense" and are viewed as a "residual." When expense budget reductions become necessary, advertising is a ready source of needed monies . . . almost a contingency fund.

For many large multinationals, the item of "advertising" is the single largest annually recurring item of *expense*. Accounting requirements aside, a strong case can be made for considering advertising to be an *investment*. While we do not wish to debate such a technicality here, we do wish to make the point that if advertising budgets were treated as an *investment* such monies would be taken far more seriously than when they are treated as an *operating expense*.

Often, a multinational's worldwide advertising budget will be greater than the funds required for constructing a new manufacturing plant the firm is considering. Yet, since the new plant is a more irretrievable decision than an annually designed advertising *budget estimate* is, the amount authorized for advertising becomes a short-term operating expense based on the additional cost the product can absorb within profit limits.

We submit that if management would accept long-term advertising objectives as an investment into the future, advertising funds would be more realistically considered in terms of return on investment. While we do not expect a fast shift in the corporate financial structure, we do believe that with more emphasis placed on *the cost to obtain specific objectives* by advertising people, corporate management will eventually take a more realistic look at what advertising can accomplish as a long-term investment.

There are at least two more problems created by the barrier of distance between subsidiary markets and home office that affect advertising budgets and that can be solved by using carefully constructed advertising objectives as a management tool.

The first is caused by using the percent-to-sales policy for establishing advertising budgets in all overseas markets. Such a policy is a delight to financial officers but is, in fact, a most inequitable measure of realistic budget requirements. With a historical record of achievement, percent-to-sale guidelines can *assist* in establishing advertising budgets in most individual markets, but national markets cannot be compared. This is so because (1) the cost of media differs greatly and (2) the "noise level," or total volume of advertising competing for attention, is quite different.

In terms of *objectives*, this simply means that, given two markets with relatively similar annual sales volume, one market will require a greater budget to achieve the same improvement on which to base data objectives than another will. It costs more to get consumers' attention.

The second problem, not unrelated to the first, is the *lead time and lag time* necessary to achieve objectives. While it is accepted as necessary that corporations must budget annually and close their books annually, this mechanical process has little to do with influencing a public by means of corporate communications. Objectives designed to establish brand awareness and purchase intentions are an ongoing, long-term process, often spanning several years.

Annual objectives must be set against annual improvements on current base benchmarks . . . for example, "improved brand awareness from 42.7 percent to 48 percent." However, the long-range objective might be to reach a brand awareness of 85 percent in year 198x, to be achieved by incremental annual and affordable goals. Any break in the planned advertising volume necessary to achieve the 85 percent awareness level is, in fact, a serious setback in achievement of this objective.

Of course, advertising objectives are in support of the total marketing objectives, and it is expected that sales increases will not lag too far behind advertising awareness progress. The point is that awareness levels and buying intention levels among consumers are unstable and can be maintained or improved only with constant investment. Should the home office management elect to not maintain the budget required to reach the 85 percent objective, all objectives must be reduced to match a lower budget level.

Advertising people should speak to their management in terms of cost versus objectives. Management should measure return on advertising investment in terms of performance to objectives.

——— Worldwide vs. Local Objectives ———

A multinational firm generally has two stages (or levels) of advertising goals or objectives. First, it will have what we have chosen to call its "worldwide" or international advertising objectives.[1] Then, worldwide objectives typically would be expected to have the following *four* characteristics:

1. They are designed to complement (and support) the MNC's worldwide marketing *objectives* and related *strategies*.
2. They are originated in the MNC's worldwide headquarters.
3. They are stated in broad terms, e.g., to increase brand awareness.
4. They serve as a basis for comparison with local or national goals and objectives.

While broadly stated owing to the differences in the level of product acceptance or company awareness found between markets, these objectives offer a degree of continuity or control that is often felt to be highly desirable worldwide.

The second level of advertising objectives . . . and the ones of primary concern in this book . . . are those that are established at the *local* (national) level. As we shall point out shortly, these objectives become highly specific, measurable targets for each individual market. In fact, the key to the MNC's achievement of its worldwide objectives lies in its ability to effectively establish and meet these local (national) goals.

It is important to reemphasize the point that much of our discussion deals with the development of local (national) objectives. We do not ignore the fact that it is *necessary* to view the larger picture, and we encourage the view that an MNC needs to present "one face" to the world. The distinction is, however, that the only way to establish truly measurable objectives . . . the kind that will enable top management to recognize advertising's real potential . . . comes via the local (national) route. It is at this level where differences in product/company awareness and market share can be isolated, where performance benchmarks can be set, and where successes or failures can be recorded.

Finally, we have taken as a premise in this book that we are talking about multinational firms that have the type of equity position, management agreement, or leverage with their subsidiaries that permits the international advertising manager to have the primary *voice* in managing the overseas objectives. This premise is reflected in our discussion of worldwide versus local objectives. Many other United States-based and foreign international firms, especially those in the industrial field, direct *all* of their overseas advertising from their home office. However, this distinction we make between types of objectives is most appropriate to them as well. While these firms likely establish worldwide objectives, it is essential that they also establish specific

---

[1] The term "worldwide advertising objectives" must not be confused with "international corporate advertising objectives." The latter is a widely used term that refers specifically to "image" advertising, and such image programs often originate in corporate communications or public relations offices. Corporate advertising is discussed in detail in Chapter 10.

market-to-market advertising objectives. Any aggregative approach to analyzing worldwide advertising efforts has the potential of *ignoring* important local differences. For example, significant local problems in terms of awareness or image could be "washed out" in employing broad or worldwide results.

—— Benchmarks: A Necessity ——

Prior to considering the types of local objectives that might be established, a word about the use of benchmarks (and longitudinal data) is most appropriate. In order to establish measurable objectives, it is important to consider "what can be effectively measured."

Most marketing objectives in local markets must, of necessity, be tied in some way to *sales*. Since the MNC should have *reliable* sales information . . . even at the local or national level . . . it is relatively easy to follow sales trends over a relevant time period (quarterly, semiannually, or annually). If an MNC's local marketing objective is to increase sales by 10 percent in the next year, the evaluation mechanism becomes quite simple: "Did it meet the target increase?" Share-of-market objectives are often difficult to measure in foreign markets due to a lack of competitive information, but some rather hard data can still be obtained.

On the other hand, international advertising objectives are usually less tangible and relate to building a state of mind regarding the product or company. When the marketing vice president or director establishes the final marketing objectives, the role of advertising . . . designed to complement these objectives . . . is assigned. The worldwide advertising objective might be to "increase product awareness"; and this could eventually be translated into a national objective for, say, Morocco, to be an increased awareness of 10 percent. This sort of local objective . . . which is a realistic measure for advertising . . . suggests the need for benchmark information, for example, what the level of awareness is prior to the campaign. The use of marketing and advertising research, including consideration of appropriate techniques, is presented in Chapter 7. However, the importance of establishing an ongoing series of benchmarks against which to measure local market performance must be emphasized prior to considering the measurable objectives.

A final caveat about such data, however, is provided by the following example (see Illustration 2–1).

Let us assume that Company A is doing a major *new consumer product* launch in France and is devoting $2M-plus to a campaign designed to achieve 50 percent *brand awareness*. As shown in Illustration 2–1, the monthly bars indicate the advertising expenditures that are heaviest from January to June. By July the company has actually exceeded its objective. If the firm took only an annual measure of each of its local markets each May 15, the planning during the remainder of the year would be based on the product having a 51.5 percent brand awareness.

— ILLUSTRATION 2-1 —
New Product Launch

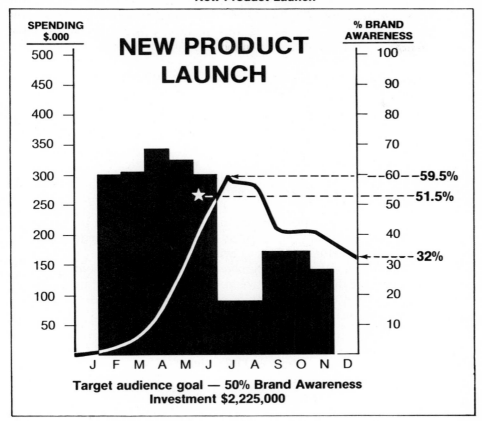

SPENDING $.000 / % BRAND AWARENESS

NEW PRODUCT LAUNCH

500 — 100
450 — 90
400 — 80
350 — 70
300 — 60 — **59.5%**
          — **51.5%**
250 — 50
200 — 40
150 — 30 — **32%**
100 — 20
50 — 10

J F M A M J J A S O N D

Target audience goal — 50% Brand Awareness
Investment $2,225,000

Unfortunately, in this case, the product's brand awareness in France has slipped by some 28 percent . . . as the advertising expenditures are reduced. Certainly, more frequent research would have caught this "slippage" and enabled Company A to make different plans for the future.

In this example, the value of ongoing benchmark research is illustrated. We recognize that conducting such local research may be expensive, but it does provide the *optimum* means for determining local performance. Fortunately, as mentioned in our discussion of advertising research, there are now various new research services that help to reduce these costs in many major markets.

—— Objectives Provide the Linkage ——

A typical international advertising scenario has a U.S. firm . . . based in L.A., Rockport, or Stamford . . . marketing its products in a wide range of developed and developing countries. It may have production facilities in some markets and only a sales office in other areas. The director of international advertising, based at the home office, must somehow coordinate the advertising programs in these various markets. (Most firms see some coordination as important if for no other reason than the desire to *protect the company's trademark brand name*.)

Such coordinative activities become especially difficult when the corporation:

- deals with multiple advertising agencies
- is involved in numerous joint ventures . . . often as a minority partner
- produces a variety of products and/or services
- heavily decentralizes its marketing/advertising functions
- is active in many of the newer national markets

Under such circumstances, the firm cannot hope to cope with the myriad of cultural, national, linguistic, legal, and so on, differences that tend to divert it from its desired marketing results . . . without clear direction. And it is here that the company's local advertising objectives, which carry home office approval, can provide the linkage between headquarters and the field. The objectives serve as the ongoing point of comparison: "How does what I am doing relate to the achievement of our objectives?"

——— Role of Objectives ———

In most books or articles on this subject, the major attention to date has tended to be given to the *nature of the objectives* and the *process for establishing objectives* rather than to the proper *management of the objectives* once they have been established. In effect, this means switching the emphasis from *creating goals* themselves to their worldwide implementation.

Viewed in this management perspective, the multinational's worldwide objectives can play an important role in all advertising/communications phases of its market-to-market:

- planning
- budgeting
- internal communications
- client-agency communications
- control

Clearly, these worldwide goals can serve as the ongoing reference point to both home office and subsidiary personnel as the local (national) objectives and subsequent plans are developed.

Planning.   Just how the local promotional objectives are developed has not been addressed . . . and, in fact, they may be initiated at the home office or at the national market level, or through some combination of home office-field involvement. Often the basic guidelines (and the worldwide goals) are initiated at headquarters (with some field input), and the actual local objectives are set by the advertising/marketing personnel in the field. These are subject, however, to home office approval. Once developed (and approved), these objectives become the focal point for the firm's advertising planning in the market. (Again, if *all* advertising planning and implementation occurs at headquarters, such steps are centralized as well.) This planning involves determining how to use appropriate strategies and tactics to achieve these local advertising objectives.

Some of the promotional efforts can, of course, be undertaken from headquarters . . . an international campaign that appears in the international editions of a United States-based publication, for example . . . or sample artwork/television commercials to use in the national markets. The central test, however, of all local planning is the extent to which it permits the achievement of its objectives, and it requires a constant management effort from the home office to reinforce this point.

Budgeting.   Similarly, through the establishment of clear-cut local advertising/communications objectives the budgeting question becomes: "What expenditures are necessary to achieve these objectives?" This question is much different than asking: "What can we afford to spend?"

Even with a high level of local (subsidiary) autonomy, it is appropriate for the international advertising manager (home office) to ask each local market subsidiary to estimate its *budget needs based on its objectives*. This effort forces the subsidiary to view advertising in specific, goal-oriented terms.

It should be added that it is extremely important for the international advertising manager to have an approval role in the budgetary process, even down to the local level. Most international advertising managers agree that this is necessary if any degree of advertising coordination from the home office is to be achieved. It is relatively simple to keep communications channels open between home office and some of the world's most remote markets before any budgets are approved. Afterward, communications can become difficult.

In addition, it is important to widely communicate the firm's worldwide and local advertising objectives to appropriate advertising/marketing/sales personnel in the corporation. This prevents misunderstandings and the development of possible conflicting objectives. Similarly, the various local objectives need to be made available to the individual agency(ies) handling this account. The local objectives become the measure against which the latter are tested as well.

Control.   Finally, most of what we have said about the importance of clearly defined local objectives becomes especially relevant when we consider the need for *control* or, in other words, for a measure of each market's advertising success. Through constant reminders of the local objectives and by testing every communications activity against these objectives, the international advertising manager has provided a basis for regularly (annually or more frequently) asking local management if the objectives have been achieved—and if not, why not. Using such an approach, advertising is no longer some sort of "ephemeral" activity that is "impossible to measure"! Rather, the international advertising manager can make judgments about the success or failure of the subsidiary's advertising efforts and can make the appropriate changes that need to be made in order to bring the communications activities "on target." *Note to the reader:* This is the reason advertising objectives are communications objectives. Advertising may be doing its job right: "something else" is the sales problem.

―――― **Steps in Managing Through Objectives** ――――

In order to effectively manage through objectives, the international advertising manager needs to:

1. *Be involved in establishing the local objectives.* The objectives can originate at the local level and simply require headquarters approval or simply be passed down from the home office. As noted earlier, the worldwide objectives and the guide for local advertising objectives often provide a starting point for the locals. While these alternatives are not exhaustive, they suggest that the international advertising manager's involvement may be *direct* or *indirect*. Under whichever approach is adopted, however, it is essential that he or she be an active participant in developing local objectives.

2. *Be involved in the budget process.* As with the local objectives, it is critical that the international advertising manager be actively involved in the local budget development. A frequently employed approach is to provide a form (or set of guidelines) that can be used in each market and submitted for home office approval. Although the home office can simply *allocate* to the local markets, this fails to demonstrate the relationship between objectives and budgeting to the locals.

3. *Be responsible for the approval of all local market campaigns.* The international advertising manager should have approval authority over local campaigns. The particular test should be the campaign's consistency with its predetermined objectives. While having such authority, however, many international advertising managers simply receive examples of all campaigns and "spot check" for consistency.

4. *Be responsible for establishing and conducting control procedures.* The international marketing manager is responsible for choosing and employing the procedures designed to determine whether or not the subsidiary programs achieve their objectives.

By following these steps, the international marketing manager can maintain effective coordination and control of the MNC's international advertising efforts. These steps in no way diminish the local or national level of advertising preparation and planning that many firms prefer. Rather, they suggest a "prudent" use of the MNC's resources.

——— What Are the Potential Measurable Objectives That ——— Might Be Appropriate for the International Advertiser?

Earlier we indicated that advertising lacks respect in some management circles, especially in the international arena. This fact can partly be attributed to the advertising community, since too often advertising seems to *lack any measurable objective*. Before evaluating *any* advertisement, for example, one needs to ask, "What is it intended to do?" and "Who is its target audience?"

The clearer the objective and concomitantly the better the audience is targeted, the stronger the advertisement or campaign and the more likely its success can be measured. In the United States, TRW, a Cleveland-based MNC, has had a most successful campaign designed specifically to improve its corporate awareness with business leaders. To determine whether or not it was successful, the company measured business executives' views before, during, and after the campaign. As a result, the company had *evidence* of the success of its campaign and a basis for its communications decision making, that is, advertising became more than just an unmeasurable quantity . . . a reality rather than a hope.

Our goal, therefore, is to identify realistic, measurable local objectives. Such objectives may be directly product- or service-related, or they may be related to the overall corporation. They may be measured in terms of attitude or awareness shifts; or, if they involve retail or direct orders, they may be measured primarily in terms of sales changes. Such communications goals may include:

- increasing consumers' or buyers' *awareness* of the *product* . . . either generally or comparatively
- improving the product's *image* among consumers or buyers . . . either generally or comparatively
- increasing a target group of opinion leaders' or consumers'/buyers' *awareness* of the company . . . either generally or comparatively
- increasing the company's *image* among a target group of opinion leaders or consumers/buyers . . . either generally or comparatively
- increasing the product's *sales* or *market share* among consumers or buyers . . . either generally or comparatively (these objectives are more appropriate for retail or direct response advertising)

Each of these objectives has an important characteristic—each is measurable. However, there are a number of inherent problems in using changes in sales or market share as a direct measure. Product advertising directed toward *immediate* sales, such as advertising to support local retailers or direct order advertising, may be measured in terms of sales or market share. On the other hand, longer-term local advertising campaigns more typically represent only *one* element in the total market effort.

The other marketing mix elements that are needed to make sales (and profits) on the company's products or services include:

- product quality (and having the right product)
- product appearance (including packaging)
- corporate salesmanship (sales to resellers in the consumer goods field or "selling in")
- retail salesmanship (sales to consumers in the consumer goods field or "selling out")
- direct salesmanship (sales to purchasing agents or industrial buyers)
- pricing (to attract target demand—appropriate for product positioning)
- product distribution (dealer development in consumer goods field and/or physical product delivery efficiency in both industrial and consumer goods)
- *advertising* (all levels)
- point of purchase (attention and persuasion ten feet from the final sale for consumer goods)
- sales promotion aids (local dealer advertising and consumer traffic-building devices for consumer goods or brochures and other sales aids for industrial sales force or selling agents)
- publicity (editorial recognition of new goods or services available)

In other words, these are just a few of the marketing ingredients necessary to make the sales . . . which in turn make the profits. Each type of product and selling organization will require refinements to this list of functions that are specific to them. To illustrate this, an advertising official of DuPont Chemicals in Geneva, Switzerland, recently noted to one of the authors that having the proper direct mailing list was a most essential ingredient in that firm's European sales efforts. In a multimarket program these ingredients will take on different degrees of importance and emphasis for the different national markets.

A Word about Sales. Still, it is inevitable that the international advertising manager will examine sales results and market share when evaluating product advertising. Such information is especially valuable when the local advertising expenditure change (increase or decrease) is *substantial*, while very little else has changed in a market. However, his or her major attention and evaluation procedures must be directed to the objectives of the campaign.

Finally, to determine what effect a promotion program might be expected to have *prior* to its initiation, a corporation may test it in a particular portion of a national market under tightly *controlled* conditions. Doing this would give some indication about what proportion of sales in a subsequent *national* campaign may be attributed to advertising.

——— **Awareness** ———

Again, communications goals could be referred to as different degrees of share of mind of a collective public . . . or of a specific target consumer group. The following will illustrate the mental process an advertising manager must perceive when anticipating the effect of the firm's local advertising on a public. These are the classical communications points that need to be recognized when seeking to achieve a given product (or service) local objective:

1. *Awareness (unaided).* When people in a specific target market think of a specific kind of product:
   a. Which manufacturer's names do they think of?
   b. Which brand names do they think of?
   c. Which brand names do they recall being advertised?
   For low brand share products, these questions can also be asked by offering a list of companies and brand names—aided recall.
2. *Comprehension.* For the brands the potential buyers recall as seen advertised:
   a. Where did they see it advertised (media)?
   b. What do they recall about the advertisement appearance (illustration)?
   c. What did the advertising tell them (copy)?
3. *Conviction.* For the brand (or manufacturer) names recalled, how do they perceive each brand in terms of:
   a. Associating brands with (suggested) quality values.
   b. Associating brands with (suggested) performance values.
4. *Action (intention to buy).*
   a. Brand preference—"If you were going to buy (type of product) today, which brand would you buy?"
   b. Brand acceptance—"And which other brands would you consider?"
   c. Negative acceptance—"Which brand would you be least apt to buy? Why?"

These questions provide meaningful, measurable benchmarks for establishing reasonable performance goals to be achieved through advertising. They need not be reestablished with every new advertising campaign. The trend data from previous campaigns for the same kind of product should extend from one campaign to the next. However, this is not to say that trend data for *different kinds of products* under the same label are usable. Some brands have greater consumer acceptance for one kind of product than for another.

It is generally accepted that there is often considerable lag time between the appearance and desired customer action of national brand advertising—the period between "awareness" and "action," even for an established, well-accepted brand name. A high-impact, attention-getting campaign, well targeted to the "significant" audience, with a high-frequency media plan can greatly reduce the lag time. However, customer action is anticipated by corporate management much faster than it can be achieved. Therefore measurement of achievement becomes critical.

—— Image ——

Like awareness objectives, image objectives require an identification of the product or company *image* prior to the beginning of the advertising program. Further, this objective is most appropriate when a particular target audience (or audiences) can be identified.

Undoubtedly, one of the classic image campaigns (overseas) was undertaken by ITT in the early 1970s. In 1974, ITT in Europe found itself with a particularly unique image problem. Research indicated that "there was a high awareness of the initials ITT linked with hostile attitudes [due to alleged activities in Chile]".[2] At the same time, there was little general knowledge about the company's major commitments in many European countries or about its favorable impact on the various national economies.

ITT countered with a corporate communications program that was targeted to high-level opinion leaders (in business, government, and education). Its campaign in Great Britain illustrates the direct nature of its messages—for example, "Does ITT give a damn about Britain's balance of payments?"—designed to demonstrate its impact on national economies (see Illustration 2–2). This and similar advertisements appeared in the *Daily Telegraph*, the *Economist*, the *Financial Times*, and similar papers during late 1974 and early 1975.

Postcampaign measures, including mail response and formal research, suggest that the campaign was a success. But perhaps the most interesting success indicator was a statement made in the House of Lords. A British lord stated that a full-page advertisement in *The Times* of London showed how much the British owed one U.S. company.

In this example, ITT demonstrates how a false image, such as the effect of a foreign MNC on the national economy, can be countered through advertising. Certainly, the company had a high public awareness . . . it was a matter of trying to turn it in a positive direction.

—— HOME-OFFICE-INITIATED CAMPAIGNS ——

Some MNCs initiate international campaigns from their home office. As noted earlier, a number of relatively large international firms, especially those in the industrial field, conduct all phases of their overseas advertising from

[2] Nigel Row, "Unbiased AD, PR Best Approach for Multi-nationals in Europe Markets," in *Industrial Marketing*, (July 1975), p. 59.

headquarters, including campaign development and media placement. Very often the degree of involvement from foreign sales subsidiaries, production facilities, or national managements is extremely limited.

However, a slightly different question concerns the activities of the international advertising managers in the types of firms we just described in detail. Do they ever initiate a worldwide campaign themselves that is *not* tied to their local market efforts? The answer is often *yes*. The international advertising manager may become involved in the development of a worldwide campaign relating to a corporate advertising theme, for example. The MNC may feel the need to develop a new "corporate identity" . . . one that better reflects the stature it wishes to portray. To illustrate this . . . such a program may be targeted toward financial interests or influences and may employ advertising in five or six key financial or economics publications, such as the *Economist* and the *Financial Executive*. Again, however, local benchmarks are needed . . . unless the company merely wants an increased awareness among the readership of these periodicals. The corporate advertising topic will be detailed in Chapter 10, and two recent important case histories will be considered.

Retail Advertising as an Exception

National brand advertisers that are also involved in direct action retail advertising will find that setting goals for retail performance is quite different. This type of advertising is not designed to build brand preference; it is designed to capitalize on that which has been created. And, if necessary, it may attempt to overcome any lack of consumer brand preference by buying a share of the market through the use of greatly reduced *prices* compared with the prices of the leading brands.

The goal of retail advertising is to deliver more customers to the point of sale and, if possible, have an action or *sales* orientation: "This is where to buy the brand you have seen advertised on television." The strategy involves reaching potential customers at the exact time they intend to buy. With many products, timing is not too significant; they are frequently purchased items. In fact, many products seem to have some degree of seasonal buying cycles, and it is important to coordinate your advertising with these buying patterns. The infrequent purchase poses the greatest problem . . . the distress purchase, the necessity that is contingent on the unplanned wear-out or failure of a similar product owned by consumers . . . major household appliances or auto parts. Many advertisers of such products often attempt to increase sales by periodic special offers to tell people: "If you are thinking about buying (product), do it now at special savings."

Let us take the auto after market (e.g., tires, batteries, mufflers, shock absorbers). If manufacturers of such items wished to help improve the retail sales of their brand, they would most likely be looking to local newspapers where they could use local dealers' names and addresses in the advertisements in order to direct consumers to the outlets. Here research into con-

— ILLUSTRATION 2-2 —
ITT Campaign

"Who the devil does ITT think it is?"

ITT is an international group of companies owned by an American parent, but run autonomously by local management.

In Britain, ITT's major companies include such famous names as Abbey Life Assurance, Sheraton hotels, and Rimmel cosmetics.

As well as some less well-known names who produce well-known products.

Ashe Laboratories, for example, who manufacture Amplex, Sucron and other familiar household products.

ITT Consumer Products, whose somewhat formal name hardly does justice to its popular televisions, radios and record players.

And Standard Telephones and Cables, ITT's largest British company, in the forefront of world telecommunications.

Unlike Rimmel, their name may not be on everyone's lips.

But like Rimmel, their products certainly are.

ITT

"Does ITT give a damn about Britain's balance of payments?"

Facts can sometimes be uncomfortable. Especially when they shatter a popular myth.

In ITT's case, the myth is that, as a multinational company, its only interest in Britain is how much money it can get out of it.

And the facts?

Last year, ITT companies in Britain paid over £12 million in Corporation Tax and more than £73 million in wages and salaries. They invested £8.6 million in new production facilities and £9.5 million in research and development.

This year, these same companies will earn more than £50 million in exports and spend less than £30 million on imports. (And the imports are nearly all essential raw materials.)

After shareholders have been paid a dividend, the net contribution to Britain's balance of payments will still be more than £11 million.

And that's a fact.

ITT

What more

At ITT, we're happy when people talk about us.

We're even happier when what they're saying is based on facts, rather than gossip.

So, over the last few months, we've been running a special corporate advertising campaign.

You may have noticed some of the ads.

(For those of you who didn't, we've reproduced them all above.)

In the campaign, we set out some of the key facts about ITT in the UK, and in particular the relationship between ITT's operations and the British economy.

But four advertisements can't tell the whole story on their own.

So we've produced a comprehensive booklet for people who want more information.

ITT companies in Britain include: Abbey Life Assurance, Ashe Laboratories, Excess Insurance, ITT Consumer Products, Rimmel, Sheraton, Standard

— ILLUSTRATION 2-2 —
(continued)

"Why would ITT want to invest in Britain at a time like this?"

For many years now, ITT companies have been investing in the British economy in a big way.

Since early 1970, for example, their investment in buildings, equipment and machinery in the UK has totalled £43 million, much of it in Government designated development areas.

Not to mention the £76 million that went into British research, development and engineering during the same period.

All of which is long term investment, with export and employment implications stretching into the 80s and beyond.

But what about 1975 itself?

And what about all those gloomy forecasts about Britain's future?

As far as ITT is concerned, there were good reasons for investing in Britain for the last 50 years. And there are equally good reasons this year.

So ITT companies plan to invest at least another £12 million on buildings, equipment and machinery in Britain during 1975.

Which represents not only a £4 million increase on the ITT average over the last five years, but also a pretty unambiguous vote of confidence in Britain's long term future.

For further information please write to: 190 Strand, London WC1 2R 1DU.
ITT companies in Britain include:
Abbey Life Assurance, Aoki Laboratories, Excess Insurance.
ITT Consumer Products, Rimmel, Sternson.
Standard Telephones and Cables and Standard Telecommunication Laboratories.

ITT

"Why should ITT care tuppence about British technology?"

With its Headquarters in the United States, ITT might be expected to concentrate its research effort there, too.

But it doesn't.

On the contrary, wherever ITT does business, it also invests in research and development.

In Britain, for example, ITT employs over 2,000 scientists and engineers on research and development, a quarter of them at Standard Telecommunication Laboratories, Harlow, the largest of ITT's four major research centres in Europe.

Among the research fields pioneered at Harlow has been that of fibre optics, which has the potential to transmit hundreds of thousands of separate telephone conversations over a glass thread no thicker than a human hair.

Apart from playing its part in helping to maintain Britain's status as a technological world leader, ITT's research investment policy has made an impact in terms of hard cash.

Over the last five years, ITT has invested over £38 million in British research, £11.5 million in 1974 alone. And if associated engineering costs are included, the five year total comes up to over £76 million.

Which is a good deal more than tuppence in anybody's language.

For further information, including a new 20-page publication "Facts about ITT in Europe" please write to 190 Strand, London WC1 2R 1DU.
ITT companies in Britain include:
Abbey Life Assurance, Aoki Laboratories, Excess Insurance.
ITT Consumer Products, Rimmel, Sternson.
Standard Telephones and Cables and Standard Telecommunication Laboratories.

ITT

can we say?

It's called "Facts about ITT in Europe."

As its name suggests, the booklet explains where and how ITT operates throughout Europe.

How many people it employs, and where they come from.

Who runs it. How it's managed.

"Facts about ITT in Europe" is yours, free.

Please use this coupon to send for your copy.

Telephones and Cables and Standard Telecommunication Laboratories.

To: 190 Strand, London WC2R 1DU.
Please send me a copy of "Facts about ITT in Europe."

Name_____

Address_____

_____

EC1   **ITT**

sumer behavior for *your product* can be most useful. It can assist you in determining the shopping efforts/patterns *your* potential consumers employ when buying the product. For example, you can determine whether they are most concerned about specific brands or about dealer services. Next, what kind of situation must this automobile after-market producer consider, and how will it measure the results? Let us illustrate this by considering the case of one such firm desiring to reach the shock absorber market in a medium-sized town in West Germany (see Illustration 2–3). The local newspaper has a circulation of 200,000 — 30 percent own autos — the significant circulation is thus 60,000. It is known that only 2 percent of the auto-owning population buy shock absorbers each day. The potential buyers are now reduced to 1,200 consumers. If this brand's market share is 10 percent, the firm could reasonably expect about 120 customers each day without retail advertising. Therefore, the goal would be to sell more than 120 customers per day over about a three-day period from date of newspaper insertion — all other things being equal — which they seldom are.

In practical terms, advertising must share the outcome of such a retail investment with the company's various sales levels and the retailer-owner. Factors such as the ad layout, the price, the position of the advertisement in the newspaper, the date selected, the weather conditions, the point-of-sale promotion, the store's appearance, and the disposition of the retail sales clerks all may need to be in good order in order for the 120+ goal to be achieved. Last, your competition may decide to do twice as much advertising and cut the price 25 percent more than your retailers do on the same date — an

— **ILLUSTRATION 2–3** —
Reaching the Shock Absorber Market

Newspaper Circulation	**200,000**
Auto Ownership	**30%**
Significant Audience	**60,000**
Daily Purchase	**2%**
Potential Customers	**1,200**
Brand SOM	**10%**
Daily Brand Purchase	**120**
Goal	**120+**

action not likely to help you achieve your objective. Still, if carefully planned advertising is conducted, a sales measure should be employed, but it should not be the only one employed for judging the campaign.

Thus, while it may require different criteria for measuring a retail campaign as compared to a national brand campaign, one should not lose the opportunity to learn from the experience of every advertising action. The result of the campaign (good or bad) should be analyzed against the elements of the action. A rainy day could have discouraged shoppers, or your ad may have been on the same page with that of the competitor who offered the lower price. On the brighter side, perhaps you have discovered that "before-and-after" illustrations excited more action—or that a different way of expressing the price ("save $4.50" instead of "20 percent discount") sounded more attractive. Advertisers who are simply too quick to "throw the baby out with the bath water" never really know what they did *right*, much less what they did *wrong*.

It is more difficult to direct and monitor the performance of retail advertising at an MNC headquarters level. Retail advertising, like sales promotion programs, is geared to solving a specific local sales problem. It takes advantage of a specific local opportunity. It is designed to generate immediate sales . . . not simply to create awareness. Even products that lend themselves perfectly to the employment of a corporate pattern product campaign can seldom use such a pattern approach as effectively at the dealer traffic-building level.

The corporate headquarters can, however, make a significant worldwide contribution by helping local markets understand advertising's role at the retail merchandise levels by encouraging them to match advertising campaigns with periods when consumers want to buy; by cycling retail advertising to take advantage of the brand awareness peaks created by national product advertising; and by setting up accountability measurements, which in this case should indeed involve sales to ultimate consumers. It cannot be overemphasized that in retail advertising critical analysis is important on a day-to-day basis so that effective adjustments can be made immediately to improve on the performance of each succeeding ad insertion.

—— Get All Promised Goals in Writing ——

To anyone promising to produce a given performance, the goal of anticipated performance must be agreed upon by both headquarters and individual overseas subsidiaries. Each must agree that the goal(s) is obtainable and affordable and that the anticipated result is worth the required investment.

Accountability is the root of a successful and profitable worldwide advertising operation. To a multinational corporation, setting goals and measuring performance to those goals is, in the final analysis, the only way a headquarters operation can justify a high advertising investment. The problem multiplies when the investment is segmented in many markets and under the control of so many different people, their opinions, and their variety in forms of logical decision making. Because of this, systematic measurement is simply a must.

Reducing to a formula the methods for setting advertising goals—and producing more accurate reporting on attainment of those goals—and proving that profitable lessons can be learned and applied in future actions represent an enormous step forward in gaining confidence from the corporate executive management. Further, it emphasizes to the local or regional managers that advertising is important and must be properly employed.

This means that we are at least approaching the area where we can offer to management advertising by the pound or by the meter. By analyzing each market as compared with its own levels of communications achievement, there is the possibility of more accurately predicting a specified return on a specified amount of investment and to do it in a language even financial directors will understand.

—— 10 KEY POINTS ——

1. Setting objectives is the *only* way the advertising function has to "tell" its management what it will receive for the money we are asking them to spend. Measuring attainment of those objectives is the *only* way to isolate advertising from all other marketing functions. This is the *only* way advertising can receive appropriate *blame* or *credit* for the way things have turned out.

2. Setting measurable objectives compared with recognized benchmarks is a recommended method for getting advertising campaigns to be considered as more than art shows.

3. People who propose advertising campaigns (programs and budgets) to an executive management need to understand the perspective of that management (know your customer). In an international situation, executives seldom live in the environment of their own advertising. They need more management information than does a monomarket management.

4. A worldwide corporate objective is seldom measurable for performance accountability in numerical terms; however, a corporate worldwide objective is needed to set the direction for individual local market measurable objectives.

5. The simple act of requiring local markets to establish advertising objectives for measuring performance is of little constructive value without also the willingness to invest in sufficient research to establish benchmarks and continuous evaluation research.

6. Advertising objectives should become the basic communications vehicle between headquarters and its network of worldwide subsidiary companies.

7. Headquarters should *not* attempt to establish an infinite amount of detailed information from each market through accountability measurements ... only sufficient benchmark trend data to indicate whether or not predicted progress is being achieved.

8. Awareness scores in research should also be examined qualitatively for image profile. A high awareness score does not automatically mean a positive image.

9. Objectives for retail advertising can assume more responsibility for ultimate sales results than can product or brand advertising.

10. An advertising objective should be considered as a contract with management and therefore should be *stated clearly in writing*.

3

Developing an Advertising Campaign

— INTRODUCTION —

As in every chapter, the authors are positioning the reader as an MNC headquarters director of advertising responsible for the advertising produced by all or many overseas subsidiary companies. However, in this particular chapter we are recommending that you think in terms of *teaching* to achieve a desired result rather than contain overseas management by prescribing a predetermined solution for the advertising campaign.

Your involvement is to direct the procedure for finding the right solution and not to direct the implementation of the procedure. You are looking for the professional approach, and you must be willing to accept any resulting creative approach that can prove itself by professional pretest procedures. Your objective is to *cause to be created* an advertising campaign that meets these criteria:

- standard of quality required by the corporation
- truthfulness and accuracy for the product or service involved
- in strong support of an accepted local marketing strategy
- positions product compatible with long-range marketing plans
- proven effective locally by acceptable pretesting procedures
- cost of campaign represents an appropriate and equitable investment for obtaining a realistic objective
- does not violate corporate policy, or place in legal jeopardy any of the registered brand or corporate names

To aid you in directing toward such ends, we offer these topics:

- the headquarters role in developing creative concepts

- multimarket creative strategies
- analytical guide for monitoring creative development
  - the marketing strategy
  - the advertising goals
  - agency response to brief
  - review of creative presentation
- corporate involvement in the creative process
- what is best for the corporation?
  - aiding a single market
  - working on a regional basis
- the worldwide pattern
- summary—advertising creative strategy

One cannot set to policy or command creative excellence. One can only provide an environment where creative excellence can germinate constructively—and one must be prepared to recognize and accept the genuine article on evidence.

Samuel Johnson (1758)
The trade of advertising is now so near perfection, that it is not easy to propose any improvements.

Claude Hopkins (1923)
The time has come when advertising has in some hands reached the status of a science. It is based on fixed principles and is reasonably exact. The causes and effects have been analyzed until they are well understood. The correct methods of procedure have been proved and established. We know what is most effective, and we act on basic laws.[1]

Vance Packard (1957)
In *The Hidden Persuaders* (1957), Vance Packard contends that advertising is such an advanced science that it can direct the destiny of people's lives through producing subconscious thought control.

To most active advertising practitioners today: The "noise level" of advertising, even in many lesser developed world markets, has become so great that it is almost impossible to attract the attention of consumers—and, if one can catch the eye of a public, it is a real problem to organize a communication that is sufficiently persuasive and creditable to sell a product.

[1] Claude Hopkins, *Scientific Marketing* (New York: Lord & Thomas, 1923), p. 1.

To designate advertising as even a pseudoscience might be to exaggerate. Proclaiming that all truly great advertising was the brainchild inspiration of unencumbered creative minds can be an equal exaggeration. The true explanation lies somewhere in between. Of greater importance is an element that too often goes unnoticed: Behind every truly great and successful advertising campaign was an advertiser who could identify the problem, establish a well-targeted advertising goal, and *recognize a truly great advertising concept when presented with it.*

Too often the advertiser is a businessperson, schooled in direct and concise communications. He or she fails to recognize a well-calculated oblique approach designed to disarm consumers' suspicions and defenses. The result is that many advertising agencies still have some of their greatest creative products on the shelf because clients did not recognize *the good idea.* But it is also the shrewd advertiser who can sort out the clever, contrived, gimmicky approach from the effective *different* approach.

Normally, the development of an advertising theme or creative concept is considered to be the responsibility of the advertising agency — and rightfully so, under the normal conditions of a one-on-one situation between the advertising agency and the advertiser/client. But this discussion is directed to the methods of the advertiser's management of multinational markets and many different agencies. It would be self-defeating for the client (the home office or headquarters) to allow every national agency to succeed or fail without becoming sufficiently involved to aid in contributing to each agency's success.

The national (or local) advertiser, which in our context is a subsidiary company of a multinational corporation, represents to his local agency a two-headed client . . . the performance of this agency must be acceptable to his local client and his client's headquarters management. To what extent the "two clients" come into the picture will depend upon the amount of central advertising control required by the parent corporation. The greater the amount of central control required, the more the headquarters of the advertiser should support the local agency in aiding it in servicing the account. The local agency needs to understand the corporation's policy; goals; long-range objectives; and, in effect, all of the taboos and requirements for the style of advertising *acceptable* to the headquarters management. At the same time, the home office must keep an open mind that will recognize a local stroke of genius that does not fit its pattern.

—— THE HEADQUARTERS ROLE IN DEVELOPING —— CREATIVE CONCEPTS

The role of multinational corporation headquarters in developing international creative concepts is a critical and important "tightrope-walking act," to say the least. It often requires some critical personal evaluation and self-adjustment by decision makers at headquarters to avoid overdirecting while still maintaining their enthusiasm. The ideal role is one that involves sufficient input to effectively add the catalytic ingredients that aid in blending corporate requirements and local marketing goals.

It requires more than just being a catalyst, of course, as it also requires the ability to constantly and consistently apply the basic principles of advertising appropriate to each situation. The international advertising manager needs to apply knowledge of corporate requirements and to stay updated on the advertising and marketing situations in the market(s) under consideration. Finally, this home office decision maker needs to apply all of these skills with a subtlety of an effective teacher rather than acting as a line autocrat. The home office–local market relationship is sensitive at best, and it is essential to maintain rapport as well as line authority.

—— ORGANIZING MULTIMARKET ADVERTISING —— STRATEGIES (CREATIVE)

How actively should the MNC headquarters (a management company) be involved in the development of a creative advertising strategy to be used by an operating subsidiary (the actual advertiser)? The very least involvement that could be expected from headquarters would be to supervise and monitor the procedure used by local subsidiaries in developing their creative approaches. This involves the formal preparation of planning materials by both the local subsidiary advertising/marketing executives and the local agencies. In answer to any whys, it must be remembered that the international advertising manager may be responsible for the MNC's advertising efforts in 30+ countries. This executive must be certain that company standards and policies are maintained and that the locals' promotional objectives/strategies are consistent with those of the home office. Further, the monitoring should be sufficient for headquarters to be in the picture so that it may intelligently critique the resulting recommendations. The checklist below should prove helpful (and indicates what should be formally written and forwarded to the home office for review).

—— ANALYTICAL GUIDE FOR MONITORING —— ADVERTISING CREATIVE DEVELOPMENT

1. *The Marketing Strategy*
   To protect the work entered into by a local advertising group (advertiser and agency), the international advertising manager must make certain that the local marketing strategy is explicit regarding the role advertising is to play. The marketing strategy should nominate specific products to be advertised, the primary benefits and features to be exploited, the current marketing profile related to each prod-

uct, and the *goals* advertising is expected to achieve. In particular, a system also needs to be developed to ensure that the company's local efforts begin in the right direction.

2. *The Advertising Goals and Strategies*

The advertising goals and strategies should be analyzed to determine how well the advertising department understood and translated their responsibility to support the marketing strategy. Since the advertising program is the "how to" performance for reaching assigned goals, it should specify the following:

a. Individual projects involved, assigning responsibility and production schedule (preferably using a critical-path schematic to diagram the time span and relationship of one project to another).

b. *The agency brief* (specifications to advertising agency). Depending on the division of work responsibilities assigned between the agency and local advertising department, it is reasonable to assume that all advertising requirements will not be performed by the advertising agency.

The agency brief can take many forms depending on the nature of the campaign required. For example, the brief can be "exploratory"—requesting the agency to study a broad but well-defined problem. The objective in this case is for the agency to submit ideas for an original strategy approach. After this submission (and approval) would come a second brief, similar to that prepared for the continuance of an ongoing campaign. It would specify the number of different kinds of print ads and TV commercials, and it would possibly specify related collateral promotion materials.

Specifications for all work should relate to the overall time schedule, or critical-path schematic.

While a brief should be specific, it *should not* write the copy or design the campaign. Plenty of latitude should be left for the agency to use its "creative genius" and to improvise on the plan. Always stay open and receptive to a better idea—but insist that original instructions are always carried out as well.

c. *Goals should be aggressive yet obtainable.* When developing the promotional effort at the local level, it is important to remember that markets' current levels of attainment affect the firm's ability to reach its communications target.

3. *Agency Response to Brief*

The third document of significance will be the agency response to its written brief. This will usually be in the form of an agency "call report" . . . playing back the instructions as it interprets them, reassigning the various segments within its organizations, and setting up deadlines for each element in order to arrive at an agreed-on client presentation date.

The "call reports" from agencies handling local subsidiary advertising are a vital source of information to head office advertising (see Chapter 6). The "call report" confirms the quality of communications between client and agency.

In this case, one should look for two elements: (a) Did the agency correctly interpret the instructions it received? (b) Did the agency note that information or further action is required from its client before it can complete its assignment? Too often clients do not take their responsibility too seriously, and this can lead to later breakdowns in the overall plan.

Call reports need to be clear and concise. This is the first test of communications synchronization. If the advertiser is not completely satisfied that his or her instructions are well understood and the problem well defined, the result could be a brilliant creative answer to the wrong problem and/or end up with mutual embarrassment over resulting costs.

When the firm is dealing with smaller local agencies in some overseas markets, especially in developing countries, it must recognize that the agencies may not be aware of the need for such reports. It is essential that this planning stage be completed in order to eliminate the sort of confusion that could wreck the entire campaign.

4. *Review of Creative Presentation*
    Since the home office is simply directing by monitoring progress, the review of a locally accepted creative presentation is the *only* opportunity headquarters will normally have for their input. The headquarters decision makers, essentially the international advertising manager and staff, will need to ask themselves such questions as:
    a. Does this campaign meet corporate standards for quality of advertising?
    b. Does it conform to corporate policy in its identification of brand and company?
    c. Is the brand positioning consistent with local and home office long-range marketing plans?
    d. Is it indeed a campaign? Is it a format that can perpetuate itself over a long enough period to create a desired product (or service) image? Or is it just a clever ad idea?
    e. Has the campaign been satisfactorily consumer-tested to indicate positive strength in communications?
    f. Is the anticipated consumer result sufficient to approve the required investment?

This is not to say that a campaign presented to headquarters by a foreign subsidiary company can only be second-guessed on the basis of a value judgment. An experienced international headquarters can establish norms and minimum performance requirements based on the six questions (Review of

Creative Presentation). These requirements can provide reasonable assurance for success in advertising products and services that remain fairly unchanged for long periods of time.

—— Corporate Involvement in the Local Creative Process ——

Few advertised products and services, though unchanged in themselves, really experience an unchanging market. One can rationalize that life insurance has not changed, that an airline still flies passengers, that gasoline is gasoline—and that Coca-Cola has been the same soft drink for generations. Why should the advertising change?

Yurtle the Turtle was master of all he surveyed. But, being a turtle, he couldn't see very far. The international headquarters needs to be the corporate window on the world, a center for collecting and analyzing performance data of the total corporate and competitive activity. The international advertising manager, like all international marketing executives, is in the unique position to use the experience of each national market for the assistance of all national markets. An international headquarters could produce *less* than a minimum contribution if it merely sat in judgment over the efforts of subsidiary companies. Executive *leadership* and middle management *push* from an international headquarters group should be critical inputs into a dynamic international marketing system. Certainly advertising, the most conspicuous of marketing tools, should contribute heavily to the overall dynamics.

Before we discuss methods for a constructive contribution by multinational headquarters, it is important to add a remark on the obvious—occupying a desk at headquarters does not automatically make an international advertising expert. One must bring to this job not only a thorough working knowledge of advertising but also an open mind capable and willing to use the world as a classroom for learning the peculiarities of advertising in different world markets as well as a capacity for absorbing his or her own corporation's long-range marketing objectives and aspirations. The international advertising manager must know in advance that his or her opinions often become decisions and must be supportable.

Stimulating a corporate marketing program, and keeping it vital and progressive, means constantly updating one's understanding of the dynamics of change that surround these markets. A corporate manager must provide direction based on a creditable understanding of existing conditions. Internally, the uniformity of product or service offered—and externally, the similarity of markets advertised in—establish *how* an international corporation should approach involvement.

Involvement here is used to imply *help* and *assistance*, not only to an operating subsidiary company, but, at the same time, to the corporation as a whole.

——— WHAT IS BEST FOR THE CORPORATION IN ———
DIFFERENT SITUATIONS?

1. A new product is developed especially for the Australian market. The Australian company has had little success in developing a campaign that corporate headquarters will accept. Logic says that headquarters involvement is needed in Australia, that is, assistance for a single local market.
2. A new product will be introduced in all European markets. For this type of product, all European consumer markets react similarly. Logic would dictate a Pan-European campaign under headquarters supervision.
3. A worldwide airline plans to introduce a new type of service on a new type of aircraft. Logic suggests one international campaign out of headquarters.

Since one man's logic is another man's paradox, it would be impossible to consider all the exceptions that might be introduced into any general example. Therefore, we will look at three general situations calling for a corporate headquarters to participate in the creative development of subsidiary advertising.

Assisting One Market. This requires no special organizational technique. It merely amounts to adding additional creative talent, a fresh and objective point of view, and the broad experience learned from developing campaigns for similar products in many parts of the world. This experience, combined with the local management's knowledge of the local people in the local market, should add greater leverage in solving a problem. (The need for such involvement could be initiated either at headquarters or at the local level.)

On the surface it might appear that the level of involvement may be obvious, but it can have dimensions of greater depth, particularly as it affects the "psychology of management." The first example mentioned that the market, Australia, had thus far been unable to develop a campaign acceptable to headquarters. This does not automatically mean that the local agency's creative director or copywriter could not put together a decent advertising theme or campaign (although that might have been the case). Nor does it imply incompetence on the part of the subsidiary's advertising manager. The problem could be one of misunderstanding of corporate goals.

The first approach of home office advertising management at the local market (Australia) should be to review the marketing strategy and briefings documents that are part of any campaign submitted to the home office for approval. Such a review should involve everyone in the local company who manages or has approval responsibility for local advertising. While this review could take place at either headquarters or a regional site, in this instance it would preferably be held in Australia.

This is to retrace all the thinking that went into creating what became an unacceptable campaign. It is essential to ask questions of a local management: What was the quality of your input? Were your instructions correct, and were they clear? Here are some specific areas to explore:

1. Marketing strategy. Was the assignment given to advertising appropriate to advertising? Was the role for advertising clear and well defined? Were the goals more appropriate to retail advertising in Sydney, Melbourne, etc., rather than in a national product campaign?
2. Agency brief. Did the advertising manager properly interpret the marketing plan in the instructions given to the agency?

These points are rather academic and not difficult to determine by simply reading the documents. More in-depth analysis requires more discussion with local management.

3. By reading through all documents with the local management, it might be determined that while everyone was in general agreement on a plan, they did not agree with the plan as it was finally written — and had not been adequately involved in the final draft. (The author of the final draft may have been clever with words but not very communicative.)
4. Perhaps after seeing two or three earlier efforts by the agency, the entire direction became redirected without changing the written strategy.
5. A senior executive, who took no part in any marketing planning meetings, may now be giving ad hoc direction to the agency during presentations. (The local agency, of course, must respond to this local executive's directions.)
6. It is not unusual to find that, no matter what had been written down, two or more principal executives disagree among themselves as to what the creative execution should actually communicate.
7. The agency might have not understood the brief — though it is a good brief — or simply may not have been able to solve the problem.

The summary to this discussion should be obvious. No one from headquarters should descend on a local subsidiary company and start to create advertising for it. Doing so would create a never ending problem, that is, the local subsidiary and agency would always be looking over its shoulder. The international advertising director's (or his or her representative's) first job is to find out where the problem lies and to clear up any faulty lines of communication. If necessary, the home office executive should aid in developing new specifications that *everyone* agrees to and should help the locals start over again to develop a new campaign.

If the problems lie with the agency's ability to create an acceptable program, there are two choices: (a) if it is a local agency, challenge it to immediately strengthen its creative team—or hire a new agency; (b) if you are dealing with a single worldwide agency and this is its local subsidiary, call on the agency headquarters for additional help in this market.

Once headquarters advertising has involved itself in directing an advertising campaign for a local market, headquarters, of course, has accepted the responsibility for success. It is advisable to stay with the problem until it has a satisfactory conclusion . . . satisfactory to the local management and satisfactory to headquarters. Anything less will discredit headquarters advertising expertise and hinder some future problem solving.

A truly successful conclusion to such an exercise is when headquarters advertising management are able to subtly direct a local market to a successful solution to its own problem. When headquarters finds it necessary to take credit for the final campaign, then headquarters has failed—failed to train that market to successfully create its own campaigns in the future.

—— Directing Advertising Development ——
on a Regional Basis

If the entire European region (seven or eight countries) is to launch a new product simultaneously, a great many people from the sales and marketing functions will be involved. With regard to developing a Pan-European campaign, a first consideration will be to organize a joint advertising development committee that is thoroughly representative and yet manageable in size. The latter factor is essential for constructive deliberation. Also, it is important to remember that creative development for group markets requires about twice the working lead time as would a single market development process. Therefore, another consideration is to persuade each market to do its individual homework (marketing planning) much earlier than might otherwise be required.

Of course, corporate organizational structures differ widely, affecting corporate management policies and philosophies. We must set up a hypothetical operation in order to discuss the procedures. However, a firm's home office management would need to make their own substitutions and alterations to consider these procedures as applied to any *specific international company*. Now, let us make the following assumptions regarding our hypothetical company[2]:

1. Each of the firm's national markets is represented by a corporate-owned, locally constituted subsidiary operating company, i.e., separate profit center reporting to MNC headquarters.
2. Each subsidiary operation is independently staffed with a managing

[2] While it would make the example simpler, it would not be reasonable to assume that each subsidiary enjoys the same product market share or corporate image.

director, a marketing director, a sales manager, and an advertising manager; and each market has an advertising agency.

3. Each subsidiary is in control of its own advertising budget, once it is approved by headquarters.

For headquarters to organize the development a Pan-European campaign, every effort should be made to involve the advertising and marketing people from all the European markets. Again, headquarters should endeavor to function primarily as a catalyst to unite and stimulate these national markets to create their *own* campaign within the parameters and guidelines established by the corporate home office.

If we estimate that eight countries will be involved and that within each country about five management people have a responsibility for developing and executing the advertising program, we quickly have a committee of forty people—a committee much too large to function in a working group meeting. Therefore, it is the responsibility of headquarters advertising management to establish manageable groups, which give appropriate individual market representation and whose function will move the project efficiently toward a successful conclusion.

This outline for functional progression is general in content and is not intended to indicate that each step be a completely separate exercise or that it be done one step at a time. Several parts can be in process simultaneously, and some can be combined into one operation. It is merely a checklist to remind a corporate headquarters management of *all the elements* that need to be considered.

1. *Organize a Pan-European marketing plan.* Before moving to produce a Pan-European advertising campaign, it must be recognized that such a campaign needs direction. Actually, before a decision is made to produce such a campaign, headquarters should study the separate marketing plans of all the national markets involved. If feasible, it would be helpful to produce a Pan-European marketing plan that is substantially common—takes the common ingredients—from each national market involved.

   Direction of this project requires considerable depth of experience regarding these markets in order to determine the value and importance of the total contents of each marketing program. Vague or ambiguous statements may need clarifying but, most important, the individual contents will likely be framed in various kinds of statements if for no other reason than that of the different forms of English used by various nationalities (where English is the second language). This may cause many plans to appear to be quite different when in fact there might be great similarity among them. The frame of reference and terminology may be the only difference. To be able to proceed will require obtaining affirmative answers to these questions:

  a. Is there sufficient commonality to combine all marketing plans into one?
  b. If real and important differences between markets do exist, can they be handled as workable exceptions within the context of a Pan-European advertising campaign? Is it possible that a market such as that of England or of Sweden might present problems separate from the other Western European group? They can be an exception.
2. *Developing a Pan-European advertising strategy.* The development of a Pan-European campaign should be done under the direction of corporate headquarters, because it represents a concerned, mutual, and objective management. A situation should not exist that permits the end result to be considered as "too German" or "too British." It must represent the corporation objectively. With this in mind, then, it is the responsibility of headquarters advertising management to prepare an advertising strategy that supports the marketing strategy of Step 1. (For example, see the Henkel and Texas Instruments cases that are presented in this chapter.)
3. *Home office initiative to begin the campaign development process.* Initiating advertising creative development involves the advertising agencies serving the countries involved—and possibly the agency serving the headquarters.
  a. If all local agencies involved are part of the same agency company, there exists more latitude and flexibility to bring the agencies into a group creative development project. In fact, the corporate headquarters can establish a counterpart management function at the agency company's headquarters office so that both agency and advertiser can pull together a strong team operation.

       The new Pan-European advertising strategy becomes an agency brief that can be used by all agency offices for simultaneous creative development. The various agency offices can interchange ideas and materials; they can consult one another on their client's behalf toward pulling together a uniform creative recommendation.
  b. If each subsidiary company uses an agency that is independent of the agencies employed by all other subsidiaries, it is advisable for the MNC headquarters to take a much more involved role of working closely with each corporate subsidiary and its agency independently—or to confine the creative development work to its own headquarters agency. Group meetings will need to be confined to the firm's own advertising people.

The regional development, such as a Pan-European campaign, involves each country in making a contribution to the advertising strategy brief—and offering its ideas to the European group. Such a project can become either a cooperative and effective group effort that increases the creative talent applied to the problem or a competition between countries in which some people win their points and some must lose.

Even though the ultimate corporate objective is the strongest, most effective campaign for all of Europe, the central corporate director for developing this project does indeed have a very real psychological matter to deal with to keep all the people involved working together cooperatively and to avoid an intermarket competition that can destroy the spirit needed for success.

Every agency, whether a part of a network serving the same client or independent of that client's other agencies, must consider its local client as its most important customer. Pride of authorship and confidence in its own creative abilities prevent it from willingly accepting another agency's work as being superior to its own. And, it can not only condition its local client to expect failure if it accepts another agency's work—it can help to assure it.[3]

——— THE HENKEL *Fa* CAMPAIGN ———

In recent years Henkel Company has employed a Pan-European campaign designed to make its brand *Fa* synonymous with "freshness." The firm's basic campaign elements were:

- girl
- water
- limes
- exotic

as it sought to position *Fa* as ". . . the freshest body care line."

However, an image study conducted in Western Europe in 1979 suggested that the firm had certain problems. In particular, the findings indicated a:

- loss of absolute dominance in the *Fa*-created "freshness" segment,
- diminished consumers' identification with the brand,

- insufficient product differentiation, and
- insufficient cosmetic appeal.

In order to revitalize and reemphasize *Fa*'s "freshness," the company launched its new campaign in 1980. As shown in the accompanying *Fa* advertisements (Illustration 3–1), the campaign showed attractive girls in island surroundings . . . again using the earlier elements long associated with the brand. This more modern or upbeat style, especially capitalizing on changing European attitudes towards sexuality, was used throughout Western Europe. (In some markets, the girls were topless, while in others they were not.)

The Caribbean campaign was designed to more deeply integrate the *particular product* into the copy/visual; give the girl more personality (extroverted); use the ocean to increase the importance of "fresh-

---

[3] It is essential, therefore, to convince the local agency that the broader company campaign is not necessarily *better* than one they might develop, but rather one that has a broader, total market application.

— ILLUSTRATION 3-1 —
Four Examples of the Henkel *Fa* Pan-European Campaign

Source: The authors wish to acknowledge the cooperation of Mr. Uwe Hofer, Troost, Campbell-Ewald, Dusseldorf, for the Henkel materials.

ness"; and de-emphasize the attention earlier given to *lime*. Subsequently, testing indicated the firm had repositioned its product back to its original high "freshness" recognition in its various European markets.

It should be emphasized that with the exception of the "topless or not" artwork, the same basic campaign was used throughout the Continent. The media em-ployed varied by market, especially because television is unavailable in some markets. Major emphasis was given to consumer magazines which for example, featured such publications as *Elle, Femme d'aujourd'hui, Marie Claire* and *Mode de Paris* in France. (Henkel has employed such a standarized advertising approach in its European communications since 1968.)

───── TEXAS INSTRUMENTS PAN-EUROPEAN CAMPAIGN ─────

In September 1981, Texas Instruments' (TI) European Consumer Division launched a "Back to School" Pan-European campaign in 14 countries for its hand-held calculators. The following is the case history of the campaign presented from the perspective of the TI's international advertising agency (McCann-Erikson International, London). (The finished advertisements that were run in Britain, Denmark and Finland are presented in Illustrations 3–2A and 3–2B and reflect the standardized nature of this carefully coordinated product campaign.)

Client

Texas Instruments European Consumer Division Hand-held Calculators

Brief

1. Conduct a Pan-European campaign timed to begin with "Back to School" time in 14 countries.
2. Give the campaign a family look to increase each unit's contribution to a brand leader image.

Marketplace Strictures

1. Some countries supply calculators to students free of charge, therefore, target audience changes from students/parents to government/educational authorities.
2. "Back to School" times vary by as much as three months across Europe.
3. The product range is not constant across all countries.
4. Market position for TI varies, by market, from number one to almost nonexistent.

Advertising Response

1. Construct a "modular" campaign, built around a constant "frame" (layout format, typeface, signature position) with which each country would slot photographs and copy of the calculator(s) that its marketing sales plan demanded.

   Part of this exercise was a search for a line that could be used either as an introduction or as a sign-off. This line had to be applicable to the entire range of TI calculators from the simplest 5-function "adding machines" up to and including

— ILLUSTRATION 3–2 A —
The British Version of the Texas Instruments Limited Pan-European Campaign

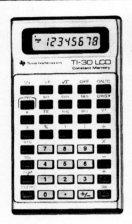   

— ILLUSTRATION 3-2 B —
The Danish (top) and Finnish Versions of the Texas Instruments Limited Pan-European Campaign

the sophisticated programmable calculators which are not very far from being mini-computers.

In addition, because of the differences in target audiences, the ideal line also had to be capable of adaptation to them without losing its basic meaning or relevance.

2. Direct this campaign in print media designed to reach:

- students
- parents
- educational authorities

depending on individual market situations.

3. Creative execution—the campaign theme line that was judged most satisfactory in answering all of the conditions listed above, was "We'll help you do better"—in the case of parents or educators, the relatively minor change to "We'll help them do better" accomplished both the objective of retaining the "family look" and of changing the beneficiary of our "do better" claim from "you" to "them." The claim itself says all there is to say about calculators or, for that matter, about any tool that has ever been invented. It will help you do better. Whether "it" is an abacus, a calculator, or the most sophisticated computer—its only reason for being is to help someone "do better."

The layout format was designed to make the machines as visible as possible with the headline and text being placed around them and the Texas Instruments logo in a prominent but not obtrusive position.

Results*

It is too early to give final results, since the campaign has been running only a few months in most countries. However, from trade sources it is felt that the Texas Instruments range of calculators has been made more visible than ever before, and the campaign is generating considerable comment from the marketplace and within the Texas Instruments organization. The next big test will come during the Christmas buying season—another seasonal peak in calculator sales.

*Authors' Note. At the time of this book's publication deadline, a complete report on the advertising campaign's success was unavailable. However, as indicated by the agency spokesman, the early results were viewed very favorably.

If the headquarters of an international agency will work in concert with the client's headquarters to integrate the entire campaign's creative development process, an acceptable result can be achieved. There should seldom be one obvious creative "author" of the concepts presented for consideration.

4. *The decision-making process for evaluating candidate creative ideas.* The home office management are now in control of creative development. They can elect to:
   a. Consider they have all the input necessary from subsidiary companies and proceed to final development of a campaign for multimarket consumer testing; or to implementing a campaign without intermediate testing.

b. Continue multimarket involvement by presenting the candidate concepts to the marketing and advertising people of all, or several important, European markets.

The purpose here is to eliminate candidate ideas and to agree on the two or three creative concepts that appear to be strongest on marketing target and most unique for attracting attention for persuasive communication. Then, by all means, these concepts should be put to consumer pretest.

Words like "concept," "execution," and "format" sometimes become confused because they are used interchangeably in multilingual settings. The word *concept* usually refers to the selling argument, or reason-to-buy idea, that is proposed as the theme for an advertising campaign. It is a statement, not necessarily advertising copy, it may or may not also have a photo or rough illustration if the statement requires it.

Concepts for a soft drink might read:

- a soft drink that is sparkling, refreshing, and *thirst-quenching*
- a soft drink with *natural fruit flavor*
- a soft drink that is refreshing and has *no calories*
- a soft drink that is *not too sweet* to drink *with food*

The advertiser wants to know which of the benefits of the product he or she should use for this advertising theme: thirst-quenching—natural fruit flavor—no calories—not too sweet with food.

Execution refers to how the agreed-on concept is developed into persuasive copy and properly illustrated to attract positive attention . . . the finished advertisement.

Format refers to the general style of the advertisement. Some international advertisers consider a format with proper corporate logotype all the uniformity necessary between markets.

In discussing advertising pretesting for this example of a Pan-European campaign, it is usually considered that all markets will test concepts (any concepts they choose) and then prepare an execution for the best concept. The execution supported by its concept test data would be the form in which each market should submit recommended candidate campaign ideas to the group. It will be left to the headquarters management to determine whether or not the original concept was valid—and whether the resulting research data do indeed support their choice of concept or support only a local management rationalization for a preselected concept idea. Objective thinking is sometimes difficult for people dominated by "gut-feel" decisions.

5. *The consumer pretest.* This step, on the surface, appears to be the easiest of all . . . simply order each market to put the approved campaign ideas to test. Actually, this is one step where the headquarters

should take complete charge, to (a) organize a very uniform test procedure and (b) take complete charge of analyzing the results—also in a uniform and objective way.

——— A Worldwide Pattern Campaign ———

We suggested that the third type of campaign development a headquarters international corporation might be concerned with (apart from single market assistance and regional development) is the worldwide pattern. An airline specifying advertising to introduce a new type of passenger service on a new type of aircraft will serve to illustrate this type of campaign.

The problem is simplified for illustration. There are no apparent national or regional differences, and we have suggested a service without traditional differences in consumer use. We are only concerned to find significant national differences and to find a creative strategy that communicates as universally as possible—and a creative proposal that will be acceptable within local advertising laws and other regulations. We have also suggested a specific assignment about which the home office would obviously have far more knowledge of the details involved than would foreign offices (airlines seldom set up overseas subsidiary companies).

Let us first examine the process from the standpoint of mechanical organization. The airline's international offices could identify some one hundred advertising locations, of which possibly ten would be considered "key markets." Therefore, we will start by working with the ten key markets. There are two types of information we must first bring together: (a) the new type of service and equipment known at the home office and (b) current corporate awareness and image data at key market locations. In the process of assembling this information, we will in effect be preparing the background to our advertising specification for the advertising agency.

Thought should be given to the organization of the investigating team formed to prepare these specifications. Different advertisers have specific reasons for circumscribing this activity:

1. *Confined to headquarters marketing.* Perhaps the overall marketing investigation process involves many more considerations than the information required for advertising. The advertising function will be given appropriate information when the market study is completed.
2. *Management personnel included.* The marketing group could include corporate advertising people and the advertising agency on the theory that the inspiration for a new campaign might come from any part of the marketing study, and that full background on all information obtained would contribute to the overall understanding of the problem.

3. *Advertising agency role.* The corporate marketing and advertising team could operate without advertising agency personnel with the understanding that the agency should consider the conclusion brief and not be burdened, or confused by information that is not appropriate to a specific problem that will be assigned to them.

We are, quite naturally, going to look at this example as it applies to determining specifications for developing an advertising campaign. We know what the new air service offers. What we don't know is which benefits will be most persuasive to potential customers.

To start the process of defining any marketing/advertising problem, it always sounds like an automatic statement to say, "Let's make a survey." This allows time for procrastination and avoids making decisions. Yes, we will need some survey work, but let us initiate some other efforts at the same time. This assumes that people involved are experienced in their work, that the problem is global, and that most of the input for a creative strategy will need to be initiated at headquarters.

Initial steps to be started simultaneously:

1. It is first necessary to prepare a creative specification agency brief for the headquarters advertising agency. Based on experience, this brief should contain all benefits and features (passenger-oriented) on the new service and equipment. Request the agency to prepare three or four experimental advertising approaches based on different primary benefits that have proven effective in the past.

2. Next, we need to request the agency to prepare two or three concept statements for each of the experimental approaches on which it is working. These concepts are to be evaluated with panel discussion focus groups in each of the ten key markets. This research would best be performed through the headquarter agency research facility, which can contract with an international market research company. Since the objective is to isolate an advertising concept, the agency should be best equipped to direct the process.

3. Finally, we need to prepare an information-gathering document to be sent to all local company managers in the one hundred foreign offices. The document should contain background information on the new service and equipment. All consumer benefits and features should be fully detailed. Attached should be a thorough questionnaire asking local managers for their opinions as to a specific list of possible customer reactions, and the degree of importance of each. Such a questionnaire should be thorough enough so that each question is framed in several different ways. This checks consistency of opinion as well as offering a vehicle for communicating back to headquarters some reassurance that responding managers did actually understand each question.

Final Steps for Completing the Pattern Campaign.   The result of this initial, three-part step can bring together a great deal of different kinds of exploratory work and worldwide opinion research at the same time.

Through a thorough distillation and analysis of this feedback, it should be possible to construct several candidate campaign executions for further evaluation. The feedback can also point to markets that have special problems that require individual attention. The new executions can now be sent to the ten key markets for a thorough consumer reaction study. The result of this final research should be evaluated only at headquarters according to procedures suggested in the section entitled "Directing Advertising Development on a Regional Basis," beginning on page 46 in this chapter.

In many respects, the development of a worldwide pattern campaign can be more direct, less expensive, and accomplished in less time than the cooperative development of a regional campaign. It would be impractical to work with one hundred markets in the same way one would with seven or eight. However, the result is not a worldwide campaign; rather, it is a *worldwide pattern campaign.* The implementation of the pattern still requires local transliteration to make certain that the intended communication does indeed communicate the intended message in terms that will be effectively understood in each country with the same strength of impact.

The implementation may require that someone from the home office agency (if a single agency organization exists) or members of the home office advertising group travel to many of these individual foreign offices to participate in the localizing effort to aid in restructuring the pattern so that it will be localized without losing its original selling strategy and pattern format.

Additional Considerations.   There will be obstacles beyond transliterating a theme campaign idea. Let us focus again on the airline mentioned at the start of this discussion:

1. *Economic factors.* What about international airline customers in many developing markets? Do we need to prepare our advertising in terms of the interest level of the average citizen if only the more wealthy, affluent, and business community represent the target market?
2. *National bias.* If ads contain illustrations or photos of people and surroundings, do we relate better with a public by using local models in local surroundings? The Heathrow Airport in London may not suggest a reality to people living in Djakarta.
3. *Legal (or advertising industry) requirements.* If television is to be used in the campaign, it is necessary to take into account that many nations forbid the use of film that is not produced in the local country (or produced by its own citizens in other locations). *Example:* Malaysia requires all television commercials to be filmed in Malaysia. The surroundings must be *typically* Malaysian. All people in commercials must not only be Malaysian but, in the opinion of the television ap-

proval board, must *look typically* Malaysian. To reach the broadest influential market, the advertiser must transliterate his message to be effective in the three local languages—Malaysian, Chinese, and English— i.e. a *content* rather than a *literal* translation.

All of these factors must be considered at the outset *and* reviewed at each stage of the pattern development.

4. *Industrial exception.* As we have noted—and will continue to note throughout the book—industrial advertising often is almost exclusively handled from the home office. This is dictated by many factors, including the nature of the buyer, the similarity in worldwide product usage, the type of foreign sales representation, and budgetary considerations. An example of directing overseas advertising from a domestic base is provided by Cessna Aircraft Company (see accompanying case history).

——— CESSNA AIRCRAFT CORPORATION ———

While many multinational firms, including Goodyear International, have extensive overseas facilities and marketing operations to provide *controls*, Cessna Aircraft maintains a uniform corporate image in an international organization composed of dealers, distributors, and Cessna Pilot Centers (CPCs). Through a careful system of annual distributor inputs (audit) to its Wichita headquarters, Cessna is able to recognize local national needs in its planning process. These are incorporated along with sales department data in its primary plans for the fiscal year.

As shown in Illustration 3-4, there are three planning phases prior to providing the company's final directions to its agency. In the first phase, the distributor and sales department inputs are considered when management establishes its primary and secondary goals for the year and does some preliminary budgeting.

Country priorities (and accompanying product mix goals) are established during Phase II. Further, a competitive analysis is incorporated into this planning stage.

In Phase III the advertising agency becomes involved, and the initial *creative* efforts are implemented. Here a single marketing theme is introduced ... along with the program designed to introduce the new model line. Final recommendations and changes in the total campaign are incorporated during Phase IV prior to the final ... *implementation* ... stage.

In Stage V Cessna's agency places the advertisements in the more than sixty business-related publications in which the company advertises overseas. This program is directed to three distinct target markets: aviation, agriculture, and general business. In addition to the journal advertisements, the home office prepares brochures for overseas distribution and directs its cooperative advertising campaign through its distributors. Again, procedures are employed to ensure that the latter conform to the overall corporate annual theme. (An example of recent Cessna campaigns in both English and translations is shown in Illustrations 3-3 A, B, and C.)

The end result is an umbrella campaign

Die Cessna Golden Eagle.

Die Reichweite, die Geschwindigkeit und der Komfort eines Turboprops — zur Hälfte der Kosten

Cessna baut mehr Geschäftsflugzeuge mit Druckkabine als jeder andere Hersteller. Und das Flaggschiff unserer druckbelüfteten Kolbenmotor-Flotte ist die herausragende 421 Golden Eagle. Sie ist einzig in ihren Leistungen unter den Kolbenmotor-Twins auf dem Markt und übertrifft auch noch einige vergleichbare Turboprops.

Die Golden Eagle ist der bisherige Höhepunkt in der Entwicklung von Twins mit Kolben-Triebwerken. Sie ist die leiseste, repräsentativste und leistungsfähigste verfügbare Cessna Kolbenmotor-Twin, und was keineswegs überrascht, das meistverkaufte Flugzeug ihrer Klasse. Es gibt keinen anderen Kolbenmotor-Twin, der schneller abhebt, schneller steigt und höher, schneller und weiter als die Golden Eagle fliegt. Und kein anderer Twin dieser Klasse kann sich mit dem leisen, erholsamen Geräuschpegel in der Kabine messen. Ein ideales Geschäftsflugzeug: Angenehm,

leise, geräumig, geschmackvoll und komfortabel. Die druckbelüftete Golden Eagle bietet 8 Personen Platz, fliegt mit einer Reisegeschwindigkeit von bis zu 258 Knoten (477 km/h) und erreicht eine maximale Reichweite von 1.107 NM (2050 km).

Leistungen dieser Art gehören bereits in die Klasse der Turboprops. Die Golden Eagle

erreicht sie mit einer Kraftstoff-Ersparnis von mehr als 40 Prozent, was bereits ausreichen kann, die sonstigen monatlichen Kosten zu decken.

Die Golden Eagle ist schnell, wirtschaftlich im Kraftstoff-Verbrauch, leise und — mit ihrem „first class"-Kabinenkomfort — luxuriös.

BEVOR SIE EIN FLUGZEUG KAUFEN, FLIEGEN SIE CESSNA. Informieren Sie sich persönlich, wie Ihnen Cessna, The World's Number 1 Business Airline, helfen kann, der Konkurrenz voraus zu sein. Für weitere Informationen wenden Sie sich bitte an

Der Konkurrenz voraus sein.

FLY CESSNA
The World's Number 1 Business Airline

Cessna Aircraft Company, Dept. E02C,
European Marketing Center, Aéroport
National de Bruxelles, B.P. 2,
Zaventem, Belgien,
Telex: 846-22502
Telefon: 7 51 81 10 / 15 / 16 / 17

Österreich
Oefag Österreich
A-5021 Salzburg-Flughafen
Tel.: 00 / 43 / 62 22 / 4 35 36
Tlx.: 63 773

Deutschland
Atlas Air Service GmbH
Atlas Airfield
Tel.: 00 / 49 / 42 22 / 20 47 oder 48
Tlx.: 249 221

E. F. G. Röder
Egelsbach Flugplatz
Tel.: 00 / 49 / 61 03 / 41 31-5
Tlx.: 415 023

Rheinland Air Service GmbH
Airport: Düsseldorf
Tel.: 00 / 49 / 2 11 / 4 21 66 21

— **ILLUSTRATION 3–3 A, B, and C** —
(continued)

The Cessna Propjets.
Compared to other turboprops, they look fantastic.
Compared to some business jets, they look great.

See the Corsair on display at the Paris Airshow, June 5th–14th.

Our Conquest and Corsair are the most sophisticated, cost-efficient propjets available today. *No* other propjet can match the Conquest's superlative performance. And *no* competitive propjet can match the Corsair's overall operating economy.

The Conquest is quite simply the finest propjet ever made. It sets the standards for the entire turboprop market; it outperforms some business jets as well. No turbine-powered airplane in the world is more fuel-efficient. And, from 31,000 feet to a certified service ceiling of 35,000 feet, it outpaces its competitors in speed while consuming less fuel.

The Conquest's high-aspect ratio wing delivers outstanding climb performance, making it possible to cruise at high, fuel-efficient altitudes even on short flights. There isn't a turboprop or small jet on the market that's able to equal the Conquest's combination of speed, fuel efficiency and luxury for eleven people and their luggage.

The new Corsair offers many of the same features found on the Conquest at an extremely affordable price. It's an ideal way for owners of cabin-class piston twins to step up

to turboprop reliability and efficiency. It carries six to eight people and luggage, quickly and luxuriously. And Corsair has the climb-to-altitude performance to let you take advantage of high-altitude turboprop efficiency even on short 200- to 300-mile trips.

BEFORE YOU BUY, FLY CESSNA. Find out why The World's Number 1 Business Airline always gives you the competitive advantage. For more information, write to Cessna Aircraft Company, Dept. K30M, European Marketing Centre, Brussels National Airport, Post Box No. 2, Zaventum, Belgium. Telex: 846-22502. Telephone: 7518110/15/16/17. Or contact one of the Cessna Dealers listed in this ad.

Get the competitive edge.
FLY CESSNA
The World's Number 1 Business Airline

IN AUSTRIA	IN ENGLAND	IN FRANCE	IN GERMANY	IN SWEDEN
Oefag Oesterr	Northair Aviation Ltd.	Fenwick Aviation S.A.	Atlas Air Service GmbH	Swedair A.B.
A-5021 Salzburg-Flughafen	Leeds/Bradford Airport	Aérodrome de Toussus le Noble	Atlas Airfield	Bromma Airport
Tel: airport-00/43/6222/43536	Tel: 00/44/532/50.22.51-2-3	Tel: 00/33/3/9568050	Tel: 00/49/4222/2047 or 48	Tel: 00/46/8/98.19.50
Tlx: 63773		Tlx: 696645	Tlx: 249221	Tlx: 19944

IN BELGIUM
Abelag Aviation S.A.
Airport: Brussels National
Tel. 751-80-78
Tlx: 24833

IN FINLAND
Finnaviation OY, Sf-01531
Malmi Airport
Tel: 00/358/0/82.11.33
Tlx: 122635 & 122659

Reprinted with the permission of Cessna Aircraft Company.

— ILLUSTRATION 3-3, A, B, and C —
(continued)

Le Cessna Corsair sera exposé au Salon du Bourget, du 5 au 14 juin.

Les *Cessna* Propjets.
Comparés aux autres biturbopropulseurs, ils sont stupéfiants et étonnants comparés à nombre de biréacteurs

Les Cessna Conquest et Corsair sont si radicalement différents, par leur haut niveau de performances, des biturbopropulseurs actuels, qu'il a fallu, pour les désigner, inventer un néologisme : « Propjet ».

Le Conquest est tout simplement le meilleur biturbopropulseur du marché mondial. Non seulement il a établi de nouveaux records de performances pour les avions de cette catégorie, mais il surpasse encore celles de nombre de biréacteurs d'affaires. Avec un plafond pratique de 35 000 pieds — 10 700 mètres ! — il vole en effet plus vite et, grâce à son rendement énergétique élevé, tout en consommant considérablement moins que n'importe quel biturbopropulseur concurrent.

Son grand allongement lui confère par ailleurs une exceptionnelle vitesse ascensionnelle qui autorise, même pour des trajets courts, l'économie de carburant du vol à haute altitude. Et vous ne trouverez pas sur le marché d'autre biturbopropulseur ou de jet de bas de gamme qui puisse vous offrir la même imbattable combinaison de vitesse, sobriété opérationnelle et confort luxueux pour onze personnes et leurs bagages.

Le nouveau mais déjà célèbre Corsair intègre la plupart de ces caractéristiques à un prix particulièrement abordable. C'est l'avion de transition entre le bimoteur à piston et le biturbopropulseur sophistiqué. Il transporte de six à huit personnes et jusqu'à 500 kg de bagages, plus vite et plus confortablement que ses rivaux. Sa vitesse ascensionnelle élevée lui permet également le vol aux hautes altitudes économiques, même sur des trajets courts de quatre à six cents kilomètres.

AVANT D'ACHETER UN AVION, ESSAYEZ D'ABORD UN PROPJET ! Vous y gagnerez de découvrir ce qui nous autorise à dire que Cessna vous en donne plus, à un prix compétitif.

Prenez de l'avance sur vos concurrents
FLY CESSNA
The World's Number 1 Business Airline

Pour renseignements complémentaires, adressez-vous à Cessna Aircraft Company Dept D12M, Lucien Tiélès, Aérodrome de Toussus-le-Noble, 78530 Buc - Tél. : (3) 956.26.46 - Télex : 696973 CESFRA.

EN AUTRICHE
Oefag Oesterr
A-5021 Salzburg-Flughafen
Tél. : aer. : 43 (6222) 43536
Tlx : 63773

EN BELGIQUE
Abelag Aviation
Aéroport de Bruxelles National
1930 Zaventem
Tél : 32 (2) 751.80.78

EN GRANDE-BRETAGNE
Northair Aviation Ltd
Leeds/Bradford Airport
Tél. : 44 (532) 50.22.51-2-3

EN FINLANDE
Finnaviation OY. Sf-01531
Malmi Airport
Tél. : 358 (0) 82.11.33
Tlx : 122635 & 122659

EN FRANCE
Fenwick Aviation
Aérodrome de Toussus-le-Noble
78530 Buc
Tél. : 33 (3). 956.80.50
Tlx : 696645

EN RFA
Atlas Air Service GmbH
Atlas Airfield
Tél. : 49 (4222) 2047 ou 48
Tlx : 249221

EN SUÈDE
Swedair A.B.
Bromma Airport
Tél. : 46 (8) 98.19.50
Tlx : 19944

Reprinted with the permission of Cessna Aircraft Company.

— ILLUSTRATION 3-4 —
Cessna Annual Planning Steps

Phase I	Foreign distributor Sales Personnel Home office	Annual goals/ preliminary budget
Phase II	Internal planners (home office)	Establishment of basic product/ country priorities
Phase III	Internal planners Agency involvement	Basic theme on corporate priorities
Phase IV	Agency preparation Home office approval	All phases of campaign
Phase V	Agency implementation/ Home office controls	Media placement, sales materials, and co-op advertising

directed from its home office that gives Cessna a *worldwide face* to its multiple publics and a high measure of *control*. It should be noted that the company retains budget approval and places the bulk of its overseas media communications directly through its United States-based agency.

——— Summary—Advertising Creative Strategy ———

We started this chapter by implying that advertising is not yet a science or, perhaps better said, it should never become a science. Advertising is best treated as a dynamic creative experience always open to the open mind . . . a constant challenge in mass salesmanship in persuading potential customers to buy and to "outstrategize" competitors. There is no end to finding new ideas . . . nor is there any end as to how often proven ideas can be reclothed to work again and again. The latter is the point most often overlooked or disregarded.

The focus panel group device is often labeled "research" and is usually conducted by research people. However, it is not designed to prove or disprove anything—it is an investigative probe into "typical consumer" minds. Although it is often necessary to use advertising ideas to lead participants into a desired line of discussion, the objective is to find arguments and rationalizations that consumers offer themselves as purchase considerations for your kind of product.

Creative people should observe this action in process. It is not unlikely that some one participant could inadvertently "drop a line" in conversation that would unlock the entire problem of effectively communicating the most important solution to effective persuasion.

Creative people are seldom "inventors" . . . they are more often people with a unique depth of perception, capable of finding the obvious beyond the natural instincts of the normally subjective mind.

A department store advertising writer can simulate the focus panel group idea simply by becoming a counter clerk for a few days and noting down questions and areas of certain product interests as they occur—no formal question structure is needed.

We suggest campaign pretesting with target market consumer groups, but testing does not create ideas. Testing helps to ensure financial investment; it provides evidence of a reasonable chance for success. People evaluating test results should also learn to evaluate the quality of uniquely different creativity.

Two U.S. campaigns will serve to illustrate "creative adventures" that violated experience-taught rules for creating advertising. Each might never have been employed had not the company's unique position been recognized.

Volkswagen—"The Beetle"—sold ugly as beautiful; the car became an enormous success by the company's criticizing its own product's features. The campaign was laughed at by competitors before they realized its sales result. This negative selling provided the right rationalization at the right time in our social and cultural development to encourage people to buy a *new* second auto without appearing to be ostentatious to their friends and neighbors.

"Avis—We're Number 2" . . . so we must try harder. "We're Number 2!" Surely, Avis was number one at *something* that would make a more positive theme for advertising this large international car rental company. The real message was: You will like Avis because they say, "We Try Harder." The "Number 2" part was a disarming admission to gain creditability for their primary selling proposition—and to get attention.

The Avis theme really caught on and became themes for political campaigns, sales conferences, and even titles for church sermons—and "We try harder," also improvised to "I Try Harder" lapel buttons—were produced and distributed worldwide.

"We're Number 2" . . . is a negative approach that likely would not research too well as a way to create a positive idea . . . "We Try Harder." After the thought had been digested by a public, it worked.

Both campaigns were creative masterpieces; both required clients with a creative understanding.

——— The Psychological Block That Eliminates "Genius" ———

Too often advertisers want to go straight to the point like a boxer throwing punches . . . they want their advertising to say, "Buy my product because it is best." They forget their customers' point of view—and the fact that customers really do not want to buy their product—they want their problems solved and they want to be happier, healthier, and wealthier—as a result of giving up their money for any product. It might be said that the advertiser's real objective (to sell the product) is almost the opposite of the customers' objective. If the advertiser becomes more interested in selling aspirin than in curing headaches, he or she can develop another psychological block. This is an especially difficult concept to "sell" to foreign subsidiaries and agencies.

For many advertisers, it is impossible to specify an advertising campaign without suggesting that (a) the campaign must be different from the competition's ads and (b) the product should be presented in a new and unique way. The question is: Does this advertiser really mean it? Can the advertiser accept, and be confident about, a "different and unique" campaign? Or does the advertiser start changing everything to revert the advertising back to the way he or she has been accustomed to seeing it for many years? In other words, companies and industries often become stereotyped in their approach to communications. The same is true of the advertising agency where the same stereotyping occurs.

Compounding the problem of introducing an innovative and creative idea is that consumer research usually will prove that the advertiser was right. Consumers are also psychologically inclined to resist change—"they do not wish to deviate from the familiar." They are also accustomed to seeing certain kinds of products advertised in a certain manner, and at first exposure it is just human nature for them to reject a "different approach." The more unique a new idea appears to be, the more pretest research should be structured to probe consumers' reactions more thoroughly. This is more obvious in industrial advertising where acceptable parameters are more evident but is more critical and more difficult to detect in consumer product advertising.

In conclusion, this is not to recommend gimmicks and stunts to get attention at all costs. A new, unique idea must have a *valid relevant concept* and a calculated constructive objective. The point is that while sound professional market planning supported by clear and conclusive communications research is vital to developing a successful advertising campaign, the resulting campaign can be right on target while at the same time hitting the consumer from an unexpected angle. In fact, you should read pretest research so carefully that you are *not* blinded by the numbers.

These obstacles to new and unique ideas are very real for any single national company's advertising development, but they become far more difficult when analyzing campaigns created in foreign countries. Unique ideas come from a play on words of a particular language or an idiomatic colloquialism of a foreign culture. Keep creativity alive. Remember . . . take the time, have the patience to be "sold" on ideas when they can be explained . . . sometimes you may need to accept a strange-looking idea on faith alone.

—— 10 KEY POINTS ——

1. Developing the creative approach to a new advertising campaign is a delicate process to direct. To direct any activity there must be ground rules and parameters—for advertising creativity, keep a "loose rein" and spare the "whip" as long as possible.

2. The headquarters role is to set marketing product position but to avoid offering specifications in the form of predetermined solutions.

3. To avoid subjective critique analysis of recommended creative strategy, use a guide system that reviews all the steps toward developing that strategy. To analyze the end result without a review of the circumstances and input is to second-guess the solution without relating the solution to the problem.

4. Headquarters can offer its most constructive input by relating local problems to the broader worldwide picture of how a market is, and will be, developing—and also by contributing proven solutions from other markets that have experienced similar situations.

5. In general, there are some ways a headquarters can become involved in the creative advertising development for a multi-market international campaign—headquarters can:
   a. Work individually with each national market. This can be accomplished by (1) establishing critical stages of development for headquarters review and approval and (2) taking to an individual market pattern materials and/or additional creative talent and becoming directly involved in the process of finding the most effective creative strategy and execution.
   b. Organize and direct a regional group of markets toward their producing a regional creative strategy.

6. If the headquarters advertising manager elects to work individually with *each* national market, it increases his or her *direct* involvement. The advertising manager must
   a. establish critical stages of development for headquarters review and approval,
   b. take pattern materials and/or additional creative talent to an individual market, and
   c. become directly involved in the process of finding the most creative *strategy* and *execution.*

7. Headquarters employment of the regional approach to international advertising management necessitates the maintenance of a group creative atmosphere in order to achieve local subsidiary acceptance of the resulting campaign.

8. The regional approach has particularly strong support in Europe where an international marketer is involved with overlapping media—one market to another—and with a transnational mobile population.

9. Headquarters' use of the worldwide corporate pattern campaign approach involves surveying to gain information from worldwide markets and then creating a worldwide campaign that satisfies all the requirements of headquarters management. (Note: The resulting pattern will require adjusting to reach the highest form of efficiency in each market, unless headquarters wishes to enforce its use as a prototype to be translated and used.)

10. Both the regional and pattern approaches involve a large production cost savings to all markets involved, especially in art, photography, and most especially in TV filming costs.

4

Managing Worldwide Campaigns

— INTRODUCTION —

When one is asked to manage a business function that he or she cannot see or touch ... one that is actually being performed thousands of miles away from the spot where the management is to take place ... it requires initiative in innovative intercompany communications. It requires a system that permits the international advertising management to become *involved*.

Involvement is what this chapter is all about. It deals with:

- involvement in the advertising planning and development processes,
- involvement in the execution processes to a point of causing some degree of corporate image consolidation and to effect important overall cost savings,
- involvement to a point of making intelligent decisions, if one has such authority, or

- involvement to a point of being well enough informed to cause intelligent decision to be made by those with sufficient authority.

To emphasize the argument being presented, the lack of sufficient involvement leaves one only in a position to criticize what was done after the advertising has appeared—and after the monies have been invested. In some management functions this might not be too serious, but the nature of advertising makes all such mistakes and reversals *very public*.

Headquarters involvement in the management of worldwide campaigns should not be designed to cast all campaigns in the same mold, or necessarily to overdirect the input. Properly organized, the primary goals are to:

- direct planning toward support of the corporate marketing and image objectives
- pool a corporate universe of creative talent to the advantage of all
- effect corporate money savings through intermarket sharing of production expenses
- assure that the resulting advertising meets corporate standards

Recommendations to these ends will be discussed in the following context:

- strategic planning
- involvement/support of all corporate heads
- planning the campaign (seven steps through headquarters direction)
- headquarters office programmed into planning procedure

- creative cross-reference
- cost savings
- management of corporate image
- qualifying home management for overseas direction (seven basic areas)
- the programmed management approach (six-step approach)
- regional campaign development (Goodyear–Europe case history)

This chapter cuts through any debate regarding the relative merits between a single, uniform worldwide campaign and locally developed campaigns. Employing the programmed management approach makes any such question unnecessary. The results of this planning process answer the question of what type of campaign is best for the corporation and how much uniformity will be effective and practical.

To standardize or not to standardize is *not* the question. The question should be: How to cause the most effective advertising to be created? "Effective" here refers to several criteria. The primary criterion must, of course, be to develop advertising that aids in selling a product or service. However, the immediate, short-term objective should be supported by policy direction that concerns the long-term future of a corporation.

To a single national corporation, these matters are looked at daily in the normal routine of administering the business. Whether guiding policies are established as a formal written checklist reminder, or become fact by virtue of traditional inheritance maintained through a gradual attrition of executive management—the resulting advertising is understood as the shaper of markets and the molder of a corporate image.

To a multinational corporation, policies that characterize a successful corporate heritage need to be monitored more closely and expressed through a management system that will sustain the continuity of success at the ends of each far-flung tentacle of the operation. Such monitoring can either take place as input to the initial development of advertising done by each foreign subsidiary, or it can take the form of second-guessing/criticism of advertising that results from local initiative. To leave monitoring unattended is to invite corporate deterioration—to anticipate success by the odds of roulette and to ultimately assume a corporate profile of mediocrity, at best.

—— STRATEGIC PLANNING ——

The question as to whether a corporation should use a standardized uniform advertising campaign over all, or many, national market programs should be answered as a result of careful strategic planning. It should not be decided as a general operating policy beforehand. However, since such opportunities for uniform advertising strength and intermarket cross-fertilization of creative output do exist (and many firms have successfully followed such an approach), headquarters management should be involved in strategic planning.

Let us briefly review three reasons why advanced planning is necessary:

1. Each activity needs to be predetermined. When approaching multiple markets, the firm cannot afford *surprises*.
2. There must be clear agreements with regard to *authority*.
3. Each stage in the process must be correctly timed.

The first of these reasons may appear to be self-evident to most veteran advertising people. There simply are a myriad of activities that are involved in a single domestic (U.S.) campaign, ranging from the theme concept to the production work, from media buying/scheduling to the meeting of the various deadlines. Now, if one multiplies these activities by the number of foreign markets and then adds the communication delays that one *can anticipate*, the importance of preplanning is apparent.

Second, of course, is the matter of *authority* . . . over and above responsibility. Who, for example, has the authority to commit the firm to an agency agreement, an advertising pretest contract, or a TV production or magazine artwork "buy"? These decisions *and the proper* delegation (or retention) of authority by the home office must be made well in advance of the timing of these actions, most likely in the original determination of corporate policies regarding local or regional offices. Finally, the proper timing for the assignment and completion of each stage of the multinational campaign is a *must*. It is suggested that PERT-like (Program Evaluation Review Technique) precision is needed and that such an approach should be established. The MNC, for example, carefully plans the introduction of new products in its various subsidiaries, and complementary planning of advertising programs is essential.

—— INVOLVEMENT/SUPPORT OF —— ALL CORPORATE LEVELS

The hugeness and complexity of the tasks that are involved in multinational advertising efforts require the involvement and support of the firm at *all levels*. Top management need to be aware of the theme, the implementation strategy, and the results of the promotional efforts. It is preferable to have initial involvements . . . and perhaps criticism or even "late changes" . . . to second-guessing after the fact.

Further, if the program does not succeed internationally or even in one national market, it will be the local subsidiary managing director(s) who is initially upset and will be contacting the vice president of the international division or the president of the international operations. High-level home office support for the firm's efforts at the outset is thus a requisite, and at least tacit top management support at the regional or local level is equally essential. The latter will ensure the needed *local cooperation* at all levels.

Next, the costs involved in the international advertising efforts are such that it is necessary to reconcile the advertising and sales approaches employed by the firm. Adequate communication channels and a complementary operational environment between these two major external marketing arms of the firm must be ensured. Since the heads of the advertising and sales areas often *compete* for funds, they may have a tendency not to cooperate; it is essential, however, that their efforts be *complementary*.

—— PLANNING THE CAMPAIGN ——

Following is an outline of the *seven stages* in the strategic plan for the implementation of the worldwide campaign. The seven stages are:

1. Determining the *target* audience
   a. Understand your market(s)
   b. Seek multimarket customer similarities
   c. Recognize importance of market research
2. Determining *specific* campaign objectives
   a. Consider the problem of multiple objectives
   b. Objectives should be simple, specific, and measurable
3. Determining the *budget*
   a. Suggest initial budget prepared on task-objective principle

- determine cost versus objective
- do an intermarket comparison
  b. If budget requires reduction
  - first reduce objective
  - cost new budget task objective
  - avoid underinvestment failure
4. Determining the *media*
   a. Product of
   - objective
   - target market definition
   - budget
5. Determining the *campaign approach*
   a. Assignment of roles
   - home office
   - subsidiary
   - agency
   b. A suggested PERT-like or structured approach
6. Developing the *campaign*
   a. Creative development
   b. Pretesting to evaluate
   c. The final assessment . . . last chance for change
7. Determining the campaign's effectiveness
   a. Meeting established objective(s)
   b. Potential for future use—modified or the same

Throughout this book we have refrained from suggesting that a head office should sit in complete *control* of overseas advertising. We have repeatedly referred to head office involvement—"involvement" to the extent that would be reasonable in the case of any major corporate investment and "involvement" to the extent of contributing service and experience. And the current trend seems to be toward a rather strong home office involvement or *centralization* of major decisions involving *planning, budgeting,* and *regularized evaluations.*

A number of international firms, such as A. T. Cross Pencil Company,[1] Deere & Co.,[2] and Levi Strauss & Co.,[3] have recently been reported as favoring centralization. A. T. Cross Pencil Company offers an example of an international firm that basically adheres to a centralized policy. Under its reported three-layer approach, the company offers in its first layer "a uniform worldwide program of advertising exposure under the direct control of the home

---

[1] Nathaniel Frothingham, "How A. T. Cross Controls Three Layers of Media Advertising," *International Advertiser*, Vol. 2 (November–December 1981), pp. 21–23, 50.

[2] Marianne Paskowski, "Deere & Co. International Marketing Foundation for Successful Future Growth," *Industrial Marketing*, (February 1981), p. 67.

[3] Dennis Chase and Eugene Bacot, "Levi Zipping Up World Image," *Advertising Age*, Vol. 52 (September 14, 1981), p. 34.

office; second [layer], to provide similar regional programs in all major regional markets . . . ; third, to provide suitable advertising material for use with or without further conversion by Cross distributors anywhere in the world."[4] Deere & Co.'s separate international advertising department at its Moline headquarters offers "central management, guidance and coordination for [its] overseas advertising," and the department's manager directs some thirty-four people in its overseas sales branches.[5]

However, other multinational firms, including Intergold[6] and Blue Bell International's Wrangler[7] jeans company, reportedly favor a more decentralized advertising approach. A representative of Intergold, which markets the South African Krugerrand worldwide, has been quoted as saying that "about 80 percent of what we do is decentralized." In other words, the company "has adopted a localized approach to marketing with the hope of capitalizing on individual market differences."[8]

Other firms, like Hoover Worldwide and IBM, basically follow a *directed* decentralized approach, that is, maintaining certain controls/monitoring mechanisms. IBM's General Business Group/International handles marketing, as well as service and manufacturing, for office products and data-processing equipment in twenty countries.

IBM's international advertising philosophy has been described as follows:

> First, to provide counsel. Second, to serve as educators. And third, to produce advertising and promotion materials that can be used directly or adopted for local use.[9]

Its manager of advertising programs sees his or her most important activity as "constructive critiquing"—"there is no one right way in this subjective world of advertising. . . . Occasionally, the country people exceed what the headquarters staff believes to be in good taste . . . then advice and counsel tends to get a bit heavy."

Coca-Cola gathers information and opinions worldwide and produces the total campaign centrally; deviations from the corporate campaign are rare.

—— HEAD OFFICE PROGRAMMED INTO —— PLANNING PROCEDURE

Any amount of head office involvement will extend the time period needed for planning and executing an advertising campaign. This execution can best be accomplished when the headquarters establishes a planning procedure

[4] Frothingham, op. cit., p. 22.

[5] Paskowski, op. cit.

[6] Thomas B. Gething, "Intergold's 80/20 Marketing Formula," *International Advertiser*, Vol. 2 (November–December 1981), pp. 32–34.

[7] D. Chase and E. Bacot, op. cit., pp. 34, 36.

[8] Gething, op. cit., pp. 32–33.

[9] Ned Crecelius, "How to Create a Constructive Central Role in a Decentralized Organization," *International Advertiser* (March–April 1981), pp. 26–28.

with scheduled dates for different levels of achievement. Individual markets may complain about the long lead time; however, considering some of the advantages to be realized from the total effort, a longer lead time can pay off handsomely. A headquarters can program to see original creative recommendations by categories appropriate to the corporate marketing plan; that is, by product category or by geographic area, so as to make constructive comparison.

Creative Cross-Reference.   It should be assumed that great creative advertising ideas can come from any one of the possible subsidiary sources. Headquarters should examine each approach as being appropriate for the source market, as well as being appropriate and as possibly being a better idea than those submitted from other markets. Perhaps elements from one program can help to reinforce programs from other sources. In effect, a headquarters critique can be the opportunity to pool a great depth of creative talent.

Cost Savings.   One of the big problems in operating a multinational advertising program is that the total budget is first fragmented into many smaller budgets (by country) and that too often each country needs to use a large percentage of its subbudget for creative production.

Corporate coordination, via the headquarters critique, can lead to intermarket cost sharing of creative-production-integrating campaigns, that is, the use of the same art and photography wherever possible. But the really big savings can come from TV film production. With experienced, creative direction, TV filming projects can "overshoot" to provide sufficient footage for editing several different types of resulting commercials. (An example of current high television production costs is shown in Illustration 4–1).

By avoiding duplication of advertising production, individual multinational advertisers can achieve 15 to 20 percent or greater media volume from the existing budget level.

—— MANAGEMENT OF CORPORATE IMAGE ——

Quite obviously, the headquarters will use this opportunity to bring some type of standardization to all advertising (not necessarily uniformly) to conform to image policy and trademark legal protection. The opportunity to compare the work done by different markets that are promoting similar products will also aid a headquarters to make certain that product positioning is consistent with long-range marketing plans.

> "Let's face it," IBM's manager of advertising states, "the guy who struggled with his agency, persuaded his management, out-argued the marketing people and just squeezed by the lawyers is not going to be very happy with that guy from New York who can't even read the language who says that the copy is too long or the logo is in the wrong place."[10]

[10] Ibid.

— ILLUSTRATION 4-1 —

76

SAMPLING OF EUROPEAN TV PRODUCTION COSTS

	Peak-time costs	Director (Daily)	Cameraman (Daily)	Top Model	Hotel room (Daily)	Construction Manager (Daily)	35mm Camera (Daily)	Recording/ Dubbing	Editing
England	Seconds / Cost: 10 = £4,145; 20 = 6,631; 30 = 8,289; 60 = 16,587	£1,000 to 5,000	£250 (Another 250 for overtime)	£125 Minimum per 10-hour day; best get 500	£70 (Hilton)	£130	£100 (Up to 500 with extra equipment)	£100 per hour	£30 for stock editing; 40 for top editor per 30 second spot
France	Seconds: 8, 15, 20, 30, 45, 60. Channel 1: FF 50,000; 93,500; 124,700; 170,000; 242,300; 323,000. Channel 2: 34,800; 64,000; 85,100; 115,900; 164,900; 208,200	FF20,000 to 60,000 for a top name	FF2,850 to 3,500	FF5,000 per day plus 650 for each showing	FF667 (Hilton; tax included)	FF884	FF1,600	400 per hour without engineer; 550 with engineer.	FF1,800 for two days
Germany	ARD (Alliance of German Stations) 30 seconds DM75,680. ZDF (Second German Television) 30 seconds 51,800 plus 13% value added tax (Client can only book in one five-minute block.)	DM6,000 to 10,000	DM1,200	DM200 to 300 per day	DM165 plus 28% tax (Hilton)	DM500 to 600	DM500 per hour	DM200 pr. hour recording; DM250 per hour dubbing	DM700 per day
Italy	State RAI tv 30 seconds 7,000,000 Lire. Private 30 seconds up to 10,000,000 Lire	2,000,000 Lire	1,000,000 to 1,500,000 Lire	30,000 to 50,000 Lire total fee	100,000 Lire (Hilton)	N/A	200,000 Lire	210,000 Lire recording; 300,000 dubbing per 45 minutes	400 to 5,000 Lire per 45 minutes
Spain	Seconds / 1st channel / UHF: 20 = 1,950,000 Ptas. / 1,500,000; 30 = 2,925,000 / 2,250,000; 60 = 4,972,000 / 3,835,000	400,000 Ptas.	250,000 Ptas.	30,000 to 50,000 Ptas. total fee	5,680 Ptas. (Sheraton)	150,000 Ptas.	3,300 Ptas.	25,000 Ptas. per spot	30,000 Ptas. per 30 second spot

Source: Reprinted with permission from the November 1981 issue of *Advertising Age/Europe.* Copyright 1981 by Crain Communications, Inc.

We do not think the critique is employed to make people "happy," but rather to make things right. A misused logotype can create serious problems in legal protection of such a valuable asset.

IBM's advertising manager was further quoted as stating, "We try very hard to develop a cooperative spirit with the country advertising personnel."[11] We agree that success cannot come from force fitting done by an inexperienced at-home office. It is possible to set forth a few general rules for qualifying a home office management to constructively critique overseas advertising programs.

QUALIFYING HOME MANAGEMENT FOR OVERSEAS DIRECTION

We see the following seven steps as being important in qualifying home management for overseas direction:

1. *Know your markets.* The home office international advertising executive should maintain an ongoing effort to collect market data in each foreign market for his product. There is really nothing exotic about this. Just keep trying to get the same type of information you would want in your home market—customer demographics (age, sex, income level, occupation), shopping behavior, product uses, etc. Differences in individual foreign markets may become apparent when you conduct a comparative analysis of available data. This analysis, incidentally, may give you clues regarding feasibility of a standardized approach, or it may clearly signal the necessity for a highly differentiated campaign.

2. *Know your foreign counterparts.* Make it a point to know personally the executives of your foreign affiliates, operating divisions, or independent distributorships. It is important to know their strengths and weaknesses, competencies and biases. Obtaining their cooperation will be much easier if you know with whom you are dealing, and if they know you. You can also estimate from such first-hand knowledge the degree of cooperation you are likely to receive in the development of your advertising campaign.

3. *Travel in your foreign markets.* This point cannot be overstressed. Most international advertising executives are seasoned passport users. They are no longer thrilled at the thought of flying to Paris, Bonn, or Mexico City. And the responsibility is certainly an easy one to shift to younger and less experienced managers. Too much delegation of foreign travel responsibilities, however, removes the top executive

[11] Ibid.

from the concrete reality of foreign market practicalities. It becomes too easy to speculate about a foreign market when the executive conceptualizes it as an abstraction because he has become too far removed to think in concrete terms. Even worse, he may be thinking in terms of yesterday's realities.

4. *Use a network agency.* It is much more convenient (and typically more effective) to work with a large international agency having branches in each foreign marketing area than to have to rely upon separate agencies in each area. Use of a network agency enhances coordination of efforts, while use of separate agencies is likely to lead to poor cooperation and lack of communication, prompted by interagency jealousies.

5. *Know your foreign advertising account executives.* Just as it is good practice to know your foreign executive counterparts, you should know the agency and advertising personnel with whom you work. This rule is desirable whether you use a network agency or depend upon separate local agencies in each marketing area. The international advertising manager should insist on meeting *local* advertising agency account executives, and should ask to see samples of their earlier work on other accounts. It is important to learn their styles, media biases and preferences, and other unique factors. Familiarity with these local agencies permits much more realistic evaluation of their campaign suggestions. At the same time, the development of a direct relationship will help mitigate the defensive attitude that some local or branch agencies develop in the face of parent corporation advertising suggestions.

6. *Use long planning lead times.* A long planning horizon has several advantages. First, it provides time to work in trips to market areas requiring special attention. Also, the longer lead time encourages foreign ad managers to internalize stated campaign objectives. In the case of nonstandardized campaigns, they can take the time to develop a campaign that is appropriately designed for local conditions, yet is consistent with overall corporate goals. For a standardized campaign, the longer lead time lets your office get needed data to develop the campaign pattern and leaves you more time to sell the campaign to foreign divisions.

7. *Maintain home office budget approval authority.* The international advertising manager should hold on to the purse strings until he or she is satisfied that local campaigns are appropriately developed, or until the standardized campaign theme is fully understood and adopted. An amazing amount of information can be obtained from some rather remote parts of the world prior to budget approval. After such approvals, communication breakdowns may occur much more readily.

—— **THE PROGRAMMED MANAGEMENT APPROACH** ——

The first objective in establishing headquarters management as being involved in advertising decision making is to create a system of key decision-making steps that will occur in the normal process of developing a campaign. Nothing ever happens in a management process until someone with recognized authority reduces a desired end result (or goal) to written directions . . . and such directions are needed primarily to establish a precise flow of communications between headquarters and head office. One can be reasonably certain of success in a plan involving headquarters in advertising decision making if the schedule of vital checkpoints is recognized by *each* operating subsidiary—and if final budget approval rests on adherence to that schedule.

A Six-Step Plan.   This plan assumes that headquarters wants their opinion recognized *before* a large investment is made on a major new advertising campaign. It does not distinguish between types of campaigns, that is, whether the campaigns are being developed individually by each market or whether each market is giving local interpretation to a worldwide pattern campaign. The process is basically directed toward satisfying the headquarters management concerning the soundness of the investment and to assure them that the advertising in all markets creates the desired corporate image that will serve the worldwide long-range market plan.

Illustration 4–2 provides the intercommunications framework. (Dates are developed by working back from the target dates—either from the corporate budget approval date, or from the subsidiary campaign launch date.) A simple PERT diagram is all that is required to implement such a plan.

1. *Marketing and advertising strategy and objectives.* At this stage, the home office and its subsidiaries should jointly clarify their understanding of the firm's marketing objectives. In this regard, established corporate goals should be paramount. This would be true, for example, in a major new product introduction. Similarly, in any given year the corporation may establish as a parameter the necessity of stressing corporatewide public relations themes. Other possible marketing and advertising objectives would include increased brand share, repeat purchases, new customers, strengthening of channels of distribution, and larger average-order size.

   In many cases, subsidiary management will be able to offer valid and useful insights regarding proper marketing and advertising strategies and objectives. Particularly useful to the home office is the opportunity to review this type of input from several different countries. Recurrent themes may alert the home office to market problems and opportunities of which they were previously unaware.

— ILLUSTRATION 4–2 —
Goodyear Intercommunications Framework

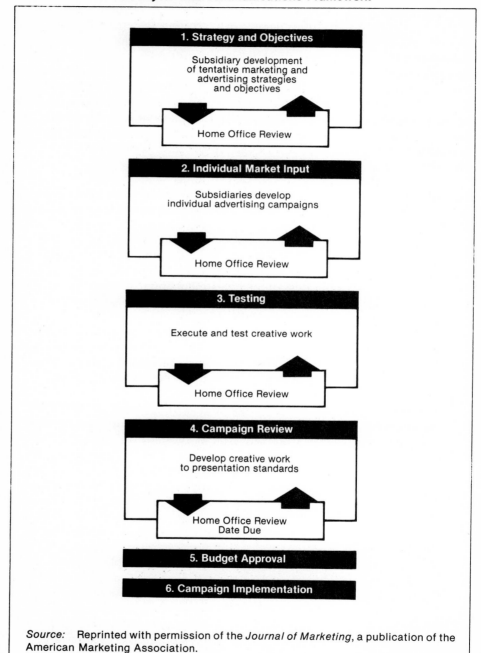

1. Strategy and Objectives

Subsidiary development
of tentative marketing and
advertising strategies
and objectives

Home Office Review

2. Individual Market Input

Subsidiaries develop
individual advertising campaigns

Home Office Review

3. Testing

Execute and test creative work

Home Office Review

4. Campaign Review

Develop creative work
to presentation standards

Home Office Review
Date Due

5. Budget Approval

6. Campaign Implementation

Source: Reprinted with permission of the *Journal of Marketing*, a publication of the American Marketing Association.

2. *Individual market input*. Based upon the home office's reaction to its strategies and objectives, each separate market builds a tentative advertising campaign. The campaign need not be developed to presentation standards, and a detailed media plan is *not* necessary at this stage. However, a sufficient amount of visual material and copy must be prepared to indicate the primary creative thrust of the campaign, and the broad types of media should be identified. The home office will review all the campaigns and offer suggestions.

3. *Testing*. Each local campaign must be market-tested in its particular country. It is preferable to use an independent marketing research firm rather than to rely on subsidiary marketing research departments, or even on the marketing research unit of the subsidiary's local advertising agency. The home office will review the test results and offer comments, criticisms, and suggestions.

4. *Campaign review*. Based upon market test results and the home office critique of those results, subsidiaries develop their campaigns to presentation standards. Each subsidiary's campaign is then submitted to the home office along with full details on media strategy for review and approval or modification.

5. *Budget approval*. Final budget approval for each subsidiary is delayed until the home office is satisfied with its campaign.

6. *Implementation*. Upon receiving budget approval, the subsidiaries have the green light to move into full-scale campaign implementation. Media commitments may be made, and final production work begins.

The overall campaign resulting from this approach may be highly standardized, or it may be a campaign that incorporates disparate elements aimed at unique market conditions. The programmed approach does not per se assure one or the other. Rather, the approach taken grows out of the interaction process; it assists in finding the right campaign approaches, and it assists management in determining whether or not one set of appeals can be standardized for the entire market area. This management system also prevents local markets from changing creative approaches too often—and eliminates the possibility of inconsistent or widely differing actions by local managers who become overly obsessed by temporary market frustrations.

REGIONAL CAMPAIGN DEVELOPMENT EXAMPLE: GOODYEAR–EUROPE

Goodyear International Corporation scheduled a new product launch throughout western Europe for the spring of 1976. It was strongly believed by corporate management that the advertising campaign to introduce this new product was of vital concern. On the other hand, there was no pressure directing that there be a single campaign for all markets in the European region— only that all campaigns be in harmony with each other regarding consistent product benefits and that they be consistent with a policy of corporate image.

The resulting campaigns were excellent in quality and impact. While there were perceptible differences between many campaigns, there was also a high degree of uniformity that was compatible with what Goodyear sees as a total European market that is highly mobile across borders, with considerable consumer media overlap, and one that approaches the buying of their products from relatively common considerations for this product. Goodyear was pleased with the success of this management framework and expects to use this system whenever the opportunity presents itself.

Illustration 4–3 shows the management flowchart initially designed by Goodyear in 1976 to direct and coordinate the development and implementation of its advertising campaigns in eleven Western European markets— Austria, Belgium, Denmark, England, Germany, Greece, Holland, Italy, France, Sweden, and Switzerland. The chart, covering the period from April to September 1975, was distributed to each European subsidiary. (Such advance planning—for example, for the spring of the following year—is obviously necessary for the scale of advertising employed by Goodyear International.) The chart is also furnished to each country's network advertising agency, all members of Interpublic Group's Campbell-Ewald International. All personnel involved were made aware of the importance of adhering to deadlines established via the flowchart.

Shown on the chart are two sets of responsibilities—home office and subsidiary actions. The light-shaded rectangles denote home office (Akron) activities, and the black rectangles indicate subsidiary (field) activities.

The flow of activities moves through discrete sequential steps from field input regarding strategy and objectives (in April) to home office approval to execute the approved campaign (in September).

The procedure and planning dates indicated by the framework are described as follows:

April 17.   The home office forwarded to each field office a questionnaire requesting a one-year marketing plan covering the 1976 period. The local office furnished documents, due in Akron on May 5, that cover objectives, strategy, and general theme of the local advertising campaigns. This stage proved to be extremely valuable. Preparation of this report assisted the subsidiaries in clarifying and formalizing their own thinking and gave the home office insight into both the unique and common problems facing each market area.

Notice the two flow paths through the chart. The flow path on the right (creative flow) signifies the fact that the field offices may initiate their creative work immediately upon dispatching their marketing plans to the home office. *They did not need to wait until receiving home office comments prior to beginning this work.*

— ILLUSTRATION 4–3 —
Goodyear Management Flowchart

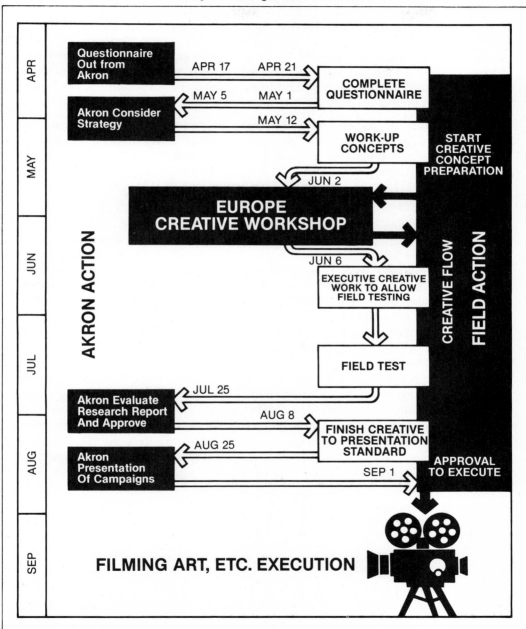

May 5. The home office began its review of the subsidiary plans on this date, completing the review by May 12. The home office provided each local office with a detailed critique of its plans. This review enabled Akron to detect and correct weaknesses in subsidiary market planning in such areas as product and brand name emphasis, media strategy, and other broad policy areas. In the 1976 campaign, for example, the home office found that several field areas were taking a short-run attitude toward sales growth and had not grasped the corporate market expansion strategy.

May 12. This was the final date designated for the subsidiaries' receipt of home office market plan critiques. These local offices, which by this time had already initiated their creative work, studied the critique and incorporated home office comments and suggestions into their campaigns. The subsidiaries then spent the last half of May working up their campaign themes and rough artwork to field presentation standards.

June 2–6. The European creative workshop, attended by the home office international advertising executive, the advertising managers from the six largest European markets, Interpublic's Campbell-Ewald representatives from each market area, Campbell-Ewald's European coordinator, and creative people from the agency's U.S. headquarters focused on overall European policies and objectives. Each market informally presented its advertising plans and creative concepts to the other attendees. A loose, informal atmosphere prevailed, encouraging a free and open exchange of views, opinions, and concepts.

The creative workshop, held in a European resort area, has proven to be a highly successful communications forum where a sense of unity of purpose is sought. Quite often the workshop results in improving all the campaigns. One or more markets may discard their original ideas in favor of suggestions offered by other markets or in recognition of an overriding corporate objective. The workshop offers the headquarters representatives an opportunity to reestablish direct contact with foreign market representatives and advertising agency representatives. The workshop also enables the Campbell-Ewald European coordinator to work directly with local agency representatives collectively, as a special account group. The agency coordinator and Akron executives in effect act as informal leaders of the client-agency symposium.

June 6–July 25. Following the creative workshop, the individual markets developed their campaign proposals more thoroughly, based upon inputs obtained during the workshop. During this development stage, the "cochairmen" traveled and worked with individual markets. Revised campaign concepts were then to be refined to a stage sufficient to permit consumer testing. This meant that artwork and storyboards were to be developed sufficiently to convey the advertising message in a market test environment.

Next, the individual market areas field-tested their campaigns. Each market area utilized independent marketing research organizations for this work rather than performing the test work themselves or permitting their local advertising agency offices to do the work. In general, three to four versions of the campaign were tested, using four to six consumer focus groups for each version of the campaign.

Psychological probing was utilized on occasion to determine underlying consumer attitudes toward the campaigns being tested. The market testing focused upon one of Goodyear's identified key markets, men in the twenty to forty age bracket. (The target market in the more affluent European countries tends to be somewhat younger than in less affluent countries. The German key market, for example, tends to be somewhat younger than the Italian market.)

July 25. This was the deadline for the formal presentation of the various comprehensive campaigns to the Akron home office. The Campbell-Ewald coordinator traveled to Akron to present all the foreign market campaigns along with market test results. At this stage, he had available TV storyboards, experimental films, and other roughs adequate to fully present each market's campaign concept. The coordinator, in effect, presented the campaigns including each market area's reasoning for developing its campaign and for altering it in accordance with market test results.

This formal presentation was made to an assembled group of home office corporate executives and advertising specialists, who had the opportunity to ask questions and to make further technical and policy suggestions. The end result was home office approval of the campaign, with possible suggestions for further modifications.

August 8. Home office approval of the research results and the campaign themes now permitted the subsidiaries to begin to develop the campaigns to finished presentation standards, incorporating any modifications needed as a result of the home office review of research results. The individual market areas now must also develop media schedules, campaign cost estimates, and proposed advertising budgets. This work had to be completed in time for a final review in Akron by August 25.

August 25. The home office reviewed the campaigns, generally suggesting some changes even at this late stage. The home office also will later review each country's overall campaign plans—media schedules, media mix, advertising budget, and the like—and may request changes in these areas as well. The creative flow line, as shown in Illustration 4–3, was actually released on August 8. The subsidiaries thus were free to develop finished creative work beginning at that time. Therefore, this second review by headquarters tended to focus more heavily upon implementing strategy (media planning and budgeting) than upon creative content. The Akron home office did, however, review such finished artwork as was available at this date. Corporate headquarters advertising executives eventually reviewed *all* finished creative work for approval prior to release to the media.

September 1. This was the deadline established for home office approval and funding of each market campaign. This approval permitted the subsidiaries to begin making the financial and other commitments necessary to implement the campaign during the following calendar year, 1976. From this point on, Akron continued to monitor local market performance. Each market is required to furnish quarterly progress reports, samples of materials produced, and consumer research reports in the form of trend data.

——— THE GOODYEAR PAN-EUROPEAN CAMPAIGN ———
"PILATUS"

The campaign that resulted from the Pan-European joint planning procedure explained in connection with Illustration 4-3 was known as the "Pilatus Campaign." The creative strategy was to demonstrate that a new Goodyear steel radial tire was both

— ILLUSTRATION 4-4 —
The Basic Pattern Form for the Goodyear Pan-European Campaign "Pilatus"

— ILLUSTRATION 4-5 —
Germany

Goodyear G 800 S. Der Autoreifen, der so sicher und stark ist, daß ein Flugzeug darauf landen kann.

Immer und immer wieder haben wir auf dem G 800 S ein 12-sitziges Flugzeug mit über 2 Tonnen Gewicht aus 3000 m Höhe mit einer Geschwindigkeit von 280 km/h landen lassen – ohne einen einzigen Reifenschaden.

Diese phantastische Leistung war möglich, weil der G 800 S Stahlgürtelreifen von Goodyear anders ist als alle Reifen, die Sie kennen. Er ist der erste Stahlgürtelreifen aus Polyester.

Warum fahren Sie noch herkömmliche Reifen? Einen sichereren Reifen als dem G 800 S von Goodyear gibt es nicht. Der einzige Reifen, der die Vorteile von Polyester und Stahl verbindet.

Der Reifen, der stark genug für ein Flugzeug ist.

GOODYEAR Deutsche Spitzenqualität

safe and strong enough to use for landing a twelve-passenger airplane. The airplane used for the demonstration was the Porter model made by the Pilatus aircraft manufacturer of Switzerland.

The basic pattern form for the campaign is shown in Illustration 4-4. Adaptations for local execution are shown as: Germany, Illustration 4-5; England, Illustration 4-6; and France, Illustration 4-7. Illustration 4-8 shows the basic pattern television commercial for the campaign. The commercial was "overshot" (much more footage was available than needed for the one commercial). This provided local option flexibility for individual national editing to correspond to print ad adaptations.

The campaign appeared in all European countries as one campaign, locally transliterated. It appeared in many countries outside Europe as well. Noteworthy of the experience was the necessity to refilm for television in certain countries.

South Africa and Mexico each required that filming be done locally because of a legal requirement that all products used in demonstration be the actual products sold locally. These countries manufacture the product.

Australia also required refilming, but for another reason. This country requires that all television commercials be filmed by local film producers.

— ILLUSTRATION 4-6 —
England

Goodyear G800 Supersteel ...
the new car tyre so safe, so strong we
landed an aeroplane on it.

"Frankly, I was sceptical when Goodyear asked me to land an aircraft on their new car tyres," says Hans Galli, Chief Test Pilot for Pilatus aircraft.

But he accepted the challenge, landing over and over again from 12,000 feet in a 12 passenger 170 mph aeroplane.

And the new Goodyear G800 Supersteel radial car tyre stood up to it every single time, even when Galli touched down with power on, and immediately applied full brake pressure.

"Now I'm impressed," says Galli, "very impressed."

And so will you be. Just imagine how many times stronger aeroplane tyres are built, and you will realise what a feat this was for car tyres.

prevent the tread distortion (we call it squirm) that happens in most tyres over 50 mph. Squirm is the major cause of tread wear at high speed.

Steel is also a rapid heat conductor, so the tyres operate at lower temperatures. We proved this on the aircraft runway where tyres run at far higher temperatures than on the road. Lower temperatures mean longer life.

G800 Supersteel stronger for longer life
The remarkable aeroplane test shows quite clearly how the G800 Supersteel radial outperforms other tyres. But there's more to it

than that. It also considerably outlasts fabric-belted radials, and more than doubles the mileage of cross-plys.

What makes G800 Supersteel unique?
The G800 Supersteel is the first tyre to combine the dual reinforcement of steel belts under the tread surface and polyester cords in the sidewall.

This combination has all the advantages of

the ordinary steel-belted tyre – and none of the disadvantages. The addition of polyester means that the harshness of the normal steel tyre is eliminated, and you get a much more comfortable ride. Plus the flexibility to avoid sudden high speed breakaway when cornering.

Why Steel?
Steel is the main mileage ingredient of the G800 Supersteel. It has the rigid strength to

Why Polyester?
Polyester is even stronger than steel and far more flexible. Polyester gives the G800 S Supersteel a more comfortable, quieter ride and extra sidewall strength to combat curbs, potholes and stones.

Get the G800 Supersteel strength working for you.
Whatever make of car you drive, chances are there is a G800 Supersteel tyre to fit. Next time you buy tyres ask for G800 Supersteel. No other tyre is so strong, lasts so long and is so safe you could land an aeroplane on it.

Mileage Comparison	Fabric Radial	G800 Supersteel
Cross-Ply		

G800 Supersteel   GOOD⫶YEAR

— ILLUSTRATION 4-7 —
France

— ILLUSTRATION 4-8 —
The Basic Pattern Television Commercial for the
Goodyear "Pilatus" Campaign

sound; music in background . . .
male voice: INTRODUCING . . .

. . . G 800 . . .

. . . SUPERSTEEL . . .

. . . BY GOODYEAR . . .

. . . CAR TYRE . . .

. . . THAT IS POLYESTER SAFE . . .

. . . SO SAFE . . .

. . . SO STRONG . . .

. . . WE'RE GOING TO LAND . . .

. . . AN AIRPLANE ON THEM . . .

sound; tyre skidding . . .

. . . .

. . . REMEMBER . . .

. . . THESE ARE . . .

. . . CAR . .

(continued)

— ILLUSTRATION 4-8 —
(continued)

.. TYRES ...

... FROM ...

... GOODYEAR ...

sound; tyres ...

... skidding ...

....

... IF A PLANE ...

... CAN LAND ON ...

... THE G 800 SUPERSTEEL ...

... IMAGINE ...

... HOW SAFE ...

... HOW STRONG ...

... THEY'LL BE ON YOUR CAR ...

Sound; music in the background to end ...
... THE GOODYEAR ...

... G800 SUPERSTEEL ...

—— Conclusion ——

The programmed management approach is not designed to take anything away from local market initiative; rather, it is designed to add resources to it by giving each market the benefit of creative work done by all other markets. It can also add long-term objective thinking and decisions to what might otherwise become providing solutions only to short-term problems.

We recommend the programmed management approach as a useful framework for the coordination of international advertising campaigns. It cuts through the "standardized versus localized" debate and offers a method for determining and implementing effective advertising campaigns in several market areas simultaneously.

Additionally, it offers the home office the opportunity to standardize certain aspects of the campaign, if this appears desirable, while at the same time permitting maximum flexibility in response to differing market conditions. This approval greatly facilitates communication between the home office and each foreign market as well as among the individual foreign markets. This communication process and the other safeguards built into the programmed management approach, such as the creative workshop and the required independent market research, help to ensure that effective campaigns are developed and that valid corporate policies and objectives are implemented.

The programmed management approach represents a hybrid prototype—a cross between close corporate control and local option management. It can result in a product that reflects teamwork—a blending of effort by corporate, local market, and agency representatives. The end result can be an effective international advertising campaign, one that is well designed to meet local market conditions and yet one that is in harmony with the corporation's long-range objectives.

As the Goodyear International Corporation campaign of 1976 development illustrates, a high level of interaction between the home office and subsidiaries is necessitated under the programmed management approach. Both the home office and local advertising representatives (and their agencies) are required to "defend" their positions and to stand the test of peer and superior criticism. The final objective, of course, is the development of the most effective campaign these joint inputs can produce.

—— 10 KEY POINTS ——

1. Central control of the management of multinational advertising is *not* synonymous with producing a uniform standardized multinational advertising campaign.

2. Centralized advertising management requires longer lead time in planning in order to involve headquarters in the planning process.

3. Headquarters executive management must agree to becoming involved in analyzing field advertising in order to give the process sufficient authority for a successful conclusion.

4. Creative cross-referencing can aid in strengthening all campaigns by pooling creative ideas.

5. Major cost savings can occur if duplication of similar artwork in several markets can be avoided. The biggest cost saving will occur from "overshooting" television commercials to accommodate editing requirements for several markets.

6. Persons assuming central management control of multinational advertising must be qualified with both advertising and international marketing experience (seven areas of qualifications).

7. The "programmed management approach" requires a precise system of intercompany communications based on a PERT-type procedure plan.

8. The most effective way for headquarters to become involved in the creative process is to establish creative workshops involving several markets plus headquarters management.

9. The single most important element in centralized management is "people management"—getting people from many world markets to work cooperatively for the best interests of the total corporate future.

10. Headquarters management's working attitude must be to add to the input of all overseas markets and to not take anything (initiative) away from them.

5

Positioning the Advertising Function

MNCs vary widely in the organizational approach they take to their worldwide markets. Practically speaking, this is partly due to the equity position they hold in their various subsidiaries or foreign operations. An international advertising manager may find, for example, that his or her role is limited in certain markets owing to the firm's *minority* position.

Even if they have wholly owned subsidiaries, however, MNCs may prefer to decentralize their marketing . . . and advertising . . . decisions. Others, however, tend to exercise a strong home office role in all or part of their marketing activities. In this chapter, we explore the various organizational relationships and indicate the extent to which firms tend to decentralize specific international advertising decisions.

A typical reporting line within the international marketing division/section is suggested, along with the duties of the international advertising manager. In addition, the factors that influence the size and composition of the MNC's advertising staff at the headquarters level are discussed.

Other topics covered in the chapter include:

- the composition of the local headquarters unit
- the use of promotion handbooks
- the importance (and protection) of the corporate brand/logo
- the training role of the headquarters personnel

Advertising, as well as merchandising, is all coordinated by Toledo head-quarters. Of course, advertising messages and media vary from country to country, depending on market conditions, etc., but there is great uniformity of image around the world.[1]

The organizational structures of many, if not most, MNCs have evolved over time, and rarely is it the precise form suggested by textbooks. While attention is often given to differences between, say, the divisional, the geographic, and the product line approaches, there are really two key questions or considerations that tend to draw the operational lines that direct the MNC's activities. These are the extent of *equity* the firm has in its various subsidiaries or foreign operations and the degree of headquarters control/involvement the firm wants to have in local decision making. (Obviously, these two factors are not necessarily mutually exclusive.)

In other words, if a firm has a minority position in a subsidiary (or subsidiaries), it has limited control over its management — unless, of course, it has a management or marketing contract to allow it to handle the managerial decisions. Similarly, if the firm wishes to allow the local (national) management to make the decisions irrespective of its equity position, that is, decentralized management style, this again will influence the character of the organizational structure.

While we may concern ourselves here with the organization of the marketing and advertising functions, the degree of influence the international advertising manager will have over the various issues is dictated largely by the firm's overall operational philosophy. Rarely, if ever, would the structure of the worldwide advertising operations of an MNC be organized very differently from those of its other marketing activities . . . and, in fact, the same general structure would likely apply to financial and production matters as well. However, while the "form" might be the same, the willingness to delegate responsibility could vary.

—— **The Equity Question** ——

The specific approaches that international firms take in organizing their overseas advertising vary greatly, as do their methods for entering individual markets. As noted earlier, however, a key consideration is the amount of

---

[1] George Galster, V.P. International, Champion Spark Plug Company, interviewed in "World's Number 1 Seller," *The Spirit of Champion*, November 3, 1979, p. 3.

equity they hold in their various subsidiary or branch operations. And this amount of equity often varies from market to market.

Some firms, for example, prefer to enter developed markets through wholly owned subsidiaries, whereas they prefer joint ventures or licensing arrangements in developing countries. Others may enter the latter markets only through exporting from the United States or Europe. The question of entry is crucial to the international advertising manager because it affects the degree of potential control he or she has over the firm's worldwide advertising. This factor becomes crucial when questions such as budget approval are at issue.

For example, Hoover Worldwide did not enter all markets on a wholly owned basis, but it does have *majority equity* in its subsidiary operations. This permits it to establish corporate advertising policy centrally and to maintain headquarters control of key decisions. The company headquarters can establish the local budgets, review proposed campaigns, and maintain reporting authority. On the other hand, the locals can make media decisions, including specific allocations and copy. Hoover may view its local management as being in the best position to understand local customs, people, language, and needed marketing strategy, which accounts for the decentralization of media-related decisions. It is the firm's entry approach, however, that largely permits this determination of corporate versus subsidiary roles.

We recognize, of course, that there are exceptions to the "equity rule." Through persuasion, recognized expertise, and so on, minority holders can have a major role in advertising/marketing decisions. And a management (or marketing contract) helps. Another possibility is that the overseas subsidiary's equity is so fragmented that a *minority* holding affords control . . . but this type of organization is the exception. (Celanese has been mentioned as an example of a firm's controlling policy and decisions that are based on such a fragmented arrangement.[2])

Decentralization Issue

Let us see how this locus of the decision-making question, that is, home office versus local, has been described:

> Regardless of the international organizational structure, an important question arises with regard to the location of marketing decision making. In many firms the home office marketing executives retain many (or all) of the major decisions (centralization), but in others most of the marketing decisions are made at the regional or local level (decentralization). Factors that influence the location of decision making include: (1) the level of local cultural differences, (2) the level of local nationalism, (3) the desire to maintain the morale of its local employees, (4)

[2] John D. Daniels, Ernest W. Orgram, Jr., and Lee H. Radebaugh, *International Business: Environments and Operations,* 2d ed. (Reading, Mass.: Addison Wesley Publishing Company, Inc., 1979), p. 382.

familiarity of local personnel with products and markets, (5) the firm's method of entry (i.e., the home office may be able to exercise little control where it holds minority equity), (6) regulations on employment of nationals, and (7) whether the area is developed or undeveloped.[3]

Regarding the extent of headquarters management participation in local decision making, Ryans and Wills, in an article from the *European Journal of Marketing*,[4] suggest that differences are found based on the *type of decision to be made* (see Illustration 5–1). In fact, their research among a number of United States-based MNCs revealed that the home office typically participates more actively in planning and control activities (establishing objectives and budgets) than it does in strategy areas (creative and media). Further, earlier research on this general topic suggests that MNCs employ more advertising decentralization with regard to developed-country subsidiaries than they do with subsidiaries in less developed countries.

—— ORGANIZING AND STAFFING THE —— ADVERTISING FUNCTION

Having now taken a rather broad look at the way MNCs approach these organization design matters, let us look specifically at the organization of the advertising function. In particular, let us consider several typical approaches that are currently being employed, and let us also consider the staffing/training and personnel concerns that follow.

International Advertising Manager. The international advertising manager may have either a *line* or a *staff* position. This individual often reports to the vice president for international marketing or to the international marketing manager. However, in a few firms he or she will report to the international sales manager or vice president or to a domestic advertising or marketing manager.

One very typical approach would employ a reporting line that has both the international advertising manager and the international sales manager reporting directly to a vice president for international marketing (Illustration 5–2). There are many advantages to this approach, as it places sales and advertising on an *equal* footing in the organization. Since the advertising and sales functions often tend to compete for the same limited promotional budget totals, this approach helps to ensure that neither is particularly favored in such allocations.

---

[3] Richard T. Hise, Peter L. Gillett, and John K. Ryans, Jr., *Basic Marketing* (Cambridge, Mass.: Winthrop, 1979), pp. 538–39.

[4] James R. Wills, Jr., and John K. Ryans, Jr., "Analysis of Headquarters Executives Involvement in International Advertising," *European Journal of Marketing*, Vol. 11, No. 8 (1977), pp. 577–84.

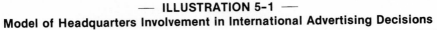

— ILLUSTRATION 5-1 —
Model of Headquarters Involvement in International Advertising Decisions

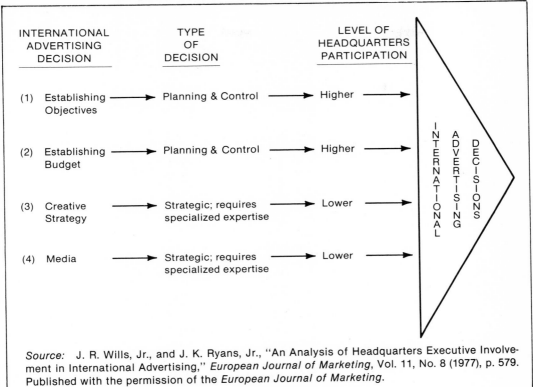

INTERNATIONAL ADVERTISING DECISION	TYPE OF DECISION	LEVEL OF HEADQUARTERS PARTICIPATION	
(1) Establishing Objectives	→ Planning & Control	→ Higher →	
(2) Establishing Budget	→ Planning & Control	→ Higher →	
(3) Creative Strategy	→ Strategic; requires specialized expertise	→ Lower →	
(4) Media	→ Strategic; requires specialized expertise	→ Lower →	

Source: J. R. Wills, Jr., and J. K. Ryans, Jr., "An Analysis of Headquarters Executive Involvement in International Advertising," *European Journal of Marketing*, Vol. 11, No. 8 (1977), p. 579. Published with the permission of the *European Journal of Marketing*.

However, a determination of an optimum "organizational chart" location for the international advertising manager or director goes well beyond the scope of our analysis here. The actual position within the line-and-staff network will vary by company, and the decision with regard to the position is typically based on other considerations, such as how *all* the home office personnel relate to the overseas staff/managers in the same functional areas. For example, the international finance manager (home office) may have line responsibility for the overseas local or regional financial managers or may simply serve in a staff role at headquarters. Similarly, the international finance manager may have line responsibility in some markets and only a staff role in others. The same is true for the international advertising manager or director.

The overseas subsidiary advertising personnel may differ in their reporting lines as well. In some firms they may have limited or "dotted-line" responsibilities to the home office. In other firms they may report directly to headquarters and have "dotted-line" local reporting lines or, in contrast, may have

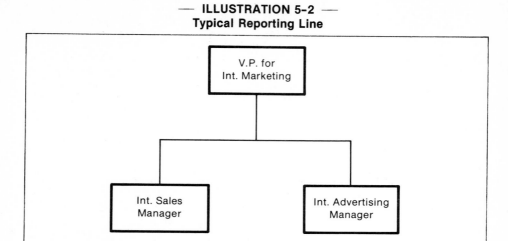

— ILLUSTRATION 5-2 —
Typical Reporting Line

no formal reporting lines to central corporate headquarters. Hopefully, the overseas advertising people will have at least "dotted-line" reporting links to headquarters if any semblance of *control* is to be maintained.

Of greater importance to us, however, is the identification of those advertising activities that should be the responsibility of the international advertising manager. Some of these activities should merely require his or her approval or concurrence; others should be initiated (and conducted) at the headquarters level.

Advertising Manager's Duties.   As mentioned elsewhere in the book, it is *essential* that the international advertising manager have the budgetary authority/ responsibility for all nondomestic advertising expenditures by the firm. This includes the initial allocation of the total budget to *all* overseas subsidiaries *and* a subsequent approval of the budgetary plans submitted by each regional or local manager. From his headquarters vantage point, the international advertising manager has a clearer understanding of the total corporate marketing objectives *and* of the advertising allocation needed to achieve these objectives.

Further, by having budgetary authority, the international advertising manager is better able to control the efforts of the locals. On the other hand, once the overall allocations have been made, he or she needs to allow the local manager some discretion in the use of the allocated funds. Doing this not only provides a morale *plus* but also takes advantage of the *cultural* and local *market* expertise of the local manager.

In addition to the budgetary role of the international marketing manager, he or she needs to have some degree of involvement in the following decision areas:

- the establishment of international advertising objectives and policies
- the nature and type of advertising/marketing research conducted at the local level
- the selection of the local or regional advertising agency (if or when a network agency is not utilized)
- the criteria for, and selection of, the local advertising manager
- the creative strategy employed at the local (as well as international) level
- the media selection decisions, especially those that have overlapping concerns with other markets
- the reporting and evaluation procedures, i.e., subsidiary or branch to headquarters
- the direct handling of all international promotion

Again, the appropriate involvements range from complete authority (the first two items in the above list) to consultation and/or approval (the third and fifth items). A complicating factor occurs when the corporation's overseas branches or subsidiaries are not wholly owned; the joint-venture partner may even have veto authority.

International Advertising Manager Evaluation. While the international advertising manager's authority parameters may be quite rigid, there is clearly a tendency for him or her to be held responsible for all advertising carrying the company logo. This can be quite unfair, especially when the individual performs in a staff function or with little overseas authority. Yet, recognizing this "reality," the international advertising manager needs to employ either formal or informal controls that are least provide him or her with a voice at the local level.

A further complicating factor results from top management's allowing the subsidiary head to have the ultimate authority. This individual may not appreciate advertising, marketing and advertising research, and the like, and could restrict all promotional efforts that affect his *bottom line*. For some international advertising managers this has proved to be a continuing concern.

Basically, the international advertising manager should be held responsible *only* to the limits of his or her *authority*. If this executive is to be charged with achieving the firm's international advertising objectives, then the authority needed to develop and implement the appropriate strategies and tactics is needed.

Advertising Staff (Headquarters). Obviously, there is great variation in the size and composition of the advertising staff at the international headquarters level. Factors that influence the staff size/composition include:

- the type of product/industry and the firm's total international sales
- the size of the advertising budget and the type(s) of advertising employed

- the nature of the market(s), including the number of countries where the firm operates and the types of customer(s)/client(s)
- the degree of decentralization of the promotional efforts
- the type(s) of advertising agency(ies) used and the role(s) assigned to this (these) agency(ies)
- the creative strategy(ies) and the media employed
- the scope of the firm's advertising and marketing research
- the level of competition that the firm faces overseas

At one extreme, we may have the relatively small industrial products firm that has a few highly identifiable customers or potential customers worldwide. These individuals may be reached most effectively by *direct mail* and by a limited amount of business press advertising. These customers may be served from only two or three regional sites . . . say, for example, a Western Europe (Geneva) headquarters and a Far East (Hong Kong) headquarters. Much of the promotional effort may be centered at the headquarters level, with some translation and/or production work done locally. In this case, the international advertising department would either have a full complement of creative and research personnel or could allow its advertising agency to handle the bulk of the advertising work and maintain a small in-house staff. In fact, in some organizations the headquarters serves as an in-house agency.

At the other extreme, a large MNC in the consumer goods field could be quite decentralized; it would have a fully staffed advertising department in each regional or local headquarters. At the same time, it could maintain a large home office department to assist the local heads in their creative and research efforts.

At a minimum, most larger firms would need to have certain *functions* performed at the headquarters level. These functions are primarily the planning and control activities that should be centralized. Whether or not separate individuals/positions are needed to perform each of these activities would, of course, depend on the total advertising efforts of the firm. These functions include establishing advertising objectives; determining and allocating the budget; coordinating and evaluating the creative themes/materials prepared by the agency(ies) or the locals; approving the media strategy; supervising and coordinating the advertising research (pre- and post-); and evaluating the performance of the individual promotional efforts.

In a number of MNCs, the international advertising department includes a manager, a creative director, a budgeting officer, and a research head. In addition, other staff specialists may be employed to meet the peculiar requirements of the firm. Each of these individuals might be expected to have some foreign experience or training that would prepare him or her to deal with a variety of market differences or expectations.

Local Headquarters. The composition of the local headquarters advertising unit will again depend on the degree of decentralization, as well as on the importance (sales and advertising volume) of the subsidiary or branch. For purposes of discussion, let us assume that this market (or country) is sufficiently important to the firm that it has a local production facility and a full marketing organization, including an advertising department. The latter is managed by a local advertising head. Given these assumptions, what decisions need to be made regarding the local manager and his staff?

The decisions include:

- the qualifications and training requirements for the position(s)
- the duties to be performed
- the nature of the authority/responsibility to be assigned
- the use of expatriates and/or nationals

Once the centralized versus decentralized decision outlined earlier has been made, the importance of the position is identified. The decision as to whether to employ an expatriate or a national tends to be part of the firm's overall personnel policy, although the issue may be pursued more fully by the international marketing manager if he or she has reason(s) to support one or the other approach. Finally, the duties and responsibilities of the various positions reflect the optimal qualifications for the position and the type of training needed.

As a policy, some major MNCs prefer to promote from within the international advertising area, that is, to move local managers to more important country assignments as openings occur and to replace them from existing staff. Others consider an advertising assignment as a step in the local executive hierarchy leading to more responsible marketing or general management positions. Still others prefer to hire advertising professionals from the outside—local agencies, media, competitors, and so on—or inexperienced individuals who they must train for the position. Similar policy could be followed regarding staff personnel, including local creative, budgeting, media, and research staffers.

The overall compensation approval line of the firm often dictates the extent to which locals may be attracted to the local advertising manager position. As a general comment, however, it must be recognized that using expatriates in these positions, especially those brought from a home office assignment, is often the most expensive approach. Further, local conditions, such as nationalism, entry-permit restrictions, or "local-hire" mandates, may affect the selection decision. Regardless of the approach followed in hiring the local manager and his or her staff, however, some training will generally be necessary.

——— Use of Promotion Handbooks ———

Many firms now employ a promotional or advertising *handbook*, which describes in detail corporate practices regarding advertising, as well as the proper use of the firm's brand name or logo. In addition, the firm's relationship with its advertising agency and a host of other guidelines may be included. Novo Industri, for example, has a handbook that contains illustrations of promotional materials, reporting forms, and many other related materials. Cessna uses its advertising handbook to tightly control all aspects of its advertising overseas, including cooperative advertising.

——— Corporate Brand Name/Logo ———

Even firms that employ rather loose home office organizational controls over their overseas communications make an exception in regard to their corporate brand/trade name/logo. Westinghouse illustrates this importance by stressing the development of a common logo for its Westinghouse *do Brasil* affiliate as its "first step" in its subsidiary communications program. This common logo—based on its familiar circled "W" symbol in the United States—will be used by all its Brazilian companies.

After a trade name is securely protected with legal documents, the description of the mark found in the registration must be followed almost slavishly to maintain that protection. A registration is more than the name itself. It is also the style or design in which it is registered to appear—the letter style; the overall word proportions; sometimes the color(s) it is to appear in; and, of course, the type of product classification for which it is registered.

The registered corporate trademark of The Goodyear Tire and Rubber Company is "GOOD (Wingfoot symbol) YEAR" (see Illustration 5–3). On a very regular basis this company receives employees' suggestions that company typewriters be equipped with one key for the Wingfoot symbol. The suggestion violates a corporate policy never to use the trademark in the context of a sentence in any printed material, because it will also require a registration symbol (R) plus a footnote, "Registered Trade Mark, The Goodyear Tire & Rubber Company"; and it would be in violation of the registration description. The registration involves a particular letter style for the "GOOD" and the "YEAR." An entire letter typed in such a letter style would look very strange indeed.

Care must be taken to never use a trademark in any manner that can be construed as being a generic description for your type of product. This can give competitors the right to use it in the same way. Usually, this refers to the use of the trade name within the context of a sentence where reference implies a generic category of product, for example, "To improve the clear picture image of your Sony (television) set, adjust the antenna. . . ." Without the word "television," Sony might be considered a generic reference.

Finally, in some countries, such as Germany, it is difficult to register letters alone. A company must take the appropriate steps to protect its trademark and/or brand name in every market . . . to do otherwise would be irresponsible management. For example, let us take a simple "bow tie"—a black one, no less. That would appear to be (1) value*less* and (2) unmemorable. Yet, through its advertising and sales promotion worldwide, Champion Spark Plugs has given it high recognition and *value*.

— ILLUSTRATION 5–3 —
The Proper Use of the Goodyear Tire and Rubber Company
Registered Corporate Trademark

GOOD YEAR

GOOD YEAR

GOOD YEAR

GOOD YEAR

GOOD YEAR

GOOD YEAR

GOOD YEAR

—— HEADQUARTERS TRAINING FUNCTION ——

It would be unusual to suggest that an international advertising headquarters could be equipped to conduct basic advertising training. But it is a most practical thought. Indeed, it is imperative that such a headquarters consider a training program for foreign subsidiary advertising managers as a basic corporate function . . . training to perform according to the international corporate guidelines. In fact, "teaching ability" should be one basic requirement for anyone assuming a position to direct an international advertising operation.

—— Operational Teaching ——

The international consumer communications network must be staffed with professional communicators—communicators training to communicate in different and specific languages within different and specific cultures.

Therefore, we must bring several elements of experience and training together. "Your man" in Italy or Thailand or Peru must be able to combine these talents:

1. A basic understanding of, and reasonable experience in, the fundamentals of an advertising operation. Such a specification will produce a wide variety of qualities of talent, because of levels of advertising sophistication in many countries, vis-à-vis a home office's standards for performance. Regardless of such comparison, it is still advisable to take the best of what is available locally and attempt to upgrade rather than to import talent to such countries. The goal is still effective consumer communications, not advertising sophistication.

2. An intimate knowledge of the culture(s) within a particular national market. Communications taught in language schools is seldom sufficient to be creditably persuasive in developing effective advertising. Simply stated, your communicator must be able to think as the people he or she is communicating with think. However, in some countries, this ability is not automatically acquired by acquiring a person born in the country in which he or she operates.

   Social class distinctions and the many levels of ethnic/social/economic/education sophistications in some countries cause groups within a country to isolate themselves from each other.

3. A sense of marketing and experience in market research development.

   In some countries there exists little distinction between the arts of advertising and public relations (or journalism). Marketing-oriented advertising experience teaches the target market concept more thoroughly . . . or using a knowledge of the differences in different groups within a single national society to direct effective, persuasive communications.

4. An understanding of modern advertising and sales promotion techniques. This requirement will be found in a wide spectrum of degrees. The additional training required will need to be assessed by individual national markets—and with respect to each new person assuming the advertising function.

5. A thorough knowledge and understanding of your corporate advertising practices, policies, and objectives. Obviously, this requires on-the-job training.

Putting these five points together, each individual national market will require individual assessment in regard to the amount of training required. However, aside from point 5, none of this training need be considered as requiring special, formal training programs if a talented person is selected in the first place.

Even in the case of point 5, corporate advertising, training should not be attempted on the first day for a new hire. The significance of what is to be learned will not be apparent until a newly hired person has sufficient time to get acquainted with the job, the new company, and the problems he or she faces in daily activity—and also and until your company has an opportunity to evaluate such a person to determine if that person has a future and is worth the time and expense to train.

Training into the corporate pattern for your advertising operation should be done at the headquarters office. The entire procedure should be almost as much psychological indoctrination as it is technical operational training.

One might say the training at headquarters is to give a new person the "big picture" of your company. The size of your company and its position in its industry might appear to be rather insignificant in some of its many different national locations.

It is also important to take such a person out of his or her local environment in order to isolate that person from his or her work as it is presently being done in order to create a fresh atmosphere for how it *should* be done . . . a fresh-start opportunity . . . give a new person "a new broom." Headquarters should always consider such occasions as opportunities to improve things—not simply as boring obligations.

——— Technical Training ———

After a person is inducted into the corporation, his entire career from that point on should be considered a training program designed to aid that person to develop and improve his or her performance. The headquarters should consider it as such and avoid any attitude of simply observing and keeping score on the progress, or lack of progress, of such persons.

All actions taken or initiated by headquarters should be designed as additional "field operations training."

1. The critique done on recommended campaigns sent to headquarters should be thorough and constructive. Each campaign should be considered as a class assignment to be graded and commented on in an instructive way that will train the field operative to improve.
2. Home office foreign market counseling is a most direct form of training. Whether or not the visit to a foreign subsidiary is to assist the local market in developing a new campaign, or to audit procedures and progress, the total approach of home office management should be in the form of instruction and helping local people solve their own problems in a way that is consistent with a company's policies and procedures.
3. The regional advertising conference is basically a training exercise. If a meeting is arranged for the purpose of joint campaign planning, the home office chairman should not bring people together so that they can witness his or her solving of their problems; the chairman should lead participants by means of corporate procedures so that they learn to practice these procedures.

The regional conference can also take on the "show-and-tell" format, with each national prepared to make a thorough presentation to representatives from other markets on the programs that are in process. Such meetings provide many benefits to an international company. First is the cross-pollination of strategies, creative approaches, and forms of execution—and an opportunity to learn from others about promotional ideas that have proved successful.

In fact, they are helping to train each other in techniques and executions. Psychologically, all will strive to put their best foot forward when presenting to their fellow advertising managers and home office executives. Annual conferences of this type tend to cause each local advertising manager to think all year long about how professional he or she will appear at the next advertising conference. The conference itself will broaden each participant and expand the participant's thinking beyond his or her own local problems.

4. Training seminars that are sponsored by the industry, a professional association, or a university can also be useful for the further training and development of a company's advertising people. Such seminars are conducted in many parts of the world—in some cases, it might require travel to another country. This should be encouraged to provide the opportunity to learn problem-solving techniques away from the subjective atmosphere of those problems.

5. Depending on the amount of formal education already completed by local advertising people, consideration can also be given to their attending evening classes at local universities.

In conclusion, it might be observed that advertising is a function that requires personal vitality and enthusiasm at all times. An advertising manager who stops learning is no longer an asset to himself or herself or to the employer . . . so the education process is never really concluded.

—— 10 KEY POINTS ——

1. The MNC's *equity* position in its subsidiary(ies) generally affects the degree of control the international advertising manager can exercise. (Majority *equity* is typically needed to ensure home office direction.)
2. Most international corporations maintain some degree of headquarters control over key international advertising decisions, such as establishing objectives and/or establishing budgets.
3. There are a number of advantages to having the international

advertising manager report directly to the vice president or manager of international marketing.

4. The international advertising manager should have the budgetary authority/responsibility for all nondomestic advertising expenditures by the firm.

5. The international advertising manager should *not* have responsibility for all the overseas advertising carrying the firm logo unless he or she is given the equivalent *authority*.

6. The size of the international advertising department depends on a number of factors—particularly on the extent to which it utilizes its advertising agency(ies) and on the size of its advertising budget.

7. The composition of the local headquarters advertising unit depends on the degree of decentralization permitted by the home office.

8. The international home office should prepare a *promotional handbook* to be used by its subsidiaries.

9. The MNC must maintain *tight control* over the use of the corporate *logo* in *all its international markets*.

10. The international advertising department needs to develop a program for training the firm's overseas (local) advertising personnel.

6

Establishing the Advertising Agency Role

— INTRODUCTION —

Advertising agencies have become as much international/multinational as other types of business, both to follow and continue to service home market clients that have gone abroad and to acquire new business in markets where they believe they can offer expertise better than is locally available. An MNC headquarters can usually be more confident working with an agency headquartered in its home market because it has a common understanding of the art of communications. This is not true only of U.S. companies; Japanese and German MNCs are encouraging advertising agencies from their homeland to follow them abroad.

Most international agencies, United States and otherwise, are integrating their staffs and managements sufficiently to satisfy local clients as being a local agency and international clients as being an international agency.

Advertising agencies often refer to themselves as "full-service" agencies, indicating that they are capable of properly servicing any type of client. In fact, they are quite differentiated, one from the other—either as a result of differing philosophy/policy approaches to servicing clients, or as a result of organizing themselves to best service the types of clients they represent.

These subjects are detailed in the context of the following:

- selecting and working with an advertising agency
  - what does an advertiser want from an agency?
  - the full-service agency
  - division of responsibilities
  - international and multinational considerations
  - matching agency to client
- advertising management position in the corporation

- what kind of agency to select
  - volunteer network
  - central control network
  - lead agency concept
  - deliberate minority
- geographic match—agency/client
  - multiple-product advertiser
  - multiple-brand advertiser
- key considerations—agency selection
  - success with local clients
  - attitude toward international clients
  - attitude toward international co-ordination
  - joint creative workshops
- agency compensation
  - media commission system
  - fee system(s) explained
- agency "call report"
- evaluation of agency performance

What does an advertiser actually buy when contracting with an advertising agency?

- The professional philosophy, attitude, and experience of the agency management
- The working time and talent of its creative people
- The working time of other professional services (media, research, and production)

Basically, the advertiser buys people's time!

- The agency brokers only the buying of physical advertising materials
- The most effective client-agency relationship is a management-to-management rather than a person-to-person commitment

---

The past two decades have seen the rapid growth of the truly "international" or multinational advertising agency—mostly United States-based agencies. "Growth," however, has two important considerations. Firms such as J. Walter Thompson and McCann-Erickson were quite active in many foreign markets prior to World War II. To their good fortune they represented such clients as Ford and Exxon, which were early in worldwide expansion and provided their U.S. agencies with the opportunity to internationalize themselves.

This was an important preemptory advantage. It was a physical growth that put them onsite in future important markets before the international advertising "gold rush" of the late 1960s and early 1970s. The latecomers found it very expensive to gain entry into highly developed overseas markets during the dynamic market expansion years.

While the initial investment was most favorable for early "squatters," revenues were initially disappointing, and it was sometimes a matter of sacrifice to maintain unprofitable overseas offices in order to satisfy a profitable home market client.

The revenue growth years really paid dividends to the established international agencies as television advertising began to proliferate. The United States-based international agency had the experience and was ready to capitalize immediately. The internationals in markets without commercial television still find revenues marginal for providing expensive talent to service sophisticated international clients.

Western Europe illustrates the scale of the advertising agency business today. In 1980 total billings by the one hundred largest European agencies reached $8.217 billion, a sharp increase over 1977's $5.55 billion.[1] Germany alone accounted for ten of the top twenty-five agencies (gross income), although the J. Walter Thompson Group, Britain, was the largest single listed agency. Clearly, the day has long passed in which the lack of availability of high-quality ad agencies is a problem in most developed countries. However, some availability difficulties are still present in many developing countries.

Another continuing question facing the MNC advertisers is whether to employ a single international or network agency, that is, one with branches in all or most countries in which the MNC operates, or a separate local agency in each market. This question has been debated for many years, and the pluses and minuses of each are discussed in this chapter and in the article in the Appendix to Chapter 12. Let us consider the advertising agency selection decision.

SELECTING AND WORKING WITH AN ADVERTISING AGENCY

What Does an Advertiser Want from an Advertising Agency?

Different advertisers with different marketing strategies and different in-house functional staff organizations should be able to give different definitive answers to such a question.

An effective advertiser-advertising agency relationship should be one in which the agency supplies functions and talent as an extension of the client's own organization. There should be no overlapping duplication of functions, nor should there exist any important void for thorough operating efficiency. Before considering which (or which kind) of agency to consider—consider first the most effective division of responsibilities (or functions) and what is needed to complement your overall marketing organization.

If one is organizing a new international marketing division as an adjunct, or subsidiary, to the parent domestic company, the incorporation of functions to be assigned to an advertising agency is important in the initial organization plans. It will prevent overstaffing from within.

---

[1] Eugene Bacot, "Foreign Advertising Agency 1980 Income," *Advertising Age/Europe*, Vol. 3, Issue 11 (May 1981), pp. 2–3.

In situations where there is to be a change to a different advertising agency, the opportunity presents itself for internal reorganization as well. Over a long period of time internal advertising staffs tend to get bulky with people designated to perform functions that were given priority by certain senior management persons who have now moved on. Slimming down the advertising department can improve output efficiency.

When a new agency is being considered, reassess the division of work between agency and client. Then outline the functions to be handled by "the new agency" . . . and organize these functions according to your priorities. It is likely that when a new agency is fit into place, further organizational adjustment will be necessary.

The Full-Service Agency

"We are a full-service agency" are usually the first words used in an initial agency to client presentation. No one is exactly sure what "full service" means unless it refers to (a) "We'll attempt anything you are willing to pay for" or (b) "What we offer should be all that is necessary." Advertising agency associations have their own definitions, but "full service" to a client should include the services necessary to complement the client's own staff and perform the additional functions necessary to get the job done.

The kind of full service that most multinational advertisers require does exist within several of the large international network operations. The caution is to investigate the depth and quality of each of the services you intend to employ. Do not accept that they are competent simply from reviewing an organizational chart. Instead, examine the credentials of the personnel at the top *and* in the lower support positions.

The Division of Responsibility
between Agency and Client

Why does any advertiser need an advertising agency?—or, stated another way, Why doesn't the client (advertiser) hire all the different talents needed to work directly for the company?

The answer, of course, is that some advertisers do just that, and they have no outside agency(ies). Criteria for such a decision have little or nothing to do with the size of the company. Such organizations are usually set up as "house agencies" in order to buy media at commissionable rates and realize the difference as savings in the budget, which helps to pay the cost and justifies the decision to create a house agency. The so-called house agency does require an independent corporate identity to qualify as a media broker eligible for "agency discount."

We can think of our primary considerations in regard to the decision of which function—if indeed not all functions—should be kept in house or designated to an agency.

One—Cost Accounting Projection.   Talent for everything comes in many areas at many prices—copywriters, layout people, finish artists, sales promotion specialists, photographers, film producers and writers, point-of-purchase specialists, sales conference organizers, package designers, media people, and communications researchers—to mention a few. The consideration is simple arithmetic. Which of these specialists can you employ sufficiently to justify their in-company existence compared with the cost of equal (or better) quality performance that can be supplied by an agency. The answer will depend mainly on the amount of time you *actually need them.*

Two—Inbreeding of Talent.   Among the creative functions, it is seldom that an in-house agency can consider a variety of people in each specialty. Unique new creative development may be important to an advertiser, but with an in-house staff there is the danger of everything gradually looking and sounding alike. Materials become channeled into a single style and single format, which is the style of the person(s) who will always be doing the creative work.

Advertising agencies rarely employ people to do finished art because they do not have sufficient need for any one art style. Creative concept people can be transferred to different client accounts in order to maintain freshness.

Three—Quality of Advertising Manager.   Is the person heading an advertising department sufficiently experienced and talented to direct all creative functions? Is such a person affordable in your company? Or would the cost of such a talent be prohibitive?

Four—Maintenance of In-House Staff.   Advertising people, particularly creative people, are accustomed to moving from job to job as the primary means of advancing themselves. The location of your company would be an important factor in attracting really top professional people. They do not like to leave the primary advertising centers—which no longer means just New York—but it does mean a large city.

Even if you are located in a large city, creative people will become bored with a single product type and want to move to another challenge . . . plus, to bigger personal income. The reverse is also a consideration. Corporate employment rules (negotiated by factory unions) make releasing of people very difficult even if their work is unsatisfactory.

Through attrition of the most talented of creative people—and lack of attrition of the least-talented creative people—over a period of years the in-house agency (or large advertising department) achieves a creative level of mediocrity.

It should also be noted that truly good creative people are looking more to finding challenging outlets for their art than they are to finding security. The corporate place is most attractive to a creative person if he or she does want security.

In the case of noncreative, administrative people, the maintenance of the in-house staff is less difficult. However, most aggressive staff people will be aware that advancement can be limited in the field of advertising and may desire broader marketing responsibilities.

This is not to say that there cannot be functions that are more affordable and yield greater efficiency when handled by in-house employees. But it is necessary to identify these functions so as to establish which services will be required from an outside agency.

International and Multinational Considerations

The words "international" and "multinational" can often be used interchangeably, but there is a difference when describing the type of advertising a corporation does . . . and this difference is very important when choosing an advertising agency.

An international advertiser is one that does advertising in many countries, but does it from the home office country. The purest form of international advertiser is one that uses international magazines and trade journals. The term would also apply to the selection and placement of advertising in local overseas media from the home office.

A multinational advertiser is one that conducts local campaigns in many countries. The campaigns can be different, or they can be the same—or they can be the product of a corporate pattern direction. But typically, each country subsidiary spends more individually than international advertisers to create advertising and to buy a media schedule.

With only two variables presented it might be assumed that there are only three combinations available for comparison—international, multinational, or a combination of both. When it comes to setting up an advertising machine to cope with all the degrees of overlap, it is difficult to select an example that will fit any specific case. We are speaking of putting together an in-house advertising organization, which is combined with an agency organization to operate effectively within a wide variety of advertising policies designed to support a number of specific marketing objectives. A careful description of the agency specifications is obviously critical indeed.

We are going to look at agencies from the advertiser's point of view. Although agency structure and location are important, agencies cannot qualify for selection based on logistics alone. There must be an understanding in advance that agencies also differ in their experience with different product categories and that each may be stronger in one function than in another.

Some agencies' experience leans toward consumer packaged goods—food, cosmetics, toiletries; others toward consumer durables—automobiles, household appliances, sporting equipment; others toward travel and transportation—hotels, airlines, vacations; others toward industrials—farm equipment, industrial machinery, manufacturing materials.

Some agencies have reputations that are particularly noted for marketing strategy; some are noted for unique creativity; others are strong for being especially skilled in research; and still others for exceptional work in media analyses and buying techniques. Some agencies have had noted successes in one medium (e.g., TV) but have had limited successes in other media. Most agencies will claim expertise in all areas that are mentioned in the last two paragraphs . . . few are noted for modesty. It will be up to the international advertising manager to judge different agencies' qualifications by examining their records and present accounts and by consulting with some of their present and past clients. Or he or she may wish to employ an experienced marketing consultant to investigate the agencies' qualifications.

—— Matching Types of Agencies with Types —— of International Advertisers

1. *Advertisers in the Export Business*
   In the simplest form, exporters, by definition, do not face difficult advertising problems. The advertiser usually has only three objectives:
   a. to advertise the exporter's product availability to foreign distributors who might wish to handle the product locally;
   b. to develop an awareness of the exporter's brand in foreign markets that will help distributors sell the product;
   c. to provide an advertising service to existing distributors, usually in the form of cooperative advertising.

      This type of company can usually receive adequate advertising agency service from any agency that can also satisfy its home market requirements; or an in-house agency could handle most of the necessary functions. Brand advertising for such an advertiser would not necessarily need to have local national input, and international publications that offer broad coverage are often the best medium. The media needed to attract additional distributors would be industrial trade journals and/or direct mail.

      Cooperative advertising assistance to distributors requires many actions of a small advertising department, which must provide art, copy, and identification service, plus the necessary bookkeeping on cost-sharing for the media purchased by the distributor. The small advertising department's biggest problems relate to media, not to creativity, and it is not unusual for an export advertiser to employ an overseas agency merely for its media placement service.

2. *Advertising in the Multinational Corporation—Selling and/or Manufacturing in Many Foreign Countries*

The key to the amount of advertising agency service required and the kind of agency needed is directly associated with the basic corporate management policy regarding the amount of home office (central) control of local management that is desired as compared to the amount of foreign, subsidiary autonomy that is allowed. The ability of an international company to exercise such an option is based primarily on the extent of its overseas corporate ownership. The degree of control cannot be decided on advertising policy alone—advertising management policy generally follows the policy of all other management functions. To mention a few:

a. An international corporation in full ownership control *that desires* management control over all primary functions. Such a company may choose any type of international or multinational advertising operating procedure it wishes.

b. An international corporation in full ownership control but which leaves the marketing function totally to local judgment. This type of firm has chosen to abdicate its advertising responsibility to local management.

c. The full ownership control international corporation that holds local management responsible for bottom-line profit results only. This might well be considered as abdicating advertising responsibility. However, in some cases there do exist policy operating procedures that regulate how certain marketing procedures are to be followed and keep a type of quality control over advertising by designating an international agency to assure a continuity of quality.

d. For any international corporation with less than controlling ownership, or a licensor, or a franchiser, the question of who controls the advertising must either be agreed to as a specific consideration in the business instrument that binds them together, or the decision may be left to the party with majority control.

—— ADVERTISING MANAGEMENT POSITION ——
VIS-A-VIS EXECUTIVE MANAGEMENT

Within corporations (international or otherwise) the subject of advertising enjoys a unique personality. Too often people criticize or admire it with about the same depth of thought they give to selecting a necktie. The advertising budget is given the thorough investment "wash" that would be given any sales expense item, but the advertising product (the campaign) itself can be successfully measured in the value judgment area. Persons arriving at executive levels via the production or finance routes can seldom wait for an opportunity to make advertising decisions.

Persons from the chairman on down like to point to their company's advertising and say, "That was my idea" . . . or at least to take advertising creative judgment away from any advertising manager.

Advertising people are the brunt of many jokes. No matter how seriously and scientifically they approach their work, they are seldom given credit for anything other than failure. Their management presentations are the best attended, and they are expected to be entertaining and theatrical . . . advertisements are often judged as an art show, and all statistics used are considered suspect as coming from unqualified sources.

Therefore, in organizing an advertising operation in-company and combined with agencies — in proposing any degree of central or field control — personalities often play a larger role than logic.

——— Now, What Kind of Agency Should Be Selected? ———

Keeping this discussion in the context of international advertising, we shall consider advertising agencies that are set up to serve advertisers with varying degrees of central corporate control.

Exceptions accepted, it can be stated rather categorically that the greater the degree of corporate control desired by the home office, the greater the necessity for an international network agency. Such an agency would necessarily be responsible to the headquarters office. Each such agency must be carefully evaluated, inasmuch as all agencies that refer to themselves as an "international agency" do not truly qualify for the term. The distinction between the real network agency and the "pretenders" will become obvious shortly.

The Voluntary Network of Independent Agencies. How much ownership control does the headquarters have of its international affiliates? What is its management philosophy regarding central management control over the activities of its affiliates? These are essential to ask of a voluntary network.

Agencies sometimes form international organizations to attract international clients without exchange of ownership shares. Or a large agency will acquire not more than a clocking minority of several foreign agencies to prevent other large agencies from "using" the same small agencies to form another international network group. Each enables all member agencies to sell themselves as an "international" agency with offices in many countries.

Such arrangements are a viable selling asset to the agency when offering its services to a prospective client. However, such organizations can be costly to a client in terms of many important services and cost-saving benefits that can be achieved by associating with an international agency network. The latter type of company has a controlling interest in all subsidiaries and can exercise that control to the client's benefit.

The major strength of the voluntary agency may well also be one of its weaknesses, that is, the size of the organization. The voluntary approach permits the smaller agency to remain "independent" while still having overseas contacts (or connections).

—— The Centrally Controlled Agency Network ——

This type of agency network is the opposite of the "voluntary network." One agency company has a controlling interest in all its subsidiaries—and, if it wishes, management control in serving the best interests of an international client.

The client's requirements are, of course, the real measure of whether the agency's organization can be considered a "full-service agency." Here are some benefits to be gained by using this type of network that an international client might consider:

1. Central development of a single corporate-designed campaign—or of a pattern demonstration campaign.
2. A positive attitude on the part of subsidiary agencies toward adapting such campaigns for maximum effectiveness in each foreign market; or to develop local campaigns with the spirit and philosophy of the overall corporate strategy and policy.
3. Provide a central agency management for monitoring the quality of the services being given clients' subsidiaries through the network of agencies and to keep these services at a high level.
4. Consult with client corporate headquarters and absorb the client's marketing policies, advertising strategies, and the basic spirit of a client's business philosophies to be constantly communicated to all network agencies involved.
5. Organize, implement, and coordinate advertising or marketing research so as to keep both the procedures and the reporting results uniform and manageable for the international headquarters.
6. Develop systems for intermarket exchange of ideas developed from anywhere for the benefit of all.
7. Develop a system of exchange of basic and expensive TV film and key artwork so these can be shared at important cost savings to the client.
8. Become an important central point for gathering data on costs and results for a worldwide advertising program.
9. Be able to transfer key people from one agency office to another to strengthen creative or account service. This can be accomplished on decisions made between client headquarters and agency headquarters without embarrassment or arousing strained feelings at the operating points.
10. Regularly schedule meetings between the two headquarters offices

to analyze progress and make broad plans for the future. This can also give a client's chief executive officer assurance that his large advertising investment is being properly managed.

11. The client can give direction to one point without attempting to work with many agencies at the same time.

12. A large advertiser can become a small advertiser if the total budget is fragmented over many markets to different agencies. By concentrating the budget with one agency organization, the advertiser keeps important leverage needed to demand the best service.

13. The qualified international agency headquarters can be an extension of the advertiser's home office staff to provide advice and counsel at the operating level and can reduce the staff needed at the advertiser's home office.

The client headquarters agency in a voluntary network would, of course, have much less direct supervision over member agencies . . . no control over the quality of local agency personnel . . . and the profit motives would be stronger than growth motives when considering client expenses.

In all fairness to the many important advertising agencies that do not fit the two extremes of full management control or voluntary nonequity networks, we should recognize that there do exist successful agency management philosophies with alternatives that could find a "best-fit" relationship to a specific advertiser's own management philosophy. The key is for both the client and the agency to recognize the reason(s) for the *fit*.

⎯⎯ The Lead Agency Concept ⎯⎯

This type of international agency, usually with substantial equity or controlling interest, deemphasizes its own home office as an international client control point. The client's international agency coordination, and the supervision of quality and service in all markets serving that client, are the responsibility of the "lead agency" . . . or of the local agency office that acquires the account initially.

The "lead agency" concept can work well for some clients. However, it is our observation that it works best for clients that happen to be located in the same market as the agency home office. There is little assurance that every local agency office will have international expertise—people sufficiently familiar with how to initiate and control an advertising campaign in multiple national markets; have the executive authority to gain sufficient needed cooperation from all other agency offices, including the headquarters; or have the facility to physically track progress in all markets.

An international advertiser should look closely at these cautions to make certain that the absence of a qualified and experienced international agency executive coordinator is not due simply to a desire (or need) to reduce agency overhead.

—— **The Deliberate Minority** ——

The deliberate minority should be discussed as a philosophy, not as a structure. We would warn the reader that this is a delicate and highly sophisticated achievement to accomplish to the mutual advantage of both agency and client.

International agencies can buy local national agencies. When they buy such an agency, they are usually buying the local agency's name, and hopefully they will gain its quality people and have an opportunity to retain its clients. Certainly, the mere physical assets of an agency are often minimal. If the agency employees stay and the clients remain satisfied, the international agency has a new unit from which to grow. (Healthy growth would include more local clients and expanding international clients into another national market.)

What we are describing as a "deliberate minority" begins with an international agency selecting a new member agency that is an outstanding local independent. It acquires a maximum minority (49 percent) in order to ensure substantial international network involvement; and yet, to ensure continuity of local experienced talent and management, it leaves the local agency equity control. Also, of course, this approach maintains continuity of clients. The delicate balance, so far as the international client is concerned, is the ability of the international partner to cause the new agency to wholeheartedly respond to its new role as an international team member and still maintain its original high-quality stature. The psychology of leaving local management with equity control aids in preventing the loss of key talent and local clients that might otherwise object to a "foreign takeover." This can be a very desirable situation, but it is one more often attempted than genuinely achieved.

—— **MATCHING ADVERTISER'S LOCATIONS TO** ——
AGENCY'S LOCATIONS

International advertisers cannot always find appropriate network agencies to match their subsidiary locations. The solution to this difficulty often depends on how close a match can be made for the most important foreign markets. However, today there are a sufficient number of large international centrally controlled agencies with offices in all the important market countries to satisfy most international companies. The exception would be firms heavily committed to developing areas.

What do you do if there are no branches of your agency in a given country? In all except a few lesser markets there are only two choices: (a) the advertiser can allow the corporate agency to make a volunteer associate arrangement with an acceptable local agency, then hold the corporate agency totally responsible for the performance of that agency, as it is for its own subsidiary agencies; or (b) the advertiser can make its own selection of a local agency. The latter alternative will separate an individual market from agency management control, and it is the advertiser's responsibility to cause such agencies to conform to corporate policy and strategy.

Multiple-Product (or Brands) Advertisers. The one-advertiser, one-product, one-agency viewpoint helps to explain how the agency network system works. In practice, however, many international advertisers find their activities multiplied by having to place advertising for their different product lines, or different brand labels, through different agencies. Such instances can only add to the value of an agency network system.

The Multiproduct Advertiser. This advertiser is concerned with many different kinds of products that are under one brand label and can think in terms of agencies that are large enough to provide sufficient experience and talent for advertising all its products. A problem, however, will be to find an agency without *competing products.* The international advertising manager may need to categorize products in terms of types of consumer target markets and have a different agency for each category.

In some firms, separate product division advertising departments administer the advertising, but all report to a central corporate advertising director. For example, a large electronics manufacturer might divide its internal product divisions in such a way as to make the division of agency service clearly separate.

- hand-held electric appliances
- large home appliances (white goods)
- sound equipment—radio, stereo, TV
- industrial electrical equipment

If such a company were advertising in twenty-five countries, wanted to keep in close touch with the performance of its worldwide advertising, and did not employ qualified international agencies, it would be attempting to follow the work being done by a minimum of twenty-five agencies to a possible one hundred agencies. Under the network agency system, the advertising investment could be monitored through one to four agencies.

The Multibrand Advertiser. This term refers to companies that advertise competing brands, for example, soap, cosmetics, foods, and beverages. Such companies often operate internally under the brand manager system. Agencies are appointed by brand, and the brand manager is totally responsible for agency performance.

The internal marketing structures of international companies can be quite complex. The agency should represent a natural extension of any existing corporate organization. In smaller companies, or in large companies in which the product line is not complex, the top-level executive officers can, and usually are, interested in overall advertising policy and performance. The international network agencies can be held accountable to the heads of the advertiser's corporate management. Where product and brand lines become so complex as to warrant sharp divisions of marketing groups, the international agency principal should be determined, for accountability purposes, at the highest level of total marketing responsibility. So long as there exists a headquarters marketing management responsible for international marketing performance, there is a need for headquarters to express advertising policy in terms of maintenance of product positioning and corporate personality. For example, Novo Industri (Denmark) has a formal corporate advertising handbook covering its policies. The advertising agency can play a key role in internal marketing communications.

It is unlikely that a large multinational corporation will have strong advertising people in every country. In each of its subsidiaries it needs an individual who understands and can implement sophisticated marketing strategy. Chances for success are increased if the corporate head of international marketing can create a strong line of communications between himself and his counterparts in each country . . . and if he can communicate through one strong executive of an agency headquarters who is able to parallel such communications to his counterparts in local subsidiary agencies.

The Resulting Advertising

One argument often voiced against the international agency system is that it might not produce the best advertising in each market. As in the implementation of any sophisticated marketing procedure, one must assume competence on the part of the people organizing the plan.

The selection of the *right* agency is all-important, and the advertiser's management philosophy/psychology is important to the performance of such a structure.

An international agency can have a network of properly located subsidiary offices and sufficient equity for management control to suit the purposes of the advertiser, and yet it might not be right for the firm's successful operation.

A NEW WAY TO SELECT AN ADVERTISING AGENCY

In some countries, it is now possible to thoroughly review up to ten preselected advertising agencies that match your specifications—and do it all in one afternoon—and remain anonymous to all concerned. This is the promise made by Advertising Agency Register, Inc. (AAR), headquartered in London, with offices now in New York and Paris . . . soon to open in Frankfurt and other major European cities.

In our opinion, this type of service fills a long-sought need by advertisers, not only in reducing the time and expense necessary to do an agency search, but by adding greater thoroughness and, most important, avoiding proliferation of confidential corporate information, which is often necessary to allow several prospective advertising agencies to understand a prospective client. (For a description of how the AAR operates, see the article from *International Advertiser* in the appendix to this chapter.)

—— Some Key Considerations in Selecting ——
an International Agency

1. *Success with Local National Clients*
   When agencies expand into additional national markets, they sometimes do so simply to accommodate large international clients. They
   staff primarily from their home market people, do not solicit local
   clients, and in fact ignore the local advertising fraternity. Such agencies cannot demonstrate their ability to communicate to local consumers. They can demonstrate only their ability to satisfy the home
   office of their clients.

   Agency subsidiary offices should be staffed largely by local nationals—particularly in the creative areas. They should also show
   substantial billing from prominent local advertisers in order to
   demonstrate competence to communicate in each market.

2. *Agency's Attitude toward International Coordination*
   This is almost the opposite of the first consideration but will indicate
   the delicate balance necessary for a successful operation. A positive
   attitude toward an international client's policies and philosophies
   must exist both at the headquarters and among the foreign offices of
   the agency.

   On occasion, international agencies will resist the international
   coordination because: (a) they do not wish to staff their international
   headquarters with sufficient competent people to handle effective
   administrative and creative coordination; (b) proper coordination
   saves the client money and lowers the revenue of individual agency
   offices; and (c) it is a burdensome agency responsibility.

   They attempt to dodge this service either by asking a coordination
   fee, which they know will be prohibitive, or by establishing a policy
   that holds that interference with their local operations would destroy necessary local creativity.

   While local components will sometimes be less than cooperative
   toward an international coordination because of possible loss in
   revenue, they may also have a psychological block. Creativity is
   their business, and corporate campaigns or pattern book campaigns
   circumscribe them sharply. They prefer pattern campaigns only
   when their agency creates the pattern. Local agencies will immediately feel that they have two clients to satisfy with each campaign—the local client and the headquarters of the local client.

3. *Advertiser's Attitude toward International Coordination*
   Definitions of corporate operating policy are most important to a
   successful agency-client relationship and to reaching the advertiser's
   goal. These definitions should be stated very clearly when first approaching any agency to discuss an international agency network
   and the degree to which you want uniformity of the advertising

product in all foreign markets. Just the words "pattern campaign" can sound like a confinement no agency would care to be a part of—without a more complete explanation.

As an aid to defining an advertiser's objective in setting up specifications for international advertising coordination, read down the list below and draw a line where you think coordination for your company should stop.

- use of corporate logotype
- consolidated report on advertising spending through agencies
- regular home office presentations on advertising being created around the world—review and analysis
- provide for home office approval on all campaigns before they appear
- administer a common theme and product-selling proposition in all advertising around the world
- require agency headquarters to organize regional client-agency creative workshops to design and agree to a common theme and format. The theme and format are then to be approved by client headquarters for use in regional advertising, that is, a joint effort to create a pattern program
- require agency head office to provide an advertising pattern guide for each product and keep each of its foreign agencies within a reasonable limit of the guide
- require agency headquarters to create and develop a complete finished worldwide campaign and to direct its use in each market—allowing only necessary transliteration

The point being made is that even a consistent use of a corporate logotype requires monitoring and supervision. Registration for corporate logos have been lost legally because of improper use.

If advertising is important to a company's marketing success and represents a large investment, home office executive management need to be concerned about it. Positioning products in the total mix is important to long-range new product planning. This is usually understood best by headquarters. At the same time, it is important that all advertising effectively and persuasively communicate to each consumer public. Worldwide advertising should not be overdirected, so that it loses its ability to communicate; yet twenty-five foreign subsidiaries can easily go in twenty-five different directions without supervision.

The Coca-Cola Company and the Exxon Corporation are two of the largest and most experienced multinational advertisers. They both employ the same international agency network system, but differ in their international advertising philosophy. Coca-Cola develops prototype campaigns in the United States for worldwide distribution—a complete package of English language materials for use in different media. The *local* Coca-Cola operation then produces a local campaign from these prototype materials . . . making any

— **ILLUSTRATION 6-1** —
**Each year Coca-Cola produces and distributes, worldwide, dozens of
finished art advertisements to keep the Coke and the theme constant
throughout the world.**

Source: Reprinted with the permission of the Coca-Cola Company, owner of the trademarks
"Coca-Cola" and "Coke."

translations or adaptations that are necessary for the particular market. Further, U.S. headquarters involvement (and approval) is required only if the local operation desires to deviate widely from the prototype (see Illustrations 6-1 and 6-2). Exxon leaves campaign development to the discretion of its overseas management and charges the agency area coordinator with the responsibility to supervise for quality and efficient management of overall performance. Often the headquarters does not see their international advertising until it is presented by the agency as a year's end stewardship report. Still, both companies find important values provided in agency network system supervision.

How much supervision—how much central conformity and by whom—is now the question international advertisers should ask themselves.

They must also question *any* decision as to how it might affect the morale, incentive, and enthusiasm of the company's local foreign managements. Again, this is a delicate balance situation in the implementation of sophisticated marketing techniques, which can be handled only with well-defined lines of authority and communication.

Let us see how this might work. Let us suppose that there has been a corporate policy decision to "draw the line" after the sixth item in the list on page 123 to establish the desired degree of central coordination. This item is a regional joint effort to create a pattern advertising campaign—plus all specifications of all items preceding it.

— ILLUSTRATION 6-2 —

I'd like to buy the world a home and furnish it with love;
grow apple trees and honey bees and so I'd settle down.

I'd like to teach the world to sing with me in perfect harmony;
I'd like to buy the world a coke and keep it company.

It's the real thing
I'd like to teach the world to sing in perfect harmony and

I'd like to buy the world a coke and keep it company
It's the real thing, what the world wants today

It's the real thing, what the world wants today
It's the real thing.

"I'd like to buy the world a Coke" has been recognized as a "classic" both in the United States and abroad. Even though Coke produces several TV commercials each year for international distribution, this one, produced originally for the U.S. market, has such a strong international flavor it was a natural for worldwide exposure.
Source: Reprinted with the permission of the Coca-Cola Company, owner of the trademarks "Coca-Cola" and "Coke."

A new product is to be launched, and all national markets involved have been briefed by mail on this product and given marketing strategy specifications. The brief and specifications were drawn up jointly by the home offices of both the advertiser and the agency. This information is issued to the foreign operations through two separate channels—the advertiser's information and instructions to the advertiser's operating counterparts and the agency's headquarters to its opposite members in foreign markets. Everyone involved can now proceed to prepare themselves to be ready at a designated date and place to participate in a joint creative workshop.

Joint Creative Workshop.   During this entire procedure care must be taken to avoid any action that would make it appear that the advertiser's foreign offices are taking instructions from the agency's home office—or that local agencies are taking instructions from the advertiser's home office. The local agency's client is the advertiser's local subsidiary. At the group workshop, the home office director of the advertiser is the chairman, assisted by his or her headquarters agency. Individual personality strengths can sometimes swing the weight of authority out of balance. It is up to the workshop chairman (home office advertiser) to keep authority well balanced in order to arrive at a conclusion that is accepted well enough for future genuine performance.

The workshop itself can be stimulating and highly productive if sufficient instructions are advanced and good homework is prepared, and if the chairman can steer it to a strong conclusion that avoids weakening compromises.

The primary point is that such a joint effort to assemble a great amount of creative talent and to do the overall corporate job jointly with the markets involved would be virtually impossible without a one-agency network involved to support and cooperatively implement the preparation of one regional campaign. Be it only one theme and format for future local national interpretation, the total corporation has made important progress.

—— AGENCY COMPENSATION AGREEMENTS ——

If there does still exist such a thing as a "standard agency agreement," or normal remuneration system between client and agency, it would have to be the 15 percent commission from media and 17.65 percent added commission for other agency services provided to the client. The situation where the client looks to commissions realized by his agency from buying advertising media on his behalf as the major source of revenue needed to compensate his agency for its creative services is gradually becoming obsolete. With the more sophisticated client requirements and the agency's greater involvement in the entire marketing process, these simple standard agreements have undergone much revision and are being replaced with more realistic agency compensation systems.

In actual practice, there should be no such thing as a standard, or uniform, compensation arrangement for all clients of any agency—there should exist only a standard checklist of paid-for services to be considered according to the specifications for those services as required for each client.

Referring again to the discussion of the division of responsibilities between advertiser and agency: What services does an advertiser require of the agency? What are the depth and frequency of such services? What is the advertiser's priority of importance for each service that will indicate the quality (cost) of talent the agency will be required to provide?

The ultimate test for arriving at a good (acceptable, equitable, sound) agreement will be the advertiser's value judgment as to whether the cost is worth what the advertiser anticipates receiving. Such arrangements are not comparable to the purchase of physical goods. It is in no one's best interest to bargain down prices if you feel this is the agency you want to use. The advertiser is purchasing only the time of talent—for less money the advertiser will receive less of each. It is better to select another agency with lower "overhead" than to cut into the quality of your number one choice. If "bargaining" is the word, the only real areas open for investigation are the factor used in plussing up the cost of talent and overhead (the "factor" is sometimes negotiable) and the means of accountable auditing for the client's charges.

If the advertiser is satisfied that the agency's financial practices are sound, fair, and equitable, but that the services cost more than he is willing to pay, the advertiser can reduce the number of services required.

——— Basis for the Media Commission System ———

The media commission system that still prevails in most advertiser-agency agreements is based on these basic elements:

1. The agency calculates its income from a client based on the volume of media that the client authorizes the agency to purchase on behalf of the client rather than the services the client will purchase from the agency. The standard agency media commission is 15 percent. The publisher (or broadcaster/telecaster) publishes its advertising rates to advertisers, with the notation, "15 percent commission discount to recognized advertising agencies." The agency contracts with the medium on his client's behalf; the medium invoices the agency for the advertising space at the published rate, less 15 percent; the agency bills his client at the full published rate. The difference is the agency's gross profit.

    It is understood by the media and the advertiser that the agency must perform certain services in exchange for a privileged purchase price. In theory, the agency is bringing the advertiser and the medium together with the promise of creating the advertising that will be used in the medium. As we shall see later, the client must pay additional costs before the advertisement can appear.

2. Nonmedia creative work is performed by the agency, i.e., designing collateral promotion materials. This is charged to advertisers on an agreed hourly rate for talent time.

3. A commission is added to costs for work performed on behalf of a client by a third party—finished art, photography, graphic arts production, film production, etc. It is customary to add a commission of 17.65 percent to the invoice of the third party and pass it on to the advertiser (17.65 percent added equals a discount of 15 percent from a quoted price).

4. Usually the agency has other services it can sell to its clients, such as various forms of market research that are priced on a project quotation (or estimate) basis.

5. Recovery of out-of-pocket costs incurred by the agency on a client's behalf—this would really classify as reimbursement, not income—including such things as travel, postage, long-distance telephone, etc. (this is mentioned only to indicate that there do exist charges from an advertising agency for which a commission cannot be added).

An agency-client agreement based primarily on commissions paid by media bears very little relationship to the advertiser's service requirement, or to the agency's service costs and overhead expense. Therefore, for those parties that insist on clinging to this system, modifications have had to be instituted.

1. *Minimum billing clause.* An agency has fixed costs in overhead, salaries, and benefits. Every client adds to those costs, and if revenue from a client does not cover its share, the agency is actually losing money to maintain that client. If the agency calculates that any client that does not provide a revenue of at least $30,000 a year is unprofitable, it translates that into 15 percent media commission terms and inserts a minimum billing clause of $200,000. This means that if any client fails to order $200,000 in media, the agency has the right to charge the client the difference in commissions not received.

2. *Fee added clause.* The analogy is the same as above. Only the method of payment is different. Instead of a year-end settlement regarding minimum revenue, the agency establishes certain added fees for the client service, usually prorated monthly.

Media Billing	Fee (Annual)
$300,000 & above	No fee
$150,000–$299,000	$10,000
$100,000–$149,000	$20,000

Methods of agency compensation vary from agency to agency. Many agencies use different arrangements with different clients. In an interview in *Advertising Age/Europe*, Keith Monk suggested that the agency commission rate should be based on the *achievement* of the advertiser's objectives.[2] He said, "if an agency is not doing a good job, it would be paid 14 percent commission—and given a warning. A success under his arrangement would get 16 percent.

—— **Fee System Explained** ——

First, there is no "fee system." At least, there is not *a fee system*. To say that a client is on a "fee system" is to imply that the agency is not retaining the media commission. The agency is passing on its media commission to its client, and there must be another type of agreement for agency income.

The principle of a fee system is to ignore how much money the agency spends on behalf of its clients in the media and to consider only what services (amount and quality) the agency provides for its client. The fee can be arrived at from different, or combinations of different, points of reference, all based on agency expenses for serving a client.

1. *Hourly rate.* It is possible to establish an hourly rate schedule for every agency employee from the chairman to the mailboy. Such rates can include salary, social and personal benefits, retirement funds, and share of operating overhead. A profit-plus factor is agreed to, i.e., cost per hour times an agreed-upon factor (x times 2.5 or x times 3, etc.). The client is charged for every hour that is devoted to working on the account.
2. *Fee plus hourly rate.* A flat fee may be established for managing the account, and only creative and production talent is charged on the hourly rate. The division between functions covered by the flat fee and those on an hourly rate can have different definitions.
3. *Fixed annual fee.* With a long history of an agency-client relationship, it is possible to agree on a total annual fee, to which both parties agree at the beginning of each year. The fee will be an estimated cost for all client service requirements.

Most fee arrangements are estimated at the beginning of each year, based on the schedule of work assignments and paid to the agency on a prorated monthly basis, with quarterly or annual adjustments made according to actual audit.

In today's world it is difficult to understand how the media commission system of agency remuneration evolved in the first place. Advertising agencies are professional consultants and creators of advertising, yet living off

[2] "How to Improve Advertising Efficiency," *Advertising Age/Europe*, Vol. 1, Issue 5 (May 28, 1979), p. E-4.

media commissions is not in any way comparable to any other system for paying consultants or talent. But, originally advertising agencies did not do marketing evaluations or creative advertising. They were not even the "agent" for advertisers. They were the "agent" for the "media," and the medium referred to was magazines. Newspaper publishers sold space directly to advertisers because newspapers were a local medium and were located near the advertiser. They paid no selling agent commission; and they still do not, except in the case of national brand advertisers, which pay a much higher rate for space than do local retailers.

Most magazines were circulated over a large region and eventually nationally. Publishers had the choice of hiring salesmen to travel the territories, or of paying independent agents in different locations to represent them in selling space to advertisers.

As an agent could accumulate the rights to exclusively represent more and more magazines, business grew. But one of the obstacles to his growth was the fact that even though there were potential customers who wanted to advertise in the agent's publications, the customers had no one to design, write, and arrange for engravings for their ads. It was customary for the advertiser to hand the magazine agent finished engravings.

"Run till forbid" was an often-used phrase advertisers put on purchase orders when they handed the magazine agent the engraving for their ad—which was often a page from their product catalog. The agent received a 15 percent commission on the magazine space each time the ad appeared, and the ad did run until the agent was told to stop it.

Such a practice did not increase business for agents. Thus, the more imaginative agents offered to produce advertising *ideas* for potential customers—sometimes they produced ideas ahead of time to whet the appetites of possible customers—and they still got only their 15 percent from publishers.

Of course, over the years agent service has become far more sophisticated. But the one most significant change is the definition of the "agent." The agent is no longer the publisher's agent—he or she is now the advertiser's agent, and the agent buys advertising space from another media agent, or from a direct representative of the publisher, for his or her client and still collects the agent's 15 percent—which means that a publisher must now pay two selling commissions.

What does an advertiser receive for the 15 percent media commission he or she causes the agency to receive? To start with, not as much as some advertisers expect to receive. In principle, the advertiser receives marketing advice for promoting the product, creative concept ideas in the form of copy and rough layout, and a media recommendation. Beyond this the advertiser must pay hourly charges, fees, and commissions added for additional services.

In practice, the advertiser received a depth and breadth of services affordable by the agency consistent with the amount of revenue received by the agency on the volume of media purchased. One must keep in mind that the media commission revenue must also cover the agency overhead expenses and, of course, a profit.

One of the greatest sources of irritation in many agency-client relationships occurs over differences of opinion as to how to "share" the media commission.

Let us suppose there are two clients in the same agency. Client A—an insurance company—orders four print ads that are to appear in *Time, Newsweek, U.S. News & World Report, TV Guide*, and a host of Sunday newspaper supplements for a media budget of $3.5 million. The agency will receive $525,000 in media commissions.

Client B is a large industrial machinery manufacturer, and it orders 48 different ads to be produced to appear in 135 trade journals at a media budget of $750,000. The agency commission would be $112,500—or $412,500 less for producing twelve times as many ads—for arranging media purchase in many more publications and probably a great deal more service overhead. Unless the agency can sell Client B additional service—for example, sales promotion programs, direct mail, or market research at good profits—the agency may also need to charge an additional fee in order to show a net profit on the account.

Client A is obviously providing a disproportionate income to the agency compared with services received and should be entitled to share in profits by receiving more services without cost.

Both accounts could strike a more equitable arrangement by having all earned commissions credited to the client and then work out a fee agreement.

Although the fee system is becoming more general in use, somehow the media commission just will not die. Some advertisers delude themselves that they are getting something for nothing—and, of course, some agencies enjoy excess profits.

The trend is definitely toward the fee system, and as it becomes more popular it is only to be expected that the media will stop paying commissions to advertising agencies. This has already happened in Sweden and is predicted to develop elsewhere in the near future.

—— Agency Compensation and the —— Multinational Advertiser

With all the foregoing discussions on standardization, central control, and agency network management, it must be observed that agency compensation is the most difficult, if not impossible, area of multinational advertising to standardize. This is because of local national uncontrollable factors . . . the differences in media commissions paid (or eliminated), local agency association agreements on percentage markup for outside services, and many other differences.

If a multinational advertiser wants to audit for stewardship of investment efficiency and to look for additional ways to effect multinational advertising volume cost controls, such an advertiser can standardize the analysis over many countries by focusing on each agency's account *revenue* (gross income), *expenses*, and resulting *gross profit*. The amount of "billing" your account represents to an agency is of little significance in agency financial negotiation.

Because of the impressive "boxcar" figures, agencies are usually characterized by the size of their "billings," meaning the amount of clients' money that supposedly goes through their hands. With more and more advertisers preferring a fee system, or buying their media direct or through separate services, an agency must calculate backward (capitalize revenue) to determine what its "billing" would have been if realized as media commissions. Many agencies no longer use billing as an in-house reference; however, the trade press will often capitalize revenue reported in order to perpetuate the traditional size ranking among agencies.

In recent years *Advertising Age* has recognized this change in analysis:

World Income Rank	1980 Agency	World Gross Income		World Billing	
		1980	1979	1980	1979
1	Young & Rubicam	340.8	249.3	2,273.2	1,921.1
2	J. Walter Thompson Co.	322.5	253.9	2,137.7	1,693.0
3	McCann-Erickson	268.7	250.4	1,792.1	1,670.3
4	Ogilvy & Mather	245.9	206.2	1,661.9	1,392.6
5	Ted Bates & Co.	210.6	181.0	1,404.1	1,203.0

Source: Advertising Age, March 18, 1981.

Finally, what type of regular reporting does the agency provide to clarify assignments and decisions? And, is there a trend toward holding regularized annual (or more frequent) formal agency evaluations?

——— ADVERTISING AGENCY "CALL REPORT" ———

The agency "call report" is normally a routine record kept by advertising agencies of the minutes taken of a meeting with their clients (the advertisers). It records and describes decisions made, affixes responsibilities to specified persons to take specified actions, and establishes the dates for completion of each specified action . . . at least, the content of an agency call report *should* include all of this information.

We bring this to your attention because too often the call report falls far short of being complete, because the advertiser pays too little attention to this document, and because of the fact that this document can be of great value to the directing of a multinational advertising operation from corporate headquarters.

——— **Content of Call Report** ———

It is not unusual for the management of a subsidiary company (a local advertiser) to immediately place the blame on the local advertising agency for an advertising recommendation that is criticized by their headquarters. The level of quality of performance of the local agency may or may not be the real problem. However, if a headquarters management feel serious enough about their criticism, they should first find the root of the problem. The file of agency call reports is a good place to start.

If it can be said that there exist qualified people on the advertiser's staff and qualified people on the agency's staff, and if the original specifications for work required (agency brief) was thorough, then we can only suppose that problems regarding continuity of regular good service result from poor communications.

Exhibit A—Call report is not too unlike many call reports. It has been written with general and vague notations, either because the agency did not want to be pinned down to details for performance, or because it was considered not important since neither party (agency or client) is accustomed to referring to this document. Better said, neither party is accustomed to referring to such a document unless there is a problem and one party wants to prove the other at fault . . . and with Exhibit A no one can prove anything.

Exhibit B—This involves the same situation as Exhibit A, except that it includes a fixed responsibility for everyone involved and fixes a precise completion date for each step—*plus* a signature acknowledgment from the client indicating agreement to the specifications and dates agreed to at the meeting.

These exhibits have been made extremely simple to make a simple point. Call reports can be several pages long, and contain dozens of actions agreed to. But the principle is the same: If the advertiser does not show interest in, and attach importance to, such a document, the agency will not consider details important, and this can lead to unpleasantness between the two parties later on.

In directing a multinational advertising operation the director should review call reports as a matter of general subsidiary audits when he consults individual markets. If he in any way has cause to believe that there is beginning to be a breakdown in communication between one of his subsidiaries and its agency, he should arrange to receive *all* call reports involving these units for a period of time as a system of concentrated audit.

Aside from keeping agency-client relationships running smoothly, call reports can serve another important service to the home office. When an important subsidiary company is undertaking the development of a major new advertising campaign, the home office usually wants to stay abreast of progress. Instead of asking for separate progress reports, simply ask to be included on the routing of all call reports (request translations, if necessary). This not only eliminates a request for additional report writing; it also puts the agency on guard to take seriously the thorough writing of these reports.

——— EVALUATION OF AGENCY PERFORMANCE ———

Many client-agency relationships are highly subjective and involve personality matches and mismatches as well as objective examination of whether or not a good job is getting done. People who must sit in judgment of the true quality of such relationships must have documented facts for constructive decisions. Rumor can be born out of offhanded, unspecific criticism that can eventually destroy an important relationship. On the other side of the coin, the advertising function can deteriorate without apparent reason, and it is important to find out if all parties involved truly understand how the agency and client are supposed to perform in relation to each other. Therefore, several forms of formal evaluation studies have been devised, which if used in combination would provide a reliable cross-reference picture of great value to a person directing a multinational advertising operation. That person's end product is the result of a complex machine of many client-agency relationships.

An Agency Evaluates Itself and Its Clients. Agencies, like most other businesses, must make business forecasts and set up growth goals. Of course, they can examine all the trend data for opportunities, but they must examine their own tools if they are to take advantage of opportunities.

It is not unusual for agency management to ask their account people to evaluate their clients. To evaluate how the client performs or fails to perform in using the agency to their best advantage, they will probe such questions as what levels of client management the agency people reach; which agency services the client requires (and rank each service in relation to importance); the quality and thoroughness of specifications when briefing the agency; the depth of marketing plans; the extent of involvement expected by the client; an appraisal of professional quality in client management, and so on—leading up to expanded business opportunities.

In one way, this gives agency management a profile on growth with present clients; in another way, this also gives the agency a profile on its own account people, how well they know their own job and their client.

To carry such an investigation further to an even more meaningful conclusion, an agency will send evaluation appraisal forms to selected clients initiating discussion that will aid the agency in providing more and better service in the areas most important to the client.

——— What a Periodic Review May Include ———

In an effort to formalize their review process, a number of international agencies have developed questionnaires that have applicability for both the client and the agency itself. They ask both the client and the agency personnel involved directly in the "partnership" to complete the form. In particular, the formal questionnaires may be completed by the advertising manager (client) and the account group manager (agency).

Let us look at a few of the concerns that are considered in this evaluation:

Creativity.   Typically, the agency wants to know if its clients are satisfied with its (a) problem solving, (b) production quality, (c) creative strategy, (d) creative work, and (e) cost efficiency. For example, it may ask how the client "rates" the agency's ability to "get to the core" of the (client's) problems.

Media.   The media are a particular concern overseas, so a special questionnaire section may be devoted to this subject. The types of questions asked here may range from establishing media objectives and plans to the agency's development of new alternatives to "taking advantage of discounts."

Other sections may dwell on account management, client-agency attitudes, research, and administration. In each area, subjective opinion—as well as objective measures—may be sought. Basically, the total exercise has not only a *control objective* but additionally a goal of trying to identify problems in the client-agency relationships that could eventually lead to dissolving the "partnership."

Finally, since the agency and the client may *both* be located away from headquarters , this information helps to bring the agency up to date on the effectiveness of the relationship.

The following article is reprinted from the November–December 1981 issue of the *International Advertiser.* The authors wish to thank the editor of the *International Advertiser* for permission to reprint it.

—— APPENDIX ——

"I hear you are looking for a new ad agency. How come?"

If an advertiser wants to change agencies, it is really no one's business; yet, too many other people want to make it their business ... either out of some special financial or other business reasons ... or, just out of a type of curiosity that can lead to needless rumors. Naturally the trade press considers a major advertiser's agency change to be "hot news." They want almost daily progress reports and often attempt to drag names into their stories in order to create personal conflict impressions. The larger the advertiser, the greater the potential for adverse *unwanted and unnecessary* publicity.

Of course, there are large advertisers which seem to have been in and out of every shop on Madison Avenue. They change agencies like Hollywood celebrities change marriage partners. Their philosophy is ... "it only hurts for a little while and besides, everyone expects it to happen anyway." Marriage can be a good analogy for a client/agency relationship. When a long-term relationship breaks up, outsiders immediately assume the worst and start speculating about which side was wrong and who is in trouble.

When an advertiser starts thinking seriously about an agency change, word invariably gets out. Its competitors speculate on the financial and/or marketing condition of its business and its junior executives speculate on their jobs during, what could appear to be, a corporate reorganization. It can even cause investment counselors to look into the company's future prospects. Simultaneously, of course, the present agency's staff gets nervous about their jobs. Competitive agencies start swarming around the advertiser to pick up the business. Competitive agencies can also use such rumors to cast doubts in the minds of the victim agency's other clients. It is a messy business which too often causes both parties to suffer needlessly.

Dean M. Peebles is director of advertising and sales promotion for Goodyear International Corporation. He is co-author with John K. Ryans, Jr. of a soon-to-be-published book entitled International Advertising Management.

A Painless Way To Screen Agencies

by Dean M. Peebles

AAR

THE ADVERTISING AGENCY REGISTER INC.

LONDON   NEW YORK   PARIS

SOME OF THE ADVERTISERS WHO HAVE USED AAR'S SERVICES IN THE UNITED STATES AND EUROPE

AIR CANADA ... AIR INDIA ... ALLIED BAKERIES
ALLIED SUPPLIERS ... BATCHELOR FOODS
BMW ... BRITISH AIRPORTS
BRITISH AMERICAN TOBACCO
BRISTOL-MYERS ... BRITISH PETROLEUM
BROOKE BOND OXO ... CADBURY
CAMPBELLS SOUPS ... CARNATION
CIBA-GEIGY ... CITIBANK ... CONRAN
THOMAS COOK ... COTY DIVISION OF PFIZER INC.
DUBONNET ... DUNLOP
ENGLISH TOURIST BOARD ... EXXON
FISHER-PRICE TOYS ... GILLETTE
GLENLIVET DISTILLERS ... HEINZ ... IBM ... ICI
IMPERIAL TOBACCO
INTERNATIONAL DISTILERS & VINTNERS ... ITT
KAWASAKI ... KNORR SWISS ... KODAK
LYONS TETLEY ... MERCEDES BENZ
MIDLAND BANK ... MOBIL ... PHILIP MORRIS
NATIONAL FREIGHT ... NESTLES
NIKE FOOTWEAR ... PEUGEOT
PHILIPS ELECTRICAL ... PIRELLI TIRES
MARY QUANT ... QANTAS AIRLINES
RICHARDSON MERRELL ... ROMANOFF VODKA
SAFEWAY FOOD STORES ... SCHWEPPES
SEAGRAMS ... STERLING HEALTH ... SHELL
SONY ... THE TIMES SUPPLEMENTS
WARNER LAMBERT ... WRANGLER ... YARDLEY

The Advertising Agency Register touts a large list of clients.

I keep using the term "needlessly" because this scenario may become increasingly less common.

Reasons for Change

There are often very good reasons why an advertiser should change agencies. To generalize: It can happen that an agency fails to grow in sophistication and depth of service required by the advertiser; or, vice versa, the advertiser fails to grow as fast as the agency and becomes an insignificant client. In other instances, an agency is too dependent on the talents of one or two people and when they leave the agency, the advertiser must suffer through a prolonged period of unacceptable advertising. Also, the advertiser, or the agency, may assume new executive management which is not compatible with those in the formerly harmonious relationship. These are just a few of the many reasons an advertiser should change agencies. But, often they do not.

They do not because of unwanted publicity; fear of being bothered with oversolicitation of other agencies; or being looked at, and into, too

*Lyndy Payne
started AAR.*

*Alain Carette
heads up the
Paris office.*

*Leslie Winthrop
opened AAR's newest
office in New York.*

critically. In addition, it means losing continuity in advertising for a long period, and, of course, it means a change of routine and the breaking up of long-time friendships. (The latter is embarrassing particularly during the search for a new agency.) There are also many advertisers which would not think twice about breasting these obstacles ... "damn spears, spur the horses." However, they have another problem.

Which new agency to choose?

Most advertising agencies maintain a rather low profile to the public and in great measure to the business world. They are supportive to their clients and what they produce is done in their client's name. Certainly, advertising people on the client side of the business could, if asked, name several large advertising agencies. There are hundreds more agencies, and knowing the name and a couple of accounts associated with those names does not mean one really is aware of the qualifications of those agencies to handle effectively the advertising requirements for particular kinds of advertisers.

There are a great many advertising agencies to consider. Just look in the classified business section of city telephone directories, e.g., in New York, 1,374; Houston, 307; Detroit, 198; Pittsburgh, 146; Chicago, 665. In a city the size of Akron, Ohio (under 300,000 population) one finds 56 advertising agencies in the telephone directory.

If one has decided to look for a new agency, it is too time consuming and costly simply to announce that one's account is up for grabs — and it is considered bad form to let it be known that an advertiser has invited more than four or five agencies to present themselves.

What to do? Now there is a better way.

The Advertising Agency Register, Inc.

The author recently visited the first three offices of AAR in London, Paris and New York. When one realizes the problems connected with making an agency change — and then looks into the AAR service — the only conclusion is, "Why didn't someone think of this before?"

If the advertiser knows what he wants in a new agency, AAR can screen all member agencies to select best matchups; then in one afternoon the advertiser's management staff can have a thorough look "inside" the 10 agencies it selects, and do it all in complete confidence. It saves the advertiser much time, much money and no one (outside the company management group) ever knows that an agency is being considered. For the advertiser, the exercise is worth the price of admission just to compare his or her current agency with alternatives occasionally — whether or not the advertiser is seriously considering an agency change.

How It Works

The Registered Agency. Before AAR has any service to offer, it must build an inventory of agencies who register with this service. Any agency can register for a fee of $4,000 a year.

The registered agency puts on file three basic documents with AAR:

(1) *A Credentials File.* This is a book of basic facts regarding the business of the agency, i.e., its clients, personnel, past experience, growth record, etc. — all organized to an extensive outline specification designed by AAR.

(2) *A Press Book.* This, for lack of a better name, is a book of print ad campaigns with information concerning objectives, strategies and results, and/or research data.

(3) *Videotape "Live" Presentation.* The only videotape specification given by AAR is a 10-minute limit to the presentation. Otherwise, a registered agency may tape anything which presents the image it wants presented. One sees some most imaginative and unique styles of presentation.

Some choose to introduce the agency management principals. Others dramatize their creative philosophy. Some use diagrams to explain their approach to marketing problems, while others feature awards they have won. Most all demonstrate their style for producing TV commercials.

These documents/videotapes may be updated or changed whenever the agency desires; however, none of the agencies are permitted to see presentations on file from other agencies.

The Registered Advertiser. The first step in becoming a client of AAR is to pay a fee of $1,500. This is what one gets:

(1) *Interview on Specifications.*

AAR starts with an exhaustive interview to find out what one is looking for in selecting an advertising agency ... types of service, special experience, competitive conflicts to avoid and sometimes marketing services other than media advertising. An international advertiser would, of course, be looking for agencies with specified foreign locations.

(2) *AAR Screening Process.* The advertiser's specifications are matched with the documents on file from registered agencies. The AAR client is then presented with a list of all registered agencies which best match the specifications. From this list, and for the fee paid, the advertiser may select 10 agencies whose presentations he or she would like to study.

(3) *Presentation of Agencies.* The management staff representing the advertiser is provided a conference room and given the three documents from the 10 registered agencies selected. In just a few hours an advertiser can have an in-depth look at the materials on the 10 advertising agencies. Other than the credentials file, these agency documents are not permitted to be taken outside the AAR offices.

This entire exercise is conducted in complete confidence between AAR and the advertiser. Only after an advertiser selects the agency, or agencies, which look to be good prospects, is an agency informed of a prospective client, and this ends the AAR service. They receive no additional compensation from any agency selected. The only services AAR refuses to give an advertiser are to recommend any single agency, or to give advice beyond the screening process.

Where Does AAR Come From?

London. The idea and development of AAR was the brainchild of Lyndy Payne who, before 1975, was an account executive for a large London advertising agency. She observed just how disruptive it was from the agency side when prospective new clients were in the offering — and, how harried those prospects looked being shuttled in and out of the agency. Ms. Payne decided there must be a better way — and she developed it in 1975. In London today, it is the exception

Most advertisers will spend an average of $22,000, exclusive of travel expenses, to make their own search among far fewer agencies.

for an advertising agency not to be registered.

Paris. Alain Carette, a long-time Paris agency executive, became Ms. Payne's first partner, opening an office in Paris in 1978. Only the name of the service in Paris is Videotheque S.A. instead of Advertising Agency Register. Mr. Carette explains that he wanted to emphasize the video presentations and he did not want to limit the service to advertising agencies. He includes public relations and sales promotion agencies as well.

Mr. Carette boasts of having registered 49 of the top 50 Paris agencies and 138 of the top 150.

New York. The newest AAR partner is Leslie Winthrop, who opened an office in Rockefeller Plaza, January 1980. This, being a very new operation, has only about 80 registered agencies at this time. First to register were the international agencies which have experienced AAR service in London and Paris.

Ms. Winthrop emphasized she is not concentrating only on the New York City-based agencies. Her target is to register most of the 375 agencies in the United States which have billings of at least 10 million dollars.

Frankfurt. A German partner is scheduled to open an AAR service before the end of 1981.

From what I have learned in visits to the three AAR offices, it appears to me to be a very valuable service to both advertisers and advertising agencies. Ms. Payne estimates that most advertisers will spend an average of $22,000 (exclusive of travel expenses) to make their own search among far fewer agencies. If a firm does not find the agency it is seeking through AAR, at least the service will have helped eliminate some candidates which will save the advertiser much time and money, and the entire exercise will have been kept confidential. □

—— 10 KEY POINTS ——

1. An advertiser does not need to think in terms of contracting with an entire agency—only in terms of acquiring an agency's services that are needed to complement the advertiser's own in-house staff. The agency is an extension of the in-house capability, not a duplicate add-on. However, sufficient functions should be placed with an agency in order to hold the agency completely responsible for the creative strategy and its implementation. It is becoming more common for advertisers to select and buy their own media in many parts of the world, as well as to handle the production of supporting collateral materials.

2. As pertains to which agency services are needed by an advertiser, this is best determined by listing all services required to handle the advertising function for a particular advertiser; then an equitable and efficient division of responsibilities is determined.

3. In deciding the type of agency that is best for each individual MNC, one needs to examine the organizational structure of the corporation and the corporate policy pertaining to central management control of advertising, the desire for uniform corporate image, and the critical aspects of brand positioning and legal protection required for trademarks. Then one can decide between:
    *   local option for individual agencies
    *   voluntary network group
    *   central controlled network
    *   the lead agency concept
    *   the deliberate minority concept

4. The minimum number of agencies is recommended by the authors. This is determined by geography of subsidiary locations and by the complexity of multiple brand names and the diversity of multiple kinds of product classifications.

5. In considering a particular agency for a multinational assignment, one must look beyond the normal considerations of credit rating, tenure of employees, length of association, and quality of present clients. One should also consider:
    *   success with local national clients as well as with international clients
    *   attitude toward working with a local client that must also satisfy an MNC headquarters
    *   attitude toward intermarket coordination

- attitude toward working cooperatively with other agencies in other national markets
- attitude toward working according to an international head-quarters specification or pattern

6. Agency compensation should take into account that a client-agency relationship is a partnership in the advertiser's market-ing function. Everyone involved must realize a reasonable profit in order to perform with the required enthusiasm. Under the media commission concept, large media budgets can overcompensate the agency, and small budgets will not pro-duce sufficient incentive to get the best work from an agency.

7. Advertising agencies are consultants selling their profes-sional time. A fee based on the time needed for creative work and supervision is recommended particularly for subsidiaries of MNCs that use headquarters creative assistance or guide-lines.

8. Local agency "call reports" can be used by a headquarters as an efficient instrument for international management informa-tion. They can substitute for, and in some cases be of greater value than, separate reports written especially for headquar-ters' consumption.

9. Headquarters can regularly institute a program to evaluate local agency performance in servicing local subsidiaries and, in the same operation, evaluate the quality of local subsidi-aries in their ability to effectively communicate with their agencies.

10. The advertising agencies evaluate the client regularly and utilize this information to determine how to serve it better.

7

Managing International Advertising Research

— INTRODUCTION —

Advertising research is not as frequently employed internationally as it is domestically. In fact, many major industrial and consumer goods firms conduct little or no advertising research in most markets where their products are sold. There are a number of factors that have led to such limited attention being given to advertising research. These factors include the many "perceived problems" of conducting overseas research.

We recognize, however, that many leading firms do conduct advertising research and are aware of its impor tance to effective advertising. The value of such research is discussed along with:

- the *quality* of overseas advertising research and research firms

- the need for *more* rather than *less* research overseas
- the *kinds* of research that should be conducted
- the importance of *coordinating research across* markets
- the *reliability* of foreign secondary data
- the basics—what the international advertising manager *needs to know* about each market
- the role of *pre- and postadvertising research*
- the *need* to *centralize* the advertising research decisions and to develop clear-cut research policies
- the "how to's" of selecting an international research firm

Advertising research plays the same vital role in the development of *effective* overseas communications that it does domestically. Many major consumer goods firms, in particular, do extensive advertising and marketing research in every foreign market where they sell their products.

Yet, many other consumer goods firms and *most* industrial goods producers do little or no international advertising research. Why? Why, for example, did a 1980 study of a sample of U.S. small appliance manufacturers find that only 21 percent conducted advertising research overseas, although *all* sold abroad? And similarly, why did a study of construction equipment manufacturers suggest that *none* conducted research abroad?

There are many reasons for this situation, of course, ranging from the high cost of conducting overseas research . . . especially with limited advertising budgets . . . to the fact that international business represents such a small share of total sales for the bulk of U.S. producers. Not the least of the reasons, however, is the widely held perception that international advertising research is fraught with problems.

This perception has left even seasoned international advertising managers reluctant to conduct such research. Also, questions we often hear in conducting international advertising management seminars are: "Where do you begin if you want to conduct advertising research overseas?" and "How do you obtain even basic information on foreign buyers?"

Owing to these real concerns and to the many misconceptions that have persisted regarding international advertising research, in this chapter we are taking a slightly different orientation to the overall management theme stressed throughout the book. While still emphasizing the management side of advertising research, we shall also briefly cover some key information sources *and* answer some of the most frequently asked questions regarding international advertising research.

Why Conduct Advertising Research Overseas?

Basically, international advertising research, like domestic advertising research, is designed to help the manager make better *advertising decisions*. Research conducted prior to the appearance of the advertisement or campaign should focus on making certain that the concept/theme and the creative material, as well as the media chosen, are effective, that is, achieve their objective(s) with the target audience. Postadvertising research or research conducted after the advertising has appeared (or while it is appearing) is designed to determine if it achieved (or is achieving) its objectives. As such, the latter type of research plays a *control* role.

Unless advertising research in a given market can assist in the decision-making process, of course, it should not be conducted. Advertising research in some form usually adds to the ability of the firm to successfully communicate with its target market, however, unless it simply is cost-prohibitive. And, as we shall see later, there are many inexpensive ways to gather useful information without conducting extensive formal field research. Industrial marketers, in particular, have found that simply asking the "right questions at a trade show" or "surveying their own sales reps" can provide valuable insights at a low *cost*.

We recommend that the international advertising manager use one particular criterion when considering the value of a research project: Will the benefits obtained from the information be greater than the cost of conducting the research? In answering the question, he or she must recognize both the short-term and the long-term value of the information and its potential use across markets.

——— Quality of Research ———

One of the myths, for example, that surrounds international advertising concerns the quality and availability of overseas marketing research firms and services. Let us try to dispel this misconception before moving on to more important questions concerning the employment of advertising research in foreign markets.

Certainly, the marketing and advertising research skills that are found in some developing countries are *not* comparable to those found in the United States or, for that matter, in Canada, Western Europe, Australia, Japan, Mexico, Brazil, and other countries. (Of course, firms in the United States are not all of equal quality, either.) Fred Bastl[1] has described how difficult it is to obtain rather rudimentary secondary and primary data in order to prepare an initial market analysis in some developing countries. Similarly, Boyd et al.,[2] in a widely publicized *Journal of Marketing Research* article, also spoke of the lack of sophistication in the developing markets. While accurate, these and other, similar views have led many to be unwilling to conduct marketing and advertising research abroad . . . generalizing from the difficulties in a few developing countries to *all* foreign locations.

In truth, many of the finest marketing and advertising researchers are

---

[1] Fred J. Bastl, "Determination of the Export Potential," *Akron Business and Economic Review* (Summer 1971), p. 5.

[2] Harper W. Boyd, Jr., Ronald E. Frank, William F. Massey, and Mostafa Zoheir, "On the Use of Marketing Research on the Emerging Economies," *Journal of Marketing Research*, Vol. 1 (November 1964), pp. 20–23.

found in the primary overseas markets. Often, they are employed by subsidiaries or branches of major U.S. concerns, but many work for highly sophisticated non–United States-based international agencies or even for totally local firms. Further, there are several foreign marketing research societies or organizations that number in their membership these same talented research individuals, as well as research experts from corporations, advertising agencies, and the media. An example of such an organization is the European Society of Marketing Researchers (ESOMAR) that has held a series of joint meetings with the American Marketing Association. The reader should be assured that in the developed countries competent research personnel are available and that research assistance similar to that found in the States can be obtained in a large share of the developing world markets— often through the local offices of major international research firms.

—— Some Research Basics ——

Next, if we were to assume that all our readers had extensive domestic marketing and advertising research experience, we might say that the same decision criteria you employ domestically in determining the need for advertising research can be used in making your nondomestic decisions. This, however, would not only be oversimplistic . . . it would be inaccurate. In fact, there are a number of factors to suggest that you will likely need to do *more* marketing and advertising research abroad. Let us consider the following research basics before taking a more detailed look at this "needs" question:

1. If the firm is planning a worldwide or Pan-European campaign, it is essential to learn at *each* important stage in the creative process whether the *message* will be viable in the *individual markets*. This calls for the use of focus group concept tests or some other type of pretest of the message in *each* market.
2. Prior to entering new markets . . . in fact, before the decision to enter the market has been made, certain basic marketing information is gathered. This will include both secondary information (available from many sources) and primary data (developed specifically for the firm). Such information is useful for advertising decisions.
3. A continual monitoring of the firm's sales records provides extensive information about the nature of its customers (industrial or consumers). This type of information gathering within the firm needs to be *regularized* so that it is not only available for *all* markets but is maintained over the years so it can be traced for historical patterns as well. This *need* has led to the wide use of tracking studies . . . often as part of omnibus studies in which data on several firms are collected simultaneously.
4. All overseas marketing research the firm conducts should be available to the international advertising manager. Certainly, consumer or industrial marketing research designed to *better target the*

market, even if it is designed to make product or price decisions, will be important for advertising decisions. There is often evidence in the United States of the different divisions of a single firm doing *duplicate research,* i.e., failing to communicate internally about marketing or advertising research that has been conducted. This practice is a costly domestic *luxury,* but it is one that simply *cannot* be afforded overseas.

5. Marketing and advertising research conducted by or for the firm is generally more *expensive* overseas. Further, it is often especially costly in relation to the *size* of a given market. By employing a single international research firm, rather than a number of individual local firms, the international advertising manager not only ensures comparable data . . . he or she also will likely have lower total research costs.

6. Full-scale test markets of advertising themes, such as MNCs often employ in the States, may not be possible in many foreign markets. Even if they could be handled cost effectively, some countries do not lend themselves to such techniques because they are "single market" countries. For example, in Venezuela, Caracas is clearly the *key* market for most consumer products. A test market elsewhere in the country is less representative, and a "test" campaign in Caracas becomes a fait accompli.

7. Pretest and posttest advertising research have entirely different objectives. Both are essential ingredients of a firm's overseas advertising programs. Pretest research is designed to determine the potential *effectiveness* of an advertising theme, a copy or campaign strategy, a particular medium, or even an individual advertisement prior to its full-scale use in a market (or markets). The research technique employed should be one that will measure what the advertiser is attempting to achieve with this theme, etc., such as building increased *awareness* or improving *image.* Posttest advertising research, on the other hand, is a *control* device, and it is designed to determine whether or not the actual theme, campaign, etc., that is now complete (or continuing) has achieved (or is achieving) its *objective.* Not only is such research necessary for measuring the degree of success or failure, but it also suggests whether this theme, campaign, etc., should be continued longer in these markets and/or expanded to other world markets.

8. The international advertising manager must often *sell* the various overseas subsidiary heads, as well as home office executives, on the value of conducting marketing or advertising research. The foreign national who is serving as the local marketing manager (or perhaps even the subsidiary or branch managing director, if he or she is involved) may have limited marketing or advertising experience. This individual may, in fact, have most of his or her experience in sales/sales management or another area of business and view each

dollar, lira, or pound spent on research as actually reducing the operating funds available to hire more sales people or to run more or larger advertisements.

"We all know people buy the lowest-price _____, so why research it?" is a refrain many local advertising managers hear frequently. This is one point where the international advertising manager located in the home office can utilize his *leverage* to assist the local advertising manager. The international advertising manager can simply require a certain amount of the advertising budget in each market to be earmarked for research, or he or she can hold back a proportion of the advertising funds and direct the research from the home office.

9. The advertising research efforts of the firm and those of its international agency(ies) need to be closely coordinated at both the international and the *local* national levels. First, the branches, subsidiaries, or local affiliates of the international agency can be helpful in the data-gathering efforts. Second, since agencies are conducting much research on their own or for other clients, some overlap of effort can be reduced and/or suggestions for joint research by noncompetitive firms might be initiated. The use of joint advertising research by two or more noncompetitive firms can be one way of reducing research costs, but unfortunately, relatively few research concerns lend themselves to such an approach.

With these basics behind us, we can now examine the sorts of advertising research needs the MNC operating as it does in multiple markets may have.

⸺ Kinds of Research ⸺

Initially, we need to distinguish between *secondary* research—that is, research available to everyone, often at little or no cost—and *primary research*, that is, data collected specifically for the firm. Because of the cost involved in collecting *primary data*, much of our attention will be focused on the use of secondary data.

In addition, of course, there are many other ways to classify advertising research, ranging from the type of product/industry being studied (consumer goods, service, or industrial) to the types of research technique being employed (personal interviews, focus groups, etc.). For our purposes, it may be most useful to consider research in terms of its source (or who developed the data base). Such a classification would include *three broad categories*, including internally generated (in-house), media-generated, and independently generated research. The latter is often company-specific but may include data collected for other firms as well.

To illustrate the types of advertising research a firm may use, let us *further* subdivide these three broad categories. These include:

1. Internally generated research
   - changes in sales (over time)
   - changes in customer type (over time)
   - brand preference or awareness surveys (over time)
   - product perception surveys (over time)
   - media preference surveys
   - competitor comparisons/analyses
   - distributor interviews (formal or informal)
   - customer interviews (formal or informal)
2. Media-generated research
   - advertising readership, listenership, or viewership surveys
   - audience profiles
   - product perception surveys
   - brand preference or awareness surveys
   - inquiries (direct response to coupons)
3. Independently generated research (often company-specific)
   - omnibus or individual tracking studies
   - media preference surveys
   - product perceptions studies (pre- or post-)
   - brand preference or awareness studies (pre- or post-)
   - concept or theme tests (pre- or post-)
   - commercial and media (etc.) tests

Few firms regularly use all of the above kinds of data; they represent many "researchable" concerns of the international advertiser. Some of this research information, such as the internally generated sales and customer data, should, of course, be readily available in-house, while other information, such as the media profiles, may be available without cost from the particular magazine, newspaper, or broadcast medium. On the other hand, the independently generated research that is company-specific, for example, television commercial tests, can be quite expensive, as will be seen later.

Reliability of Secondary Data. When using secondary data generated outside the firm, a note of caution is appropriate, because such data often vary widely in quality. In fact, before using any secondary data, the international advertising manager needs to ask the following questions:

1. Who collected the data and why were they collected?
2. What research technique(s) was employed?
3. Would the data source have any reason(s) to bias the data?
4. When? How old are the data?

While it is often difficult to obtain answers to all these questions, they do suggest that the international advertising manager exercise *caution* in accepting "facts." For example, published UN data have a bad reputation, because member countries often provide inaccurate or unsubstantiated information. Similarly, media data in a number of countries are unreliable. In regard to each of these instances, question (3), above, provides the *basis for the problem*.

—— **Knowing the Market** ——

Unlike advertising research conducted by U.S. firms in the States or by German firms in Germany, the international advertising manager often knows few, if any, of the "basics" about the country or market where the advertising will appear. With the plethora of secondary data available from the U.S. government and other reliable sources, a useful "first step" in any country often is a brief "country analysis."

Among the basics that the international advertising manager may find useful to include are:

- socioeconomic data
- political/legal information
- cultural data
- raw materials/industrialization information
- urbanization
- geographic factors
- demograpics

Some comments on *sources of information* that one of the coauthors recently presented in *Industrial Marketing* are presented in Illustration 7–1. It is recommended that the information available from the U.S. Department of Commerce (DOC) or Department of Agriculture (DOA) is often sufficient for the international advertising manager's purposes here. For example, an *Overseas Business Report* (OBR) published by the DOC typically will offer the sort of brief overview that is quite useful prior to developing an in-depth study of a market. Many companies regularly develop and maintain background reports for use in making a variety of international decisions. It is recommended that the international advertising manager determine if such reports are available in the firm and, if so, access them (or other marketing-related country data) before seeking data outside the firm.

— **ILLUSTRATION 7–1** —
Foreign Market Info Sources

The following checklist of secondary information sources for overseas marketers was compiled by John K. Ryans Jr., professor of marketing and international business at Kent State University.

At one extreme, the U.S. Department of Commerce provides a "wealth of fantastic information" through the departments listed below. But among international organization sources, the United Nations provides rather poor information, Prof. Ryans says. "There's some good UN material, perhaps from UNESCO (United Nations Educational, Scientific and Cultural Organization), but it carries a heavy political bias depending upon what help a country is seeking from the UN," he cautions.

Department of Commerce:

- Overseas Business Reports (published on a country by country basis)
- *Business America* (a biweekly journal)
- *Export* (an annual publication)
- Individual "country desks"
- Commercial attaches
- Trade opportunity programs and business counseling services

Department of Agriculture
Overseas Private Investment Corp.
U.S. State Department
U.S. Agency for International Development

International Organizations:

- International Bank for Reconstruction and Development (World Bank)
- General Agreement on Tariffs and Trade
- World Health Organization
- Food and Agriculture Organization
- International Labor Organization
- Organization for Economic Cooperation & Development
- European Economic Community

Other Sources:

- International Advertising Assn.
- U.S. Chamber of Commerce, and U.S. Chambers of Commerce in different markets
- Angel's Directory of Corporations (annual directory of companies trading overseas)
- National Foreign Trade Council (an organization of multinational corporations, based in New York).
- World Trade Education Center (New York)

Additionally, major commercial banks and advertising agencies have substantial foreign marketing information. Major transportation companies are a good source of shipping information. Certainly the governments of overseas countries should not be overlooked as sources.

Most of the above-listed sources provide free information. After exhausting those, as appropriate, data and special studies are available for sale from international trade consultants and their newsletters. Among recommended sources are: Business International, New York; The Conference Board (services available to members); the Intelligence Unit of the *Economist*, and *World Business Weekly* magazine.

Source: Reprinted with permission from *Industrial Marketing*, February 1981. Copyright 1981 by Crain Communications.

Finally, when developing a brief country analysis, it is essential that the international advertising manager give special attention to the cultural considerations. As discussed in Chapter 12, cultural concerns may play a role in the firm's success, so hints regarding the cultural "do's and don'ts" are very essential.

MANAGING THE FIRM'S ADVERTISING RESEARCH NEEDS

U.S. corporations tend to make more extensive use of advertising and marketing research than do their European counterparts (and they often differ in techniques employed). A 1977 study by Permut found that concept tests that were ranked first in domestic research importance by U.S. firms were *not* used by their Western European counterparts.[3] Other findings of the Permut study further suggest important differences in the amount (and types) of research conducted by the European and American marketers in their domestic advertising. Similar findings would be expected in studies directed to the foreign marketing efforts of these marketers.

Just *how much* and *what types of* international *advertising research* a particular firm *needs* depends on many factors. Not only are there the obvious target market differences between consumer goods and industrial producers; there are also important differences between firms within the same industry. For example, two MNCs in Industry A may have widely different levels of awareness and market share (and corporate authority) in France, but similar statistics in Italy. Thus, their overall advertising research needs (and advertising budgets) may differ markedly on these factors *alone*. Add to this the differences in advertising objectives, as well as the possibilities of *new* product introductions, and the difficulty in describing general research *needs* becomes even more apparent.

At a minimum, most firms need to have certain basic information about their various markets to assist them in making their advertising decisions. These basic research *needs* include:

- some information regarding the characteristics of their target market
- some type of continual monitoring of their *image* and their *relative* level of awareness
- some form of concept testing, as well as pretest research of their advertisements/campaigns
- some follow-up research to determine if their advertising objective(s) was achieved, i.e., a measure of control

Just how firms go about obtaining such information, however, can vary widely—as do the budgets they have to devote to research.

"I Can't Afford Sophisticated Research"

This is another frequently heard complaint when we talk with international advertisers, particularly smaller firms. For this reason, we will stress both sophisticated and "opportunistic" approaches to obtaining research insight.

---

[3] Steven E. Permut, "The European View of Marketing Research," *Columbia Journal of World Business*, Vol. XII, No. 3 (Fall 1977), p. 981

Optimally, the international advertising manager needs to carefully research each step in a campaign's development. In Chapter 10, the approaches followed by Digital Equipment Corporation and Henkel KGaA illustrate this optimum use of advertising research in their development of effective corporate advertising campaigns. And many international firms have sufficient budgets to conduct the necessary levels of *formal* research.

Let us look at one or two ways that a firm could achieve the *minimal* research needs noted above. Generally, the international marketing division/department will be developing data on the target market, and this information should be available to the international advertising manager. He or she can then convey it to the advertising agency(ies) or to in-house planners/creative staff. In the case of consumer products, these target market data could range in sophistication from consumer demographics to psychographic profiles, while with industrial products the potential industry categories could be described *or* specifics about the appropriate level of buying decision makers could be provided.

If formal target market data are unavailable, the international advertising manager may need to turn to the company's sales force for information (or to dealers/distributors for certain consumer products). While the data would be "second hand," they would offer some research guidance. Finally, considerable data are often available in the company's *sales records*; a point too often ignored.

Image/Awareness Monitoring.   The availability of omnibus studies have greatly reduced the problems many firms have had in attempting to adequately track their image changes and relative level of awareness (versus competition). Described more fully later, the omnibus studies bring economies of scale to research, that is, it allows a number of firms to participate in the *same* ongoing research and thus to drastically reduce their research costs. For example, an MNC can include two or three key questions in an omnibus study rather than having to conduct the whole research project itself. This approach is particularly useful in tracking the firm's level of awareness or image in numerous markets; if it notes a *significant* change between *time periods* in some markets, it can then conduct more extensive research study in the "problem" area or country to get at the cause(s).

Many other firms prefer to conduct their own ongoing research regarding their image and level of awareness in various markets. In this case, it is vital that the research data obtained are readily comparable.

For example, if an industrial firm cannot afford such formal tracking research, it can take actions ranging from asking visitors at its booth at a trade fair to telephoning or sending questionnaires to key customers or distributors.

Concept Testing/Pretesting of Campaigns.   The use of focus groups in concept testing is growing rapidly. While some researchers still shy away from *any* technique that does not employ random sampling procedures, it should be stressed that, conducted properly, a focus group provides considerable insight *quickly* and at a *relatively low cost*. What is essential, of course, is to select focus group participants that approximate your target audience as closely as possible.

Perhaps the biggest *plus* of the focus group, however, is the *interchange* between the participants, which often appears to produce a "geometric" rather than a "linear" growth in *ideas/views*. Other techniques such as mail or telephone surveys or personal interviews with respondents selected from the target audience can also provide helpful information for concept testing.

Similarly, focus groups or panels can be quite effectively employed in the pretesting of the campaign or advertisements. For the industrial marketer, the international trade shows and exhibits often provide excellent forums for testing concepts and advertisements or even for holding "informal" or formal focus groups. Certainly, a food manufacturer or equipment supplier could find all the potential focus group participants it needs at the Hamburg Food Fair, for example. Again, other techniques, such as personal interview surveys, can be very effective in such research for either industrial or consumer products.

Postresearch. The type of post–advertising/campaign research (or continual monitoring, if the campaign is to be continued) depends on the objective of the campaign. If, for example, it is designed to provide sales leads via requests for information (response cards or inquiries), then a predetermined level of responses may provide the *adequate* measure (or possibly the quality of the leads).

On the other hand, if a change in image or awareness is desired, a follow-up study similar to the earlier "benchmark" research would be necessary. Here, changes identified by the tracking research might prove to be sufficient.

What is essential is that the posttest research must be consistent with the desired objectives of the research. Otherwise, no real measure of the success of the campaign will be available.

Finally, before leaving the research *needs* section, it is important to stress the point that research—comparable research—is *needed* in each market where the advertising is to appear. Practically speaking, however, many advertisers often tend to try to cross borders with their findings; for example, to consider an Italian concept test to be valid for Europe. This is *highly risky* and is especially not recommended for consumer product research. More firms have been successful in "generalizing" across borders in the old Benelux area than elsewhere in Europe, but the international advertising manager should try to avoid such tempting shortcuts.

Managing the Research

Frankly, we recommend that much of the firm's international advertising research be centralized in the home office. There are many valid reasons to support such a recommendation.

In fact, we recommend a high degree of centralization of the research function *even* if the firm decentralizes most of its advertising decisions.

Why? First, many of the major international marketing and advertising decisions, especially regarding the budget, are made in the home office. Therefore, it is important that the international advertising manager receive relatively *uniform* information on the individual foreign markets or subsidiaries. Such comparable data permit the home office to spot differences that are developing regarding image or awareness *between* key markets—a change that may be less apparent at the subsidiary level. Since markets differ widely in many normal measures, the key changes are typically in relative trends, not absolute differences.

This same point can also be made (and, in fact, was emphasized in our earlier discussion of standardization of advertising) when the research is designed to *assist* in developing a theme or campaign specifically for multimarket use. Such preresearch efforts could range from concept testing via focus groups or personal interviews to less formal "interviews" at trade fairs in the case of medium and small industrial users.

Perhaps the best summation of the overall value of standardization (and centralization) in research efforts is offered by Anna Maria Sarmento, a Marplan Research, Inc., executive, who says:

> In conducting international research, particularly multi-country research, a client is mostly interested in *comparability* of research findings across countries. But it should be pointed out that the problem of comparability is not confined to surveys which are explicitly "multi-country." It is often as important in the case of a survey carried out in a single country where the results may at some time in the future need to be compared with results from equivalent surveys in other countries.
>
> To achieve comparability across countries, there are strong arguments in favor of *standardization of research methods* . . . .
>
> 1. The use of standard approaches can save time and money internationally, particularly at the design stages and the data-processing and analysis phases. And, where absolute uniformity internationally is essential, it can be obtained only by strictly standard approaches in the field.
> 2. Standardization also simplifies life for the users of research—it allows for *direct* comparison of results from different countries—while it provides the user with greater confidence in using research findings based on those standard approaches.
>
> Standardization, however, should not be pursued for the sake of standardization, and local differences must be taken into account to help reflect marketing, cultural, and environmental differences.

In organizing international research where comparability is desired (which is often), we deem the need for *firm coordination as a critical requirement.* Coordination can be achieved successfully only if a clear and recognized central point of responsibility for decisions affecting the design and conduct of the research is established. It is especially important that the respective roles, contributions, and involvement of the headquarters and of the local units—in both the client and research organizations—be agreed upon from the outset.

To facilitate the coordination process, it is necessary to develop a close relationship between headquarters and the field, that is, the various subsidiaries or local branch offices. This is particularly essential in those firms where a local has advertising management responsibilities, such as a local advertising manager or even a local marketing research head. These locals' input into the preparation of the research instruments or the decisions on research methodology, for example, can be essential in avoiding cultural difficulties.

Ms. Sarmento adds the following:

> In our experience, parallel communications must be established between the client's headquarters and local clients, and between the research company's headquarters and local research organizations. At headquarters there will be direct communication between client and research organization, the same occurring at the local level. *Responsibility for decisions lies at the headquarters level only,* although open communications between field and headquarters allows for the integration and adaptation to take into account specific local needs.

Next, the cost of research must always be an important consideration . . . and one worthy of special attention by the international advertising manager. A "golden rule" for marketing and advertising researchers would read something like, "Exhaust all secondary sources before doing *primary research* and then obtain *only* the data that you absolutely need." The firm's advertising and marketing research efforts overseas should be complementary and, if possible, additive, that is, adding to the body of knowledge you are developing regarding the particular market and your buyers generally.

As we shall see shortly, the market-to-market costs of interviewing *alone* can be quite expensive. Thus, while we are advocates of a strong marketing research program, we recognize that a dollar, a peso, or a lira spent for research is usually one less available for media purchases or creative materials. Each situation must be viewed differently, of course, but "overresearching" may be almost as *costly* as "underresearching" a market. For this reason, headquarters management are in a much better position to evaluate the *real* research needs than are those advertising managers in the branch or subsidiary locations.

Advertising Research Policies. The international advertising manager needs to develop a series of policies and guidelines for the effective management of the firm's international advertising research. These involve:

1. The budgeting process . . . as noted earlier, we recommend that this function be centralized.
2. The role of the firm's advertising agency in the advertising research function . . . we recommend a coordination of efforts, but keeping

the agency at arm's length in much of the actual research and data analysis.

3. The selection of an international or local research firm . . . we feel that final approval should rest at the headquarters level.

4. The coordination and communication of all international/marketing research conducted by the firm . . . we feel that any advertising/marketing research conducted by the firm should be *available/accessible* to *all* IM departments. (This may require a directive from the senior marketing executive to implement.)

5. The determination of the actual longitudinal (long-term and/or tracking efforts) and the special studies (campaign concept testing, etc.) needs . . . we again see the home office playing the central role in this effort with inputs from the local office.

6. The establishment of a regular reporting and routing system for certain basic data, such as sales data by product category, that is essential to all marketing decisions.

7. The careful delineation of all lines of authority and responsibility regarding the research methodology approval process.

Such policies will prevent the ad hoc conducting of advertising research at some local subsidiary that may actually be unnecessary or even redundant. It should also preclude the firm's conducting *two* internal marketing or advertising studies when only one is needed.

——— Fieldwork Costs Example ———

We have frequently mentioned that overseas advertising research can be expensive . . . even in relation to domestic research in the United States. To illustrate this with actual cost data, let us consider the case of one U.S. consumer goods producer.

During 1979 and 1980, this major MNC embarked on a worldwide awareness and attitude study that would be used in developing its regional and international campaigns. A single international research firm planned the entire project. Therefore, in each of the various locales the same questionnaire and basic methodology were employed. The costs presented in Illustrations 7–2 and 7–3 thus reflect the *fieldwork costs alone.* (The local subsidiary in each area could use either the international research firm's subsidiary or a local research firm, provided it was willing to be supervised by the international research firm.) The important point here is that the costs of conducting research abroad are equal to, or greater than, the costs of similar projects in the United States; some advertisers expect to get an all-European study for a fraction of the costs for a similar project in the United States. This is not correct, of course, and the data shown here reflect only field costs. If the research were totally localized, that is, with no central handling of methodology, planning, and analysis, the overall costs would have been much higher.

— ILLUSTRATION 7-2 —
Fieldwork Costs: 1979—South America and Asia*

Country	Number of Interviews	Local Currency		Exchange Rate	U.S. $
Brazil	650	256,000	CrS	.037	$ 9,472
Colombia	450	200,000	Peso	.023	$ 4,600
India	500	34,000	R.	.1256	$ 3,396
Japan	400	2,550,000	Yen	.0046	$11,730
Peru	800	1,803,521	Sol	.00443	$ 4,800
Venezuela	1200	60,000	Bol.	.233	$13,980

*Confidential data provided to authors by U.S.-based MNC.

— Illustration 7-3 —
Fieldwork Costs for 1980 Study*

Country	Number of Interviews	Local Currency		Exchange Rate	U.S. $
Belgium	500	296,000	BF	.035	$10,360
Netherlands	400	340,000	BF	.035	$11,900
England	850	5,875	£	2.329	$13,683
France	600	62,000	Fr	.241	$14,942
Italy	600	7,600,000	L	.0012	$ 9,120
Germany	1200	31,400	DM	.559	$17,553
Sweden	400	40,000	Kr	.275	$11,120

*Confidential data provided to authors by U.S.-based MNC.

—— Selecting an Advertising (or Marketing) ——
Research Firm

The international advertising manager has a range of alternatives available when selecting an advertising (or marketing) research firm. On the one hand, he or she could choose a research firm with a "worldwide" network of local branches or subsidiaries; on the other hand, a local research firm could be selected in *each* market.

Major international firms, such as Marplan International and Burke Market Services or Gallup International, have their own location in a host of major cities. Similarly, International Research Associates (INRA), the international division of Starch INRA Hooper, Inc., offers an associate network that spans some thirty-three countries. The use of such international research agency, networks or associate networks clearly offers the advantages of:

- cost (efficiency)
- consistency (method)
- comparability (trend not absolute)
- client relationships

Some firms, however, do prefer to use strictly *local* agencies or have occasional research needs that apply to areas not served by their international research firms (or do not require their involvement). Thus, another question we frequently hear is, "How do you select an advertising (or marketing) research firm in an *unfamiliar* market?" In these instances, we suggest taking certain key steps when selecting a foreign marketing research firm.

Step 1. Identifying the Alternatives. The "country desk officer" in the Department of Commerce handling the country in which you are interested normally can provide a list of its advertising and marketing research firms. Other possible sources for names include your own (or other) multinational advertising agencies, U.S. companies (noncompetitors), and banks with offices in the country; your own subsidiaries or branches; and the U.S. Chamber of Commerce's local branch. Similarly, organizations such as the Academy of International Business (academic); the International Advertising Association (professional); or the European Society of Marketing Research (professional) could identify their members located in the country. Finally, there are a number of local marketing research societies, such as the Japan Marketing Association or the Marketing Research Society of Australia, that could provide information on their markets.

Step 2. Contacting the Marketing and Advertising Research Firms. Having now obtained the names/addresses and hopefully a few recommendations, the international advertising manager or his or her research director can now contact several research firms directly. These firms should be required to send detailed background materials on their staff, information on their services, and if possible copies of prior studies. In particular, these firms should give you the names of their prior U.S. clients and cost estimates for the sorts of projects you are considering.

Step 3. Contact Prior U.S. Clients. As you recall, it is essential to learn how these firms actually approach and conduct research. This goes beyond their skills and is really more a matter of research philosophy or attitude. Prior *U.S.* clients can indicate not only the strengths and weaknesses of these firms but their appreciation for, and attitude toward, research as well. Do not hesitate to telephone a peer in another U.S. or Western firm to ask such questions . . . and similarly, be prepared to provide your experience to other inquiring firms yourself.

Step 4. Visit the Selected Alternatives. While a personal visit may seem unnecessary, it is wise to actually meet the foreign research firm's personnel and get your "own feel" for its ability. Further, research terms are, unfortunately, *not standard*. The authors recently discussed a project with a British research firm and found that roughly 20 percent of our terminology *differed*. If this is true of an English-speaking, developed-country research group, what might you expect in Egypt or Colombia?

Step 5. Make Your Selection. Once you have considered the available alternatives . . . make your selection. If possible, do so while still in the particular country so that you can negotiate the details in person.

This step-by-step approach may seem to be unduly laborious. However, once you have identified a highly qualified research group, it becomes an important information asset for you/your firm. The next time you need research conducted in that market . . . the job *should be* greatly simplified.

——— SOME FINAL THOUGHTS ———

No attempt has been made in this chapter to provide a detailed discussion of the various advertising and marketing research *techniques* to employ overseas. Virtually the same range of prepromotion research technique alternatives are available in most developed and many developing countries that are found in the United States. Focus groups, personal interviews, telephone and mail surveys and panels are generally available. A point to remember, however, is the research "skills" or experience of the interview*ee*. Unfamiliarity with advertising and marketing research's raison d'être may cause the interview*ee* to be wary and less than candid in his or her response. (This point is equally valid for the industrial buyer as it is for the ultimate consumer.) At a minimum, the inexperience suggests the need for more emphasis being placed on explaining the nature (and importance) of the research and to the sophistication of the techniques employed. A good local agency or the branch of an international agency can provide very useful guidance on this concern.

Naturally, the problems associated with inadequate telephone systems or poor mail systems can also affect the methodology employed. For example, the Egyptian telephone system has been notoriously bad in recent years, and the country has begun a massive effort to improve it. Therefore, a telephone survey in Cairo would simply be out of the question until such problems as long delays are corrected. Further, due to many other problems with telephone ownership and coverage, the telephone method is often a poor technique to use. Similarly, countries such as India and Colombia have long had the reputation for having a poor mail system. These, along with sampling concerns, have led many firms conducting research in the developing world to *opt* for the use of focus groups . . . where the representativeness of the participants is the main consideration. While this approach precludes the use of the usual statistical reliability tests, it often provides the international advertising manager with the sort of concept tests or other insight that is needed.

Research Restrictions.   The number of restrictions on the advertising and marketing researchers overseas are increasing rapidly. Various *privacy acts* limit the type of consumer information that may be obtained as well as the techniques that can be employed, for example, telephones in Sudan. Also, some marketing research associations have developed self-regulatory guidelines designed to preclude legislation. In Britain, for example, the marketing researcher is limited to specific occupational categories when asking the consumer questions about his or her occupation. In Germany, sales receipts names/addresses may not be used to provide follow-up consumer surveys *unless* prior approval of the customer is obtained.

The international marketing manager must be aware that each market is likely to have some research restrictions and that they often relate to income, occupation, and similar data categories. Such restrictions must be considered when developing survey instruments to employ in either individual or multiple markets.

Joint Research.   Finally, we recommend that more U.S. international firms conduct joint research projects. Very often an MNC that manufactures automobile accessories will be doing a field research project among consumers in Brazil or Western Europe at the same time that a similar consumer study is being conducted by a tire or battery manufacturer. These firms clearly are in complementary rather than competitive industries . . . yet are attempting to reach similar market segments. If the two firms were to conduct *joint* research—for example, each contribute questions to a jointly administered questionnaire—their cost would be significantly reduced.

While this seems to be a most *viable* way to dramatically lower an international corporation's research cost, surprisingly few firms have ever considered such joint research. It is recommended that international marketers, including the major MNCs, begin to identify "partner research firms" and explore the potential of such joint research efforts.

——— 10 KEY POINTS ———

1. The *need* to conduct advertising research is just as great (or perhaps greater) in overseas markets than it is domestically.
2. The international advertising manager needs to exercise *centralized* control over the international advertising research function—particularly all planning and analyses phases.
3. Advertising research is needed prior to conducting advertising

campaigns to ensure maximum effectiveness in reaching target audiences and *following* the advertising as a *control* measure.

4. The quality of overseas advertising research firms should *not* be underestimated, and "workable" projects can be undertaken in most markets.

5. The international advertising manager will find that advertising (and marketing) research is generally more expensive outside the United States.

6. The international advertising manager will often find the firm's foreign subsidiary or branch managers reluctant to devote funds to advertising (or marketing) research.

7. The international advertising manager needs to question the reliability of foreign secondary data.

8. Of special importance to most international advertising managers are *tracking studies*—which permit the monitoring of the firm's image and awareness levels, and *concept* tests, which enable him or her to determine the appropriateness of proposed campaign themes.

9. Follow-up research (postresearch) is essential, as it enables the international advertising manager to determine how successful the individual markets have been in achieving their advertising objectives.

10. If an MNC is conducting multimarket advertising research, we recommend employing a single international research firm rather than separate research organizations in each market.

8

Guiding the Media Decisions

— INTRODUCTION —

Media problems provide some of the greatest frustrations and concerns for the international advertising manager. In fact, nowhere are the differences between domestic and international advertising more apparent than in the media area. And some familiarity with changing media regulations; new media developments; and the usual differences involving media rates, availability, and selection *is necessary*, although the international advertising manager should generally be more concerned with media planning and policy than with *hands-on* practice.

In this chapter, we focus on those media questions that do face the international advertising manager as he or she develops appropriate media policies and guidelines for the home office and subsidiary operations. A requisite for the development of such media guidelines is *flexibility* ... having a flexible approach that permits the field to make appropriate subsitutions when preferred media are unavailable, are overregulated, or where the quality of the media is suspect.

Naturally, a major factor in media decision making is the international firm's budget. This clearly establishes the parameters within which the home office and field media decisions are made—particularly the media choice(s) questions. A special policy concern of the international advertising manager relates to the subsidiary role in the budgeting process. Among the other topics developed in this chapter are:

- the importance of the local *noise level* when analyzing individual markets
- the question of media *viability*
- some local variations in *familiar media*

- the need to effectively manage media selection, scheduling, and controls
- the use of media planning groups

- the potential importance of cooperative advertising to many international firms

---

The differences between domestic and international advertising are perhaps *most* apparent in the media area. Traditional problems regarding media rates, availabilities, and selection *abound*, but these are often superseded by the impact of a new regulation or by the development of a totally new medium. Just what commercial satellite television will ultimately mean to European advertising is only one case in point. In fact, similar questions are undoubtedly being asked by foreign advertisers as they watch the growth of cable TV networks and pay TV in the United States.

Couple rapid media *change*—whether it is satellite TV or the growth of newspaper color magazine supplements in Europe—with already recognized differences in *relative media importance between markets*, and you quickly see the international advertising manager's dilemma. For example, an advertising medium, such as cinema advertising, may have limited value in the United States and be a basic form of advertising in Indonesia or Kenya.[1] Thus, the international advertising manager must be flexible in his or her evaluation of possible media and not judge the media recommendations received from overseas only on his or her own domestic perspective.

There are, of course, a myriad of media problems that the advertiser faces outside the United States, particularly in the developing countries. These are especially apparent for the consumer and service industries but can be difficult for an industrial producer as well. (Some of these latter concerns are addressed in Chapter 11.) What the international advertiser must keep clearly in mind is his target market/audience and his need to communicate with it. The medium (media) selected should be less related to the international advertising manager's convenience and more to what the particular target customer group reads, hears, and sees.

[1] *World Advertising Expenditures* (Mamaroneck, N.Y.: Starch INRA Hooper, 1980), p. 45.

Role in Media Determination

As with the other topics discussed in this book, the international advertising manager in firms doing extensive overseas advertising is generally concerned with the media budget, media approval, and performance evaluation. In firms with minimal overseas advertising, he or she may have more involvement in the actual media selection process. Fortunately, in the United States a number of agencies/service groups have been established recently to assist in handling the foreign media needs of the smaller advertiser. In the past, media planning and scheduling had occupied a disproportionate amount of the advertising manager's time. Therefore, there are many pluses to using these new services.

The Overseas Media Concerns

The types of media questions facing the international advertising manager are basically the same regardless of whether the firm produces industrial goods, consumer goods, or services. Naturally, however, the answers may be quite different, depending on the firm's needs. These basic questions include:

1. What must the firm's media budget be in order to achieve its objectives in its target markets?
2. What media are *available?*
3. What is the *quality* of the available media?
4. How can my company obtain *reliable* media cost data?
5. How can my company obtain reliable media coverage/circulation information?
6. How much media *redundancy* is present in the market, and how important is this to my company's advertising decisions?
7. Should my company employ international editions of U.S. print media or regional or national editions in the various local markets?
8. Do the international and local media provide adequate, accurate research information, including reader, listener, or viewer profiles?
9. Are there media restrictions with which my company needs to become familiar?
10. How can I establish uniform controls across markets to ensure that I am obtaining optimal return on my advertising expenditure?

While this list of questions is not exhaustive, the questions are indicative of the media-related concerns the firm that is advertising overseas has.

Obviously, the international advertising manager located at headquarters level does not normally obtain the answers himself or herself unless the firm and/or its advertising budget is *small*. Yet, *media policy* should be developed to: (a) ensure that the answers are obtained and (b) provide the guidelines to follow in light of the answers obtained. For example, a policy must be established regarding the redundancy issue, that is: Should media be employed that overlaps markets, or must local boundaries be maintained at all costs? (This concern may be especially great in Western Europe where high levels of broadcast redundancy were found *even before* satellite and cable television became an issue.)

Availability.   The availability question will be considered in more detail later. However, it is important to emphasize here that any media policy needs to provide some operational flexibility. Direct mail may be an industrial advertiser's primary medium in Switzerland and virtually impossible to employ in a West African market. Similarly, the types of media, albeit *minor* media, one finds in some markets seem to be limited only by the human imagination (or by creativity). This is illustrated by the importance assigned to outdoor advertising at soccer stadiums, which undoubtedly led to the special women's gymnastic event held in a stadium in Madrid in May 1981. This "event" was staged so that strategically positioned *outdoor advertisements* could be seen on television while the athletes performed. The international advertising manager should not be shocked by a local manager's request to use sound trucks in Upper Volta or airline food trays in Sweden. Rather, the use of such advertising forms would depend on the habits of the firm's target audience and the availability (or lack of availability) of other, more traditional media.

Quality.   Even if a particular medium is available, its quality may be a relevant concern. Newsprint quality in some Indian magazines/newspapers, for example, is such that it is impossible to get a good halftone reproduction. Similarly, color television is nonexistent in a number of countries, even if commercial television is available. These facts suggest, not only the need to be aware of quality differences, but the development of policy for such concerns as well.

Coverage/Circulation.   The U.S. advertiser has come to rely heavily on the Standard Rate & Data Service, Inc. (SRDS), for coverage/circulation and accurate cost information. SRDS does offer similar audit information for Britain, Italy, France, Austria, Switzerland, West Germany, Mexico, and Canada. (SRDS does *no* research per se but publishes audit/sworn statement data.)

In several other markets, advertising industry associations have set up auditing procedures similar to those found in the United States. However, *accurate* media information is still a concern in most markets, and most frequently local nuisances in auditing procedures make cross-country comparisons difficult.[2] Unless the firm simply employs international editions of

---

[2] Rosemarie Grieb, "What the Audits Tell," *International Advertiser* (May–June 1981), pp. 45–47.

U.S. or European publications—for example, *Business Week International*'s advertising indicates that its European edition reaches 160,000 executives in Europe, the Middle East, and North Africa—it must recognize that circulation or audience data are a continuing concern.[3]

Not only has the experienced international advertiser come to expect inflated circulation and audience statistics, but he or she is faced with variable pricing for time and space. In many markets, especially developing ones, the rate card simply provides the basis for initiating the negotiation. The international advertising manager needs to ensure that the firm's local representative determines the type of pricing structure in the particular national market.

Redundancy.   Both media and people cross borders in Western Europe and in many other markets. A U.S. technical trade publication may be read by those in the same field throughout the world, while a Dutch housewife often watches a German television channel. For example, a *Datamation* advertisement stated that it is "by far the leading data processing magazine in the world"—a claim substantiated by impressive circulation details.[4] If a consumer goods firm is attempting to very effectively segment markets (and changing appeals to meet local needs), this could prove extremely frustrating, while to many industrial advertisers this may be an important *plus*. To cope with this issue, the advertiser may follow a policy calling for minimal redundancy. On the other hand, many firms consider such "media overspill" as being critical to obtaining maximum impact for a limited budget and plan to take advantage of media that do have this attribute. Certainly, this can be especially true in markets where the commercial use of broadcast media is banned, since the advertiser who feels that radio or television is essential to his or her campaign must totally rely on overspill from neighboring countries. It is in such instances where satellite and cable TV again bear watching.

The Budget.   No discussion of media would be complete, of course, without considering the impact of the budget on all such decisions. The budget is the critical link between the established objectives of the international firm's advertising and the media and control decisions. If the international advertising manager has unlimited resources with which to work, the budget decision would be made independently from the establishment of the objectives and the identification of the target market(s). In this optimal situation, the budget would be dependent solely on determining the amount needed to achieve the desired objectives for each target group. While even this approach would not be easily operationalized owing to the many uncertainties we have discussed, the funding realities of most international advertising managers' situation make the budgeting process even more difficult. It often becomes a situation

[3] *Business Week International* advertisement, *Advertising Age/Europe*, Vol. 3, Issue 3 (March 1981), p. 5.

[4] *Datamation* advertisement, *Advertising Age/Europe*, Vol. 1, Issue 3 (March 26, 1979), pp. 3–17.

in which the manager is constantly forced to make compromises between the type of media exposure that is felt to be necessary and the funds available. In fact, in many firms the budget may be established *prior* to the establishment of the advertising objectives; this is an approach that is perhaps superior only to totally ignoring the need for a budget.

Suffice it to say, then, that budgets play a critical role in both the media selection decisions and the control (evaluation) process. Policy decisions are needed regarding the subsidiary(ies) role in budget determination and media allocations and the extent to which approvals are necessary at the home office. As was indicated in Chapter 5, if the company has a worldwide "coordinated" program, the budgetary approval process helps to ensure that home office policies are followed.

Other Policy Matters.   While the adequacy of media research information and the media restriction concerns are real, they do not represent policy matters. However, any checklist or promotion manual developed at the home office for the field should make reference to them. Virtually every country, for example, has an ever increasing number of advertising regulations, and the subsidiary advertising manager needs to be aware of local laws. It may be a requirement that all television commercials must be filmed locally (Australia), that brochures cannot be imported (Venezuela), or that *all* television advertising must pass a local review board. It is essential that the local advertising managers keep the home office aware of these laws and regulations and that they make certain the corporation is not violating them.

To help ensure this, the international advertising manager may establish this type of information as part of the data regularly reported to the home office. (The nature and types of regulation that are found overseas are discussed more fully in Chapter 9.)

We will not attempt to discuss further "how to develop an international budget" or "how to formulate a plan for assigning total or individual budgets." The process itself becomes too individualized because of the many variations in organizational structure, entry strategy (export, license, joint venture, etc.), and profit center preferences employed by multinational firms. For example, the simple (and traditional) percentage of sales by product category approach so often followed domestically becomes clouded when you are talking about wholly owned subsidiaries in select national markets (e.g., France and Denmark) and export regions or about using licensees for the remainder of your overseas sales.

Making the budgetary decision even more complex, however, is an imponderable that too often receives *no* recognition. This is the difference in *noise level* between markets. Noise-level differences alone make it unwise for most international firms to develop a simple across-the-board percentage-of-sales budget allocation. If the firm is to maximize its total advertising budget, regardless of how the budget has been established, it must consider the noise-level question before making its allocations.

——— Noise-Level Concerns ———

We have repeatedly warned against comparing one national market or region to another. This has been mentioned particularly in reference to pretesting advertising concepts and in measuring consumer buying intentions. In these situations the reason given had to do with the advertiser's corporate or brand image. Almost every multinational corporation (name or brand) is perceived differently from one national market to another, and therefore data collected for each market can be compared only with that same market's historical trend.

Now we introduce the same caution, but for a different reason. The advertising noise level—or the volume of advertising within which each single advertiser's efforts must compete for attention—is different.

This situation exists for several reasons, including the availability of media and the cost of media. National markets dominated by television advertising are, for example, more expensive to advertise in than those with limited television commercial time available or without commercial television. Thus, a greater media budget may be necessary to achieve the *same* level of target market contact in one market than in another.

In the European market, only England can be said to be dominated by television—and, by U.S. standards, TV there is not *as* dominant over other media. There is commercial television in France, Germany, Holland, Switzerland, and Austria, but it is very tightly controlled to severely limit the amount of commercial time. An advertiser would find it difficult to use television as a primary medium in terms of the target audience covered. Yet, it *is very expensive* in terms of dominating an advertising budget.

Italy also has commercial television. The national channels have controlled amounts of commercial time—more liberal than the other countries mentioned—and a new dimension has been added since 1975. A court order established that the government could no longer hold a monopoly on television, and since then many short-area transmission stations have emerged. These stations are highly commercial, and their existence has greatly clouded a calculable effectiveness of television in that country. On the plus side, it makes possible local or regional use of TV . . . segmentation.

Commercial television exists in Luxembourg, Monaco, and Yugoslavia, further complicating the calculation of budget efficiency. These markets represent very small consumer potential for advertisers, but Luxembourg televises in three languages (French, German, and English) and has effective coverage over much of Germany, France, and Belgium. Similarly, Monaco exercises effective leverage over southern France and northern Italy, *and* Yugoslavia's television represents a medium in northern Italy. Thus, to make budget allocations simply on a percentage-of-sales basis for Luxembourg or Monaco or Yugoslavia would be to ignore the coverage provided from these markets.

The Scandinavian market, on the other hand, is advertising-media poor. It offers no electronic media (except in Finland), no effective national newspapers, and a relatively small selection of magazines. And it has what appears to most advertisers to be an antisocial attitude toward advertising, which is reflective of the amount of legislation directed toward it. One cannot budget heavily for fast marketing action in these markets.

To add to the budgetary allocation problem, one could also observe that there is very little relationship between the cost of similar media, with similar exposure levels, from one market to the next. Germany, England, France, and Italy would qualify as having similar populations; however, the cost of media would rank in the order listed. (Listing Italy as fourth, as least expensive, refers to actual buying prices—all published rates in Italy are negotiable.) England is often listed as less expensive mediawise than Germany; yet England, being TV-dominated, requires a higher budget than Germany does for an equally effective campaign.

Other Noise-Level Factors. We have mentioned the noise level in advertising with regard to media availability and cost. Another related factor is the national attitude toward the social acceptance of advertising and the degree of consumer sophistication found in the advertiser's audience.

This is a consideration that cannot be documented. It is a value judgment dimension based on observation and experience; yet it is of sufficient concern to recognize when establishing the advertising budget. To generalize, Latin American and East Asian markets can be said to be "noisy markets." It requires a high volume of advertising to penetrate these markets effectively. In some of these areas, the ability or inclination to read is rather low; for a mass market product, electronic media are usually more effective than print. When the international advertising manager determines this characteristic of a particular market, the budget considerations are clear; more funds must be allocated to achieve desired impact.

On the other side of the coin there are national markets with a much more conservative attitude toward advertising—ranging from respect for heavy advertisers that show good taste in presenting informative advertising to contempt and suspicion against brands that are "too heavily advertised." Thus, the advertiser would lower the allocations in such markets.

These subtleties are often confusing to advertisers when they enter a new market for the first time. Of course, they look first to their competitors' advertising and sometimes cannot rationalize their approach. This issue does provide one more important reason why the advertising to sales budget relationship cannot be employed in allocating or making comparisons between markets. Similarly, it highlights the point that effective media selection goes well beyond a comparison of circulations or even determining the media that are significant to your target market. Media decisions must include some understanding of the level of competition for the buyer's attention. "What is the noise level for your target audience?" can be the critical question for the international advertising manager.

—— MEDIA AVAILABILITY ——

The term "media availability" implies an intent to merely indicate that commercial television is *not* available to international advertisers in some countries (e.g., Nepal and Norway), or that radio is not available for advertising in Belgium. And, naturally, the international advertising manager will find markets where some medium is not present in any form or where the local government permits no commercial use of the medium.

However, it would perhaps be more appropriate to coin a new phrase . . . "functional media availability" or "media viability" . . . since the international advertising manager must look beyond simple media *availability*. He or she needs to determine whether or not the medium is available in a *quality and quantity* and at a *cost* that will permit the international advertiser to successfully employ it.

Perhaps a bit more elaboration will further clarify this point. Let us take television advertising in Australia as an example. Australia certainly has commercial television available for the international advertiser, *but* the government requires local producers for the commercial. The added cost of producing a commercial in Australia may preclude the use of Australian television by an international advertising manager who sees a *limited* market for his or her firm's product in the country and had planned to use a slightly modified United States-produced commercial there. To this international advertising manager, the question is one of "media viability" rather than of "media availability."

Next, "media viability" includes regulatory requirements that may prevent the use of a particular advertising medium *in the form desired*. A manufacturer of a food product that has *children* as its target market may find many media "unavailable" to it, although the same media are available to other advertisers. For example, the international advertising manager of a firm producing a lemonade mix for the Swiss market may wish to employ outdoor advertising and depict children drinking (and enjoying) the product. Such outdoor advertising would not be permitted in most Swiss cantons because of local regulations regarding the use of children in outdoor advertising. To this lemonade mix producer, outdoor advertising is not a viable medium in Switzerland.

Similarly, there may be restrictions regarding the amount of advertising that is permitted for a particular medium, due either to government restriction or to limits imposed by the medium itself. For example, several Greek magazine publishers recently had to turn away advertising because of the excess demand for their space—that is, demand beyond the government limits.

On the other hand, there may be other media available in a market that the international advertiser is unaccustomed to employing in the home market. To illustrate this, we suggest that the international advertising manager take a careful look at *World Advertising Expenditures*, sponsored by Starch INRA Hooper and the International Advertising Association. This annual publication presents a breakdown of advertising expenditures *by medium* in over fifty countries. It suggests some interesting questions for the international advertising manager to explore. Why, for example, is roughly 15 percent of the total advertising expenditure in Turkey devoted to exhibitions and demonstrations, or why does radio receive 40 percent of all advertising expenditures in Surinam? An international advertising manager may find it useful to obtain answers to similar questions regarding the breakdowns for the firm's own target markets. As was emphasized earlier, flexibility in regard to media is a desirable trait, and the principal question still is: "What medium (or media) best reach(es) my target audience?" We have added to this a second question: "Is this medium (or media) a viable alternative for my firm?"

—— SOME MEDIA SPECIFICS ——

The actual media alternatives worldwide seem limitless as long as one is generalizing across markets. Yet, to an international advertiser frustrated in his or her attempts to find *realistic* alternatives in *specific* markets, such a comment appears to be meaningless. While we will discuss individual media in some detail, a broader issue concerns whether or not the individual medium has the same strengths/weaknesses in every market, that is: Do media attributes successfully carry across borders? In the United States network television is the primary medium for the consumer goods advertiser desiring to communicate with the largest possible national audience. Our question, therefore, is: "Does television have the same attribute in all markets?" The answer is *no*. Regulatory restrictions aside, it must be recognized that television saturation varies widely among markets. The number of TV sets in relation to the total population (or the total number of households) thus becomes a relevant basis of comparison.

What are the traditional media attributes in the United States, and how appropriate are they for other markets? Similarly, what questions need to be asked about an individual medium as the advertising decision maker considers the available choices?

—— Television ——

Television is the most technologically sophisticated medium and continues to change rapidly. For example, the growth of satellite television in Europe, coupled with the increased use of cable television, makes an accurate assessment of television's future role there difficult. Undoubtedly, these developments will allow the major international consumer goods advertiser to make even more use of centralized planning and of coordinated but standardized campaigns. While it has been hard to *contain* television to a single national market in the past, doing this will become nearly impossible in the future.

Not only will consumers continue to cross borders, but television will also "travel more widely." Further, there will be increased competition for viewers' time as more alternative programming/stations become available.

Television is the primary medium for the broad national market in virtually all developed countries. Only restrictions and prohibitions regarding its use have stopped its development as a prime advertising medium in all these areas. And it remains the best medium for demonstrating the product's use to a wide audience, except in countries where cinema advertising or display trucks are important.

Western Europe, South America, Japan, Australia, Mexico, and New Zealand are among the countries or regions where television makes an impact (and has attributes) similar to those of the United States and Canada. Even in these markets, however, there are differences—often due to regulation—that place constraints on the advertiser.

There are almost always unique differences between markets for television advertisers. The strength of presentation, the impact of public influence and social concern for "invasion of privacy" . . . plus the fact that much television is government owned and controlled have created many obstacles for advertisers. One must deal with such problems as:

1. All commercials are confined to three or four "blocks"—e.g., running six to eight commercials at one time, three times a day. In Germany, multiple blocks must be purchased, and therefore most commercial times appear too early in the day to attract an audience for male-oriented products.
2. The number of times one commercial film can be aired during an extended period is limited. A schedule for which a U.S. television advertiser would produce one or two commercials might require seven to nine commercials for government-owned Italian TV.
3. Available (limited) commercial television time is assigned by product category. This further limits available time for each type of product and the advertiser's ability to acquire sufficient effective amounts of television time. One must build effective schedules, depending upon later cancellations (in category) and knowing that one's own cancellation may well aid a competitor.
4. Government protection of other media can make the entire process of media planning more complicated. Some countries specify a limited percentage expenditure on television compared with one's total media expenditure. This could mean that adding one more commercial to a media schedule would require the purchase of two pages of newspaper space, one more magazine ad, plus additional cinema and billboards. Indonesia is the first country to have had commercial TV and then discontinue it (April 1981) to protect other media.
5. The content of television advertising receives much more scrutiny than other forms of advertising, including: what products can ap-

pear on television; how a product can be demonstrated; documentary proof of claims; social concern for life-styles depicted; religious and nationalistic taboos.

6. Then, of course, there are the requirements that commercials be filmed locally; or, if out of the country, produced by local national production companies. This specification is becoming more widespread throughout the world and causes many quality problems.

Finally, before ruling out television as an advertising medium in those markets with a *low* proportion of sets per capita/household, one additional consideration is that many advertisers use television to segment their market. For a firm that is directing its message to an upper-income market, the presence or absence of a television set in the household may be an important indicator of its disposable personal income (DPI). In some markets, industrial producers have even successfully employed television advertising as a selling tool, especially when their primary customer is the government and their target audience is government officials. Still, in many countries television transmission is bad; the number of sets is low; the time costs are outrageous; the programming day is short; and the program quality is poor. In such areas television is just not a viable medium.

In employing television, the international advertising manager must be especially sensitive to:

1. The need to determine where the firm can optimize its television commercial production quality with production costs. (If there are no regulations regarding the importation and use of finished commercials, considerable cost savings can be obtained by "shopping around.")
2. Apparent minor television commercial restrictions that may lead to significant problems, i.e., requirements regarding the use of children under a specific age in commercials.
3. The unintended cultural blunder that can negate an otherwise effective standardized commercial campaign. (Recently, a potentially sound campaign designed to be used in several West African countries received local criticism because the actors were all seen as being "obviously Nigerian.")

—— Radio ——

Although it has recently received a rebirth in the United States, radio uniformly suffered from the rise of television in developed markets. In fact, it became at best a secondary or support medium for many major world advertisers, who saw it as providing background for the housewife doing housework or for the automobile commuter. In addition, radio has received regulatory attention similar to that for television.

Yet, many consumer and industrial goods producers have found it a most viable medium in select markets. It generally has two important attributes—cost (time charges/production) and flexibility. Perhaps even more important to many is its ability to penetrate across borders, such as Radio Luxembourg's coverage of areas where broadcast advertising is prohibited, and its ability to reach the illiterate (or functionally illiterate) customer.

When making an assessment of radio, the international advertising manager should determine the following:

1. The actual *coverage* of a particular station—and compare it with its listenership claims. (An independent assessment of coverage *by time period* is preferable.)
2. Whether the medium is considered primary or secondary in a given market. This will affect its time charges and its potential use.
3. The degree of redundancy (or overlap) between stations, even though based in different countries (and broadcast in different languages). A Dutch housewife may prefer to listen to a German station's music selections, even if it is broadcasting in the German language.
4. The listening habits of its particular target group(s), which vary significantly by market area.

—— Newspapers ——

The United States has long been characterized as a country without a *national newspaper*. Only a few specialized newspapers, such as the *Wall Street Journal*, clearly have the attributes of a national press, and these are directed toward the needs of particular markets. One could debate the issue, but undoubtedly only the *New York Times* and *U.S. Today* even approach national visibility, and they have a very limited circulation, although a very influential one. In fact, newspapers in the States are most often characterized as being the medium for local retail advertisers.

The international advertising manager needs to be aware of the possibility that there may be a national newspaper in a particular market, since nationwide coverage is much more easily attained in smaller countries. Similarly, newspapers, such as most London-based newspapers, contain a high proportion of advertising directed to a national, rather than a local, London retail audience.

Perhaps even more unique in many markets is the heavy competition among newspapers . . . based on their political orientation or affiliation. (Regarding the latter, some newspapers even have the sponsorship of a particular political party.) A good illustration is provided by Greece, where colorful newspapers are available for Greeks of any political inclination. This raises a very important concern of the advertiser: "What will be the local reaction to my firm's advertising appearing in a heavily politically oriented newspaper?"

Will the firm's local prestige be affected, and/or will there be a certain degree of "guilt by association"? (Similarly, of course, would be the reverse question of "added prestige.") These questions are often debated, and undoubtedly the international advertising manager must develop a policy on this media selection point. Unfortunately, the answer is usually not clear, unless one is considering an extremely controversial newspaper, such as one advocating violent behavior or strongly left-wing positions. Undoubtedly, the best advice may be to simply avoid extremist presses on either political side . . . even when they have the largest circulation. However, the international advertising manager's local representatives (corporate or agency) should be important sources of information with regard to this sensitive concern.

In addition, the following are concerns regarding newspapers that bear particular consideration:

1. Does the newspaper's production/newsprint quality permit the type of illustration (halftone) you wish to use?
2. Conversely, does the newspaper offer high-quality four-color production, as is found in some European countries? (Does it have a viable color supplement?)
3. How reliable are the circulation data? Take special note of subscriptions versus street sales. In some countries there are no circulation data. The only statistics available are the number of copies printed each day.
4. Does the country (or city) particularly known for having "high readership" have a population that considers the newspaper a vital part of its daily life? (If objective readership studies are available, these could be useful.)
5. Is there a true national newspaper in the country? (A distinction needs to be made here between a government press and one national in acceptance/distribution; the latter is our concern.)

Some consumer and most industrial international advertisers, of course, have the business community as their target market. Therefore, their prime concern is identifying a viable daily business publication, such as the *Financial Times* (London) or *Nihon Keizai Shimbun* (Japan). Most developed countries have either a newspaper or a magazine that effectively reaches the *Wall Street Journal* type of market. (The *Journal* itself has an Asian edition, which is published in Hong Kong.) General business readers in other markets tend to rely either on the well-known daily publications from the developed areas or on weekly business journals.

—— Magazines/Journals ——

Magazine readership is considerably higher in many foreign markets than it is in the United States. Further, this medium is increasing by offering the types of special audiences (readership) that enables the international advertiser to tightly segment its market — not only by customer type but by country/region/ city as well. Our attention here will focus most heavily on consumer magazines, since a rather extensive discussion of business publications is included in a later chapter. However, it is important to note that consumer and industrial advertisers are turning more and more to magazines (or journals) because of their ability to reach carefully targeted markets and because of the increased cost of other media.

Consumer Magazines. There are a number of alternative approaches that might be followed by the international advertising manager. These range from using a magazine such as *Reader's Digest*, either the worldwide or a local or regional edition (for which a progressively increasing discount can be realized) to using a carefully chosen local magazine in *each* market. Of course, many United States-based publications, including *Newsweek, Playboy* and *Time*, have special foreign language editions and high overseas readership. To reach a broader *localized* market, however, many consumer goods companies have turned to locally produced publications in the countries themselves. Again, the critical question concerns the international advertiser's target market. For certain segments, such as the "international sophisticate" and the expatriate, a United States publication may be appropriate. However, to reach the middle-class Greek or Brazilian housewife, a locally produced magazine is often best. (*Bunte* in Germany with over 5 million readers is illustrative of a locally important consumer publication.) Regional publications often are also important; *Hjemmet* (Denmark), for example, has long been a leading general-interest magazine in Norway.[5]

Creative concerns aside, such a country-by-country approach could produce (and often has) enormous scheduling problems for advertiser and agency alike. Naturally, many major advertisers and advertising agencies have specialists in overseas media selection and scheduling. Similarly, many larger overseas publications such as the *Financial Times*, United Kingdom, and *Sterns* of Germany, have their own sales offices in the United States (and other countries), while other publications are represented by firms specializing in such services. For example, Dow Jones International Marketing Services represents a number of business and news publications, including *Die Welt* (Germany) and the *Australian Financial Review*. In addition, a growing number of international media consulting firms include media *planning* and *buying* among their services, as well as a variety of media research offerings. These consultants have been particularly useful to the medium and smaller advertisers, although many larger companies/agencies are numbered among their clients.

Business Publications. Frequent discussions with executive-level business people throughout the world indicate that they are usually conversant about

---

[5] Geoffrey Ward, "Foreign Publishers Frolic on Norwegian Turf," *Advertising Age/Europe*, Vol. 1, Issue 3 (March 26, 1979), p. E–17.

articles/advertisements that have appeared in general publications such as *Business Week, Fortune,* or the *Economist.* Still, they are also up to date on trade publications for their industry and on their local business journals.

There are relatively wide ranges of regional or local general business publications. *Kapital* (Germany), *Norges, Industri* (Norway), *L'Expansion* (France), and *Maclean's* (Canada) represent just a few of the alternatives. Similarly, there are many United States- and foreign-produced trade publications that focus on particular industries. Several approaches for targeting industrial markets are suggested in Chapter 12, but one might generalize by stating that *local* general business (or news) publications are most appropriate for corporate advertising campaigns of either consumer or industrial advertisers. On the other hand, the industrial product advertiser may find foreign editions of U.S. trade publications to be a very *useful* medium . . . if the appropriate industries are carefully targeted. For example, the *Oil & Gas Journal* may provide not only a strong domestic segment to its advertisers but key non-U.S. decision makers in the petroleum industry as well. In such instances, the international industrial advertiser needs to carefully analyze the market to determine whether or not non-U.S. industrial journals are needed to reach its target audience.

There are, of course, other key concerns with which the international advertiser needs to be aware when considering *either* nondomestic consumer or business magazines. These include:

- the need for the same type of circulation, rate, and research information that was needed for newspapers, i.e., the dearth of media data is a continuing concern
- the questions of production quality of the journals and of special size/space requirements
- the need to determine the degree of cross-border redundancy of the various publications
- the necessity to develop some understanding of the readership habits of the target audience, e.g., the preference for local versus international publications, and/or the value of magazines versus other print or broadcast media

—— Other Media ——

Direct mail, outdoor advertising, cinema advertising, transit advertising . . . the list of other media can be extensive. While typically *secondary* media, each medium can be very valuable for select products in particular markets. Direct mail, for example, is only as effective as the quality of the *mailing list* and the *postal system.* Restrictions regarding the sale of membership or subscription rosters in some countries creates difficulties for the direct mail advertiser, as well as increasing the medium's costs. Similarly, outdoor advertising is heavily regulated in most developed and many developing areas. At the same time, there are many firms that have effectively employed each of these media.

In particular, such media provide the advertiser with alternatives, when the *primary* media are unavailable or too costly. For example, as noted earlier, serious limitations on the use of television have led to the widespread use of cinema advertising, especially in developing countries. Further, these types of secondary media can often successfully *complement* campaigns that employ a primary medium. Combinations, such as repeating a television theme in an outdoor advertisement, may be just as effective in Brazil or Venezuela as in the United States or Britain. And the use of such a combination may prove to be much less costly than an *all-television* campaign. While we realize we are repeating ourselves, we wish to stress that the international advertiser must be flexible, imaginative, and even opportunistic when making *media decisions*. Otherwise, an important local medium or the possibility of taking advantage of cross-border coverage may be totally ignored.

Stated simply, the international advertising manager needs to ask himself or herself:

1. Am I ignoring a potentially important local medium?
2. How might I reduce my costs and maintain (or improve) my effectiveness by substituting a lower-cost medium to *complement* my primary medium (or media)?
3. Are the regulations so strict or the traditional media so heavily employed by other advertisers that a so-called secondary medium would improve my product's visibility?

—— MEDIA PLANNING: SELECTION, ——
SCHEDULING, AND CONTROL

Naturally, it is difficult to separate media selection, scheduling, and control from the overall campaign planning process. Very clearly, the international advertising manager must include such questions as, What is the *most appropriate* medium (or media)? in the overall campaign decision-making process. So at this point the question really concerns: "Which magazine or journal or which newspaper will I select from among those alternatives that are available in the market?"

All other things aside, such as political philosophy or noise level, the firm would then be concerned with *cost per contact/target audience* or similar ratios *and* with the availability of particular space or time segments in the desired media. For example, the firm may wish to launch its campaign in September, but the September closing date for Magazines A and B has passed. If advertising in Magazine C is unacceptable then some alteration in planning is necessary.

Once the actual campaign has been approved, the media selection and scheduling activities for many firms are routinely handled by the corporation's advertising agency (subject, of course, to an agreed-upon approval mechanism that is part of the client-agency agreement). For the network agency, this process may be centralized or handled at the local/subsidiary level.

Many of the various foreign media may be represented in the United States or other major markets by agents or may have their own local representatives. For example, *Al-Hawadess* (Beirut) advertised that it had its own local offices in London and Kuwait, but was represented in the United States by N. DeFilippes Company and in Japan by J.A.C., Inc.[6] Such available local representation assists the international advertiser and/or his or her advertising agency in two ways. First, it is obviously convenient in terms of time and effort. Perhaps more important, however, is the fact that such local presence "acquaints the medium" with the *needs* of a United States-based international advertiser. The importance of providing media profile data and accurate rate/circulation information becomes more apparent . . . if it has not already been recognized.

Rates, of course, are a subject in themselves. In most foreign countries, paying rate card rates is comparable to paying automobile "sticker prices" in the United States. Recently, it was estimated that in France the *rubber* rates are such that three fourths of all media buys are negotiated.[7] Thus, the firm needs to ensure—often with local subsidiary or network agency help—that it is getting "a good deal."

Similar concerns relate to the circulation data of publications, as noted earlier. Media planners are often frustrated, for example, because of the difficulty of making intercountry comparisons even when the audits are conducted by reliable organizations in the countries. Grieb recently noted that despite the fact that all the audits employed in Europe provide reliable quantitative data, they "vary in the degree of detail supplied and the media categories which are audited."[8] This, of course, makes many of the quantitative comparisons that United States-based corporations are so accustomed to using domestically difficult to employ if they use local media. Yet, it is recommended that the corporation employ objective measures whenever possible in evaluating its media selection efforts.

Finally, from a control perspective, it is essential to have proof that its advertising actually appeared in print or was presented by the broadcasting medium. If the firm has subsidiary advertising managers, this can be one of their assignments, that is, requiring them to send page proofs to the home office for verification *and* to ensure that the company's requirements regarding its logo or brand name were followed. Otherwise, the local agency or network subsidiary handling the account should be required to provide *proofs of publication* and/or verifications of the broadcast messages by actual *monitoring*.

---

[6] *Al-Hawadess* advertisement, *International Advertiser* (March–April 1981), p. 5.

[7] Peter Inserra, "Paying Rate Card Prices in France? Few Do," *International Advertiser* (March–April 1981), p. 46.

[8] Grieb, op. cit., p. 45.

What should be reemphasized here is that the international advertising manager's role in the media planning area is often one of ensuring that:

- the media planning and selection is consistent with the campaign's objectives
- the procedures for buying time or space recognize that rate variations are typical and provide for appropriate negotiations
- the problems in obtaining accurate and comparable circulation data are taken into consideration in qualitative comparisons
- steps are taken to establish proof that the advertising actually appeared

On the other hand, many smaller international consumer goods advertisers and international industrial advertisers of various sizes, including larger corporations, may be more directly involved in the actual media selection and scheduling process. According to a study published in *Industrial Marketing*, only forty-eight U.S. industrial advertisers spent more than $1 million in 1980 on business publication advertising—the most common medium for most industrial advertisers.[9] Though not directly offering "international statistics," this certainly suggests the lower parameters of industrial expenditures. While a sizable portion of the larger industrial advertisers *do* use the services of an advertising agency, many medium- and smaller-sized firms make only limited (or no) use of such services. The international advertising managers in such firms may plan and schedule the advertising themselves or work with firms that specialize in media planning and scheduling.

—— MEDIA PLANNING GROUPS ——

Media planning groups (consultants) appear to be gaining in prominence, especially in their services to smaller international advertisers *and* to advertising agencies that have few or no network linkages. It would be incorrect, however, to imply that these are the only clients of these relatively new service organizations. In fact, several number among their clients some of the largest advertisers and/or agencies.

Typically, these media planning groups offer such services as media research, planning assistance, media buying/scheduling, and account management. Their most critical quality from the client's standpoint, however, is their understanding of the complexities of availabilities, data base (computer) analyses, and scheduling. Even larger advertising agencies, which have only infrequent need for a foreign media specialist or that have limited expertise in a particular geographic area, find these services to be valuable. Among the groups are: All Media Services (Britain); JDM International (Britain); Media

[9] "*Industrial Marketing's* 100: AT&T Heads Exclusive List," *Industrial Marketing* (June 1981), pp. 70–71.

Buying Services International, Inc. (United States); and Michael Jarvis and Associates Inc. (United States). The latter, briefly discussed in Chapter 11, includes among its range of services some assistance for the very small advertiser (i.e., with $25,000 or less in billings).

—— A Sample Strategy for the Smaller ——
Consumer Advertiser

Many of the recommendations and suggestions that we have made in this chapter have been primarily relevant to the large consumer advertiser that will be working with a major United States- or European-based network agency. Its programs and related strategic planning are comprehensive—and the *management* (in some instances, coordination) of all the various organizational components, including subsidiary managers, corporate line officials, and agency representatives (at all levels and in all countries)—is necessary for *effective* international advertising.

But what about the small to medium international consumer advertiser or the industrial advertiser? To assist the latter, we have devoted Chapter 11 to the special problems, concerns, and opportunities of international industrial advertising. We feel that the area of industrial marketing and advertising is sufficiently unique to make separate treatment essential. Here, to assist the smaller to medium international consumer advertiser, we have developed the following discussion, which includes a number of "how to's" about market identification, dealer relations, and the use of cooperative advertising, as well as an illustration featuring a Goodyear International program in a local market (Britain).

—— MAKING A SMALL BUDGET EFFECTIVE ——
IN CONSUMER ADVERTISING

To a great extent, we have been discussing the establishment of advertising budgets as if every advertiser had available all the money necessary to do a thorough advertising job in every country in which they market . . . which is probably seldom the case. Without such resources, it is still possible to make an effective advertising investment.

There is only one rule that must be established and never violated: *Do only that which can be done effectively.* Do not fragment a budget into ineffective segments or enter an area of advertising for which a budget will be stretched too thin to be effective.

—— Market Segmentation ——

We offer two methods of segmenting a market: geographical and vertical. With some products there will be a choice; others will be confined to one or the other. Some budgets can take advantage of both; others will need to make a choice.

Geographic Segmentation. This term needs little explanation. The strategy is simply to select only that part of a national market that advertising can penetrate effectively. Primarily, the strategy is to avoid national mass media.

The determination in this strategy requires two areas of parallel investigation: (a) segment the market into priority sales potential areas; (b) segment the market into regional/local media reach areas. The results of these two pieces of data will undoubtedly require some compromise to make a fit, with the media data dominating the decision because it will be the least flexible in the equation. The result will be one of geographic segmentation diagramed on a map and numbered according to priority of sales potential.

The media alternatives will vary greatly with different markets; but, more often than not, there will be a greater number of media to be considered than one might perceive at the outset—and, of course, that selection will also be affected by the product in question.

—— Regional Media Consideration ——

Newspapers
Regional TV
Radio
Cinema
Magazines
   (regional editions)
Outdoor boards
Buses and subways

Taxicabs
Door handbills
Direct mail
   (household)
Sponsored events
Others (indigenous to
   specific areas

When *all the facts* are considered, it is possible that aggressive promotional action cannot be taken in the number 1 priority market, or in the single most effective medium. Rather, an alternative—and often a viable one—is to *dominate something.* Perhaps it must be decided to take priority area number 3 and dominate cinema, which will "give you strength over 55 percent target audience in area number 3." But a payoff (or measurable progress) should be a targeted goal.

Perhaps it will be necessary to forsake all the major metro markets and concentrate on a selected group of rural markets. To the "giants" at headquarters, this could appear to be very demeaning, but it could also be a far better solution than doing nothing—and it could be profitably affordable.

Vertical Segmentation. This term refers to the highest potential type of consumer target marketing. Such a strategy precludes increasing aggregate demand to make more room for a new brand entry. It means driving hard at the heaviest users or most likely consumers. It means advertising in specialty publications.

To the camera marketer, it means photography magazines; to the automotive-related products, the motoring press. There are sports publications that offer endless possibilities for many different kinds of products because of the emphasis on youth, recreation, health, outdoor and indoor activities, the trend/pace setters—to say nothing of sports equipment users. This one category alone could give good exposure to toiletries, cosmetics, clothing, watches, plus food and beverages . . . and more.

All that a responsible person would need to do is to go to a large news vendor in the country in which that person finds himself or herself to study the special-interest publications offered—plus use a little imagination in regard to what kind of people read hobby magazines, home planning, travel, boating, skiing, fashion, pet care, psychiatry, bridge playing, gardening, astrology, camping (and so on, ad infinitum) magazines. All these people brush their teeth, shampoo their hair, wear underwear, travel, take vitamins, think about their complexion, drink beverages, own cars, take baths, and get hungry. But, more than that, special-interest people are usually in the higher-income group; they are alert to new ideas and are accustomed to reading for information. An advertising agency can provide information about the demographic makeup of any of these publications.

The point is, of course, to work harder to cultivate a small target audience. There can be an argument from some advertising consultants that a couple of small ads in the largest publications is worth more than many larger ads in smaller, special-interest magazines. Their primary argument is that the cost per 1,000 circulation for the smaller, specialty publications is much higher than that for larger publications. And they are right. They are also often right about the cost per 1,000 of the category of reader you want to reach in the larger publications. But, can one afford to buy that big an audience with sufficient frequency? We subscribe more to the theory that people become aware of a new product slowly and forget quickly . . . *frequently.*

Advertisers with products that have appeal to the more wealthy will find that class and club magazines give them a prestige position at relatively low cost.

Direct mail can also play a unique position in exclusive target marketing. There are often available directory lists from clubs, professional organizations, and business associations. There are also opportunities to buy participation for including your product folder with monthly statements sent out by credit card organizations and automobile clubs. Department stores are often willing to include folders in their monthly statements for products they sell.

—— Dealer-Distributor Involvement ——

A second area for consideration in making small budgets effective is to involve the reseller whom an advertiser depends on to actually sell the advertiser's product to the consumer. Here, again, we suggest two approaches for consideration.

Cooperative Advertising.   This is the most traditional form of dealer-involved advertising. This term refers to the supplier paying an agreed-on portion of the retailer's advertising. Although it can often be difficult to impose rules on a customer, cooperative advertising cannot provide an effective return on investment without the supplier getting fair treatment for the money contributed. Therefore, administrative control is a primary concern when choosing dealer cooperative advertising.

Newspapers are the most traditional medium used. Radio and local TV are also used, as is direct mail advertising. There are an endless number of forms of advertising a retailer might want to involve his or her supplier in—as there are endless types of cost-sharing agreements. We would only caution about certain elements that need to be observed in order to attempt to make such involvement profitable:

- Establish a fixed percent on the retailer's purchases as a limit to involvement.
- Establish a limit on the amount of the total cost to be shared for each ad a dealer uses.
- Establish the kinds of media to be considered.
- Establish how a product and brand name are to be treated in advertising.
- Establish a time limit between the date on which the ad appears and the application for payment (credit) occurs—avoid receiving charges over one year old. (Three months is more practical.)
- Establish the documentation required with payment (credit) application—i.e., newspaper pages (including date and name), plus media invoices. Avoid paying for the same ad more than once.
- Establish (if possible) an opportunity to see the advertising before it appears or "approval rights."

There can be other elements that should be included for cooperative advertising of certain products, in certain industries, under different kinds of distribution systems—these are basic elements for most. Nothing can be "established" unless it is printed in clear, understandable language and presented to the retailer before any advertising is entered into.

Special large-volume customers will often require special agreements appropriate to their importance to a supplier. Advertising allowances offered to retailers without serious concern for the resulting advertising do not belong in this discussion. They are only an additional selling discount.

Dealer Participation Advertising.   This can be quite a different approach than that for cooperative advertising. The rules are reversed. This term refers to the product marketer developing a retail advertising program in which the retailer participates.

The product marketer may establish a regular schedule of advertising to appear in a newspaper; prepare the ads to best present the product; and provide space for the dealer's (dealers') name, address, phone number, and similar information. We mention dealers (plural) because such a campaign can be most effective to the marketer, and most economical to a dealer, when several dealers are involved in each ad.

Such a program should be *sold* to dealers in much the same way as the product is sold . . . through the use of samples, benefits, and features designed to show a dealer how he or she can make a good investment.

We recommend the following steps:

1. Examine a trading area represented by the effective circulation area of a selected newspaper.
2. Determine the number of the kinds of dealers in that area that would be considered desirable and probably willing participants for such a campaign.
3. The cost of the newspaper space and the number of participating dealer prospects will determine the size of the ad and the number of ads one can plan into a program that will represent an attractive offer to each dealer.
4. Have a couple of ads prepared. They should be as attractive as possible—best if typeset and done with finished artwork. *This is a product to be sold.*
5. Have the names and addresses of dealer prospects already typeset in the ad. It may be difficult for dealers to refuse the deal if they know their names will be deleted.
6. Prepare a formal newspaper insertion schedule and a detail cost for the total campaign:
   a. Cost per insertion multiplied by the number of insertions.
   b. Cost of ad preparation (creative cost).
   c. Total cost of campaign.
   d. Indicate sponsor will pay preparation costs and (suggestion) one half of space costs.
   e. Indicate number of participating dealers divided into remaining space cost.
   f. One sixth, or one eighth, or one tenth of one half of the total space cost should look very attractive.
   g. When the dealer is shown the cost to participate, it can aid the *sale* to show the dealer a line diagram of how much space can be bought in the newspaper for the dealer's share amount (very small).

Alternate item 6 (an alternative to item 6 in the above list). Prepare a formal newspaper insertion schedule for the ads to appear—but show no costs. Offer participation based on the dealer's minimum order of merchandise (products) that is calculated to increase the sponsor's business sufficiently to cover the dealer's share of participation . . . or more.

Of course, all promotional ideas have their problems, particularly if a selected dealer has had no experience with the type of promotion offered. For this approach we can suggest a few obstacles that can be anticipated.

1. It may be necessary to *sell* one ad at a time—not a schedule, which would be desirable.
2. It should be anticipated that, at least the first time such a program is offered, it will not attract sufficient dealers to share as much of the cost as calculated. The sponsor will need to assume a greater part of the cost. A successful ad result and the fact the ad did appear without the names of dealers who turned it down will attract additional dealers when offered another time . . . or, still another time.
3. There may be certain dealers that refuse to have their names appear with certain other dealers in the same ad. This may require using more than one ad for all dealers, separating dealers that are located too near to each other, or eliminating a dealer that is not compatible with the other dealers.

——— Cooperative and Participating Dealer ——— Advertising Compared

The types of retail distribution that exist for a marketer/advertiser may preclude a choice between cooperative and participating dealer advertising. One *or* the other may often be the only choice. Both plans offer the advantage of expanding distribution to additional dealers, building inventories, and attracting customers to the point of sale. But it is rather obvious that the advertiser can have better control over his or her investment if the advertiser operates his or her own program.

From the standpoint of the working content of the advertising, cooperative advertising can more often include price, and might attract more customers to one retailer. On the other hand, the multiple-signature ads may attract a greater total of customers to all outlets.

This discussion is centered on alternatives for advertisers with small budgets. If dealer-involved advertising is used as an alternative to one of the segmented marketing strategies for developing brand awareness, then the dealer participation strategy has an added advantage. Since the ad is being prepared by the manufacturer/marketer, it can devote more of the space to selling the product and building brand awareness. (An example of the use of participating is the Goodyear Plus campaign, which is described in the accompanying case.)

—— CASE HISTORY ——
GOODYEAR PLUS CAMPAIGN
GREAT BRITAIN

Dealer "Plus" Campaign

British Newspapers
Full-Page Ads
April 3 and 10

Birmingham Evening Mail
Bristol Evening Post
Cambridge Evening News
Cardiff South Wales Echo
Coventry Evening Telegraph
Eastern Daily Press
Glasgow Daily Record
Hemel Hempstead Evening Post-Echo
Hereford Ad Mag
Leamington & District News
Leeds Yorkshire Evening Post
Leicester Mercury
Lincolnshire Echo
Manchester Evening News
Mersey Mart (freesheet)
Newcastle Evening Chronicle
Northampton Chronicle and Echo
Norwich Eastern Evening News
Nottingham Evening Post
Sheffield Star
Sun (London & Southeast)
Teeside Times
Wolverhampton Express and Star Group

"Plus Campaign" is an in-house term used by Goodyear to distinguish between the dealer cooperative advertising program and corporate-sponsored dealer participation advertising. The company offers an ongoing cooperative advertising assistance program that is used by dealers, at their own discretion, depending on their earned accrual co-op funds. However, the "plus" is that, in addition to the cooperative program, dealers may participate in company-sponsored and company-operated retail advertising programs that are not associated with the cooperative funds accrued by the dealers.

The "Plus Campaign" is a special retail promotion that is characterized by large space newspaper ads with multiple dealer signatures. Dealers are grouped according to the circulation area (trading area) of selected newspapers. Dealers can usually "earn" the right to participate by purchasing a prescribed minimum number of units of the product. This provides the company sponsor with a predictable return on investment before the promotion is put into action.

In this case, Goodyear in England set up a promotion that offered consumers a contest—one entry for each tire purchase (see Illustration 8–2)—for a six-day holiday in New York and travel on the British Airways Concorde, SST (see Illustration 8–3). Tire retailers were offered an opportunity to participate in this promotion.

Technically, every dealer that purchased and offered a particular brand of tire (Grand Prix-S) was participating, because delivered to the dealer with each tire was one consumer entry form . . . and the contest itself was being promoted in the national press. Beyond this, it was a matter of Goodyear salespersons encouraging dealers to increase their individual involvement.

Salespersons were organized with presentations to dealers that explained that the national market was being divided into four parts. There would be a consumer winner from each part, plus the dealers that endorsed the winning entries would receive identical prizes. Dealers were provided with co-op ads to use at their own discretion along with point-of-sale posters. Then they were offered an opportunity to participate in the full-page "dealer plus" ads. This amounted to including their name,

FIT GOODYEAR Grand Prix-S and you could fly to New York by Concorde

Goodyear Grand Prix-S tyres are a major contribution to road safety.

But now there's yet another good reason for fitting these famous tyres.

Because every tyre you buy entitles you to enter our Concorde to New York competition.

Yes, fit Grand Prix-S tyres and you could find yourself breaking the sound barrier and win a luxury six-day holiday in New York.

Goodyear Grand Prix-S
A major contribution to road safety.

Consult your local tyre specialist

Tyreservices Great Britain
Blackbird Road, Leicester
Tel: 25211

Tyreservices Great Britain
56 Leicester Road, Loughborough
Tel: 214171

Tyreservices Great Britain
56 Thorpe End, Melton Mowbray
Tel: 2485

Tyreservices GB/Kettering
206 Central Road, Hugglescote
Coalville
Tel: 32773

Tyreservices GB/Kettering
Goose Lane, Barwell
Tel: 42285

Tyreservices GB/Kettering
8/12 New Street, Hinckley
Tel: 632513

Tyreservices GB/Kettering
7 Catherine Street, Leicester
Tel: 24677

Tyreservices GB/Kettering
Leicester Road Corner, Kingston
Avenue, Wigston Fields, Leicester
Tel: 881453

Tyreservices GB/Kettering
53 Queens Road, Loughborough
Tel: 61753

Tyreservices GB/Kettering
124a Countesthorpe Road South
Wigston
Tel: 775452

E.T.C. Tyre & Battery Centre
Ravensbridge Drive, Leicester
Tel: 531877

Walkers Tyres
73 Melton Road, Leicester
Tel: 62513

Walkers Tyres
Crumble Stand, Aylestone Road
Leicester
Tel: 549534

Walkers Tyres
34 Narborough Road South, Leicester
Tel: 890890

Walkers Tyres
Melton Road, Syston, Leicester
Tel: 606271

Walkers Tyres
Bradgate Street, Leicester
Tel: 530343

GET DOWN TO YOUR GOODYEAR DEALER TODAY.

— ILLUSTRATION 8-2 —
Dealer "Plus" Campaign

Every Goodyear Grand Prix-S you buy between now and the 30th April, 1981 entitles you to a free competition entry.

How many miles is London from New York?		Flying time by Concorde, London to New York?	
6810		6 hrs	
3440		8 hrs	
2140		3¾ hrs	
Which of these is famous for its Theatres?	MADISON AVE	How many states make up the USA?	60
	WALL STREET		30
	BROADWAY		50

Use your skill to complete the following slogan:—

I bought Goodyear Tyres because ....

....

Name ....

Address ....

....

....

DEALERS NAME AND ADDRESS

№ 031020

— ILLUSTRATION 8–3 —
Dealer "Plus" Campaign

address, and phone number in two ads appearing in local newspapers. To qualify they needed to order fifty Grand Prix-S tires.

The result was that eighty-one dealers signed up for the "Plus Campaign," and "Plus" ads appeared in thirty-three newspapers (see Illustration 8–1). Sales of Grand Prix-S tires for the two months (April and May) were increased more than 100 percent for the same months compared with the previous year. Eight couples, plus a Goodyear host couple, had a beautiful Concorde trip to New York, and new sales momentum was started.

Objective and Strategy

The basic objective is obviously to boost sales rate or sale of units over a stated period. In this particular case, it is also to create greater brand awareness, not only among consumers, but among retailers also. If retailers are investing in the promotion of a particular brand, they are also concentrating their sales efforts on that brand.

The strategy is to find an effective consumer-interest promotion theme. This involves developing an attractive advertising and point-of-sale program, *and then* "packaging" the entire program into presentation form for company salespersons to take to retailers as a "benefit-and-feature" presentation. Such promotions need to be *sold* to retailers in the same manner selling a new product does. Salespersons sometimes complain that they do not have time to *also* sell promotions. In such cases, sales management has failed to train salespersons in merchandising. Merchandising can sell more products, more often than order taking can.

A direct retailer sales promotion/merchandising strategy is not common in many overseas markets. Often, traditional attitudes are oriented toward wholesale merchandising, and becoming involved with assisting in the retail process is avoided.

For international advertisers, this is a strategy that can be used in many cases as a successful promotions innovation. It is one that can catch competitors off guard. However, since effective retail promotions are usually designed to meet the peculiarities of individual markets, the strategy is better taught as a program strategy procedure than packaged as a headquarters pattern.

Common Problems of the Small-Budget Consumer Advertiser

There are proven successful strategies for applying a small advertising budget to aid constructively in building a market for a consumer product. *But* they all have some common problems, chief among which is that all these recommendations represent *a lot of hard work.* Much more effort will be needed on the part of a company's representative, who is already overworked and understaffed, who is most likely untrained in advertising, and who is a long way from head office assistance.

If this kind of problem becomes too severe for the person on the action line, he or she will undoubtedly come to the conclusion that buying a few ads in large publications at a lower cost per 1,000 rate is a good investment; or that spreading the small budget among dealers and distributors in any form of un-managed advertising allowances is equitable and good for building business relationships; or that he or she can dispense with the advertising function by putting ads in the telephone book and buying a couple of billboards.

By contrast, for people in multinational subsidiary management, assigned to large markets and having at their disposal large advertising budgets and advertising specialists, the whole process requires much less personal effort. The person working to build a market on a small budget needs much more than directives from headquarters; that person needs help to invest that small budget properly.

Help can come in the form of home office assistance in selecting a small advertising agency. And this help can include indoctrinating, directing, and supplying the agency with what is needed to perform a specified strategy. Regular working visits from home office advertising staff or the corporate agency coordinator will be needed to assess quality of advertising performance, make adjustments in a campaign strategy, or simply to keep it operating properly.

The small budget can be effective and can be made to work hard—but not automatically.

—— 10 KEY POINTS ——

1. The international advertising manager is primarily concerned with the development of media policies and procedures that will ensure the achievement of the multinational firm's advertising objectives.
2. Some flexibility in international advertising policies and procedures is necessary because of the diversity of local media regulations and the availability/viability concerns.
3. The "noise level" in a given market affects not only media availability but also the budget needed to achieve the desired level of consumer "attention" or exposure.
4. Media *viability* is perhaps more important in many markets overseas than is media *availability*. For example, television advertising time may be available in Country A, but the number of TV sets in use may make it an ineffective medium.
5. Television is the primary medium used to reach the broad national market in most developed countries, but it tends to be more highly regulated than in the United States.
6. Two critical concerns regarding print media in many developing markets are (a) the quality of the printing/paper and (b) the reliability of circulation figures.

7. Many international advertising managers are faced with the trade-offs involved when making the choice to employ international editions of U.S. or European journals or local national journals. (The latter offer quality, circulation reliability, etc., while the former potentially reach a broader, more localized base.)

8. Media selection and scheduling offer far greater concerns internationally than domestically to developed-country advertisers. This is due principally to the variable rates, the differing local market regulations, and the lack of reliable circulation/coverage and media research data.

9. A major concern of the international advertising manager is the development of *control* procedures to ensure that his or her advertising actually is published/broadcast.

10. The establishment of media planning groups (consultants) is an important development for the small advertiser and agency, which typically cannot afford employing such specialists in-house.

9

Considering Local Regulations in the World Marketing Plan

— INTRODUCTION —

Advertising regulations often differ sharply among national markets. In this chapter we highlight the types of differences that the international advertising manager may find and provide some background in terms of the "worldwide advertising regulatory climate" facing the MNC.

It is impossible for the international advertising manager to be aware of every different piece of advertising legislation—in fact, the rules are changing daily. What is important is that the international advertising manager must recognize that differences among national markets exist.

This chapter reviews:

- the impact of consumerist groups on advertising regulation
- the role of the UN and the EC in advertising regulatory efforts
- a few examples of the types of regulation that may exist
- the implications of advertising regulation for the international advertising manager

In the appendix to this chapter, Sylvan M. Barnet, Jr., offers his views on worldwide advertising regulatory trends.

Naturally, the advertising efforts of the firm must be conducted within the legislative parameters of the individual countries in which it operates. The headquarters-level international advertising manager must develop an understanding of the various legislative mandates, just as he or she must become acquainted with the cultural taboos that restrict his or her efforts. This becomes especially important if the advertising manager is attempting to orchestrate a pattern campaign that will avoid the prohibitions in one or several markets. What questions and concerns, then, must the international advertising manager be aware of when viewing the individual countries? Let us answer this question after we provide some understanding of the current regulatory dilemma.

—— Current Climate ——

Advertising is fast becoming one of the most highly regulated business practices (worldwide). In fact, if current United Nations and European Community (EC) proposals were to be adopted, it could be the most regulated marketing activity of the firm.

International marketing and advertising decision makers, as well as executives at all levels, must take care *not* to believe all "the credits" assigned to advertising by its critics. Doing so would mean accepting the premise that the advertiser can create whatever demand is desired simply by employing various sophisticated psychological techniques.

Numbered among the international critics of advertising today are a host of consumer*ist* organizations and developing-country officials. At the national level, there are already many existing laws and regulations directly affecting advertising. Basically, these restrictions deal with such topics as:

- the type of products that may be advertised
- the content or creative approach that may be employed in advertising
- the media that all advertisers (or different classes of product/service advertisers) are permitted to employ
- the amount of advertising that a single advertiser may employ in total or in a specific medium
- the use of advertising materials prepared *outside* the country
- the use of local versus international advertising agencies
- the specific taxes that may be levied against advertising

To provide a clearer picture of the intent of the regulatory efforts, let us consider the critics and the nature and focus of their criticism.

——— Consumer Organizations ———

Successes in countries such as Sweden, Australia, and the United States have offered encouragement to many national and international organizations, commonly identified as *consumer organizations*, who seek to regulate advertising. (It should be noted that many question the representativeness of these many groups categorized as consumer organizations and feel that they do not deserve the "consumer" label, but this point will not be debated here.) These organizations have become stronger and better organized in recent years, especially at the nation/state levels, through their appeal to politicians, who see their efforts as representing and/or attracting voters.

In the late 1970s a worldwide study of the impact consumer organizations have had on advertising regulation was sponsored by the International Advertising Association (IAA).[1] According to these results, the business community and the *consumerists* both felt that the consumerism movement has had a significant *impact* on the advertising industry (see Illustration 9–1). Roughly 85 percent of the corporate managers and three fourths of the consumer organization leaders in the study felt this to be true. (It should be noted that the corporate participants in this study were selected from some fourteen "high consumerist active" countries, while the consumer organization leaders were chosen from a worldwide sample.)

— ILLUSTRATION 9–1 —
Response Groups' Attitudes on Statement:
"The consumerism movement has had a significant impact
on the advertising industry" (Percentages)

Combined Groups	Agree		Disagree	
	+ 3	+ 2 or + 1	− 1 or − 2	− 3
Managers	12.8	73.0	11.6	2.6
Consumer*ists*	9.4	66.7	23.9	0.0

Source: Adapted from data originally presented in John Ryans and James Wills, *Consumerism's Impact on Advertising Regulation (Worldwide)* (New York: International Advertising Association, Inc., May 1979). Response size includes 98 consumer*ists* and 78 managers.

[1] John K. Ryans, Jr., and James R. Wills, Jr., *Consumerism's Impact on Advertising Regulation (Worldwide)* (New York: International Advertising Association, Inc., May 1979).

As one might expect, the views of the consumer organization leaders and the business executives differed sharply regarding advertising's value to consumers (see Illustration 9–2). Further, it is not surprising that the so-called consumerists seek to ban the advertising of certain products and to affect the nature and direction of certain types of advertising. Perhaps most "telling" are the fundamental attitudes that the consumerists have toward advertising in general, as shown in comparison to the views of businessmen in Illustration 9–3. Finally, it is clear that unlike the corporate executives the consumerists do *not* consider self-regulation by the advertising industry as a viable means of ending what they perceive as advertising ills (see Illustration 9–4).

As will be seen in the next section, both the UN and the EC have considered *consumer protection* measures and have been holding hearings, preparing reports, and, in the case of the EC, enacting legislation on the subject. Much of the impetus for these activities can be *directly* attributed to the efforts of consumer organizations. For example, according to *Business America*, the European Bureau of Consumer Unions, a federation of national consumer organizations of the nine member states, is playing an important role in consumer legislation and particularly is acting as an effective lobbyist with the EC.[2]

——— UN and EC Activities ———

A report is being prepared in the UN Economic and Social Council (ECOSOC) that could lead to model consumer protection legislation for developing countries. (Under a draft resolution sponsored by Kenya, Mexico, Uganda, and Venezuela, the secretary general was called upon to prepare such a report.)

— ILLUSTRATION 9–2 —
Respondents' Views on Advertising Reliability

Statement	Country/Region	Consumerists Agree	Consumerists Disagree	Managers Agree	Managers Disagree
2. In general, advertising is a reliable source of information for consumers.	a. U.S./Canada	35.0	65.0	78.0	22.0
	b. Western Europe	29.6	70.4	89.0	11.0
	c. Other	28.5	71.5	83.0	17.0

Source: Adapted from data originally presented in John Ryans and James Wills, *Consumerism's Impact on Advertising Regulation (Worldwide)* (New York: International Advertising Association, Inc., May 1979). Response size includes 98 consumerists and 78 managers.

[2] Richard Barovich, "Consumer Protection Movement Gains in Europe," *Business America*, May 7, 1979, p. 8.

— **ILLUSTRATION 9–3** —
Respondents' Views Regarding the Need for Specific Legislation
Classified by Country/Region

Statement	Country/Region	Consumerists		Managers	
		Agree	Disagree	Agree	Disagree
1. Advertising directed	a. U.S./Canada	82.1	17.9	72.3	27.7
to children should	b. Western Europe	90.9	9.1	68.6	31.4
be regulated.	c. Other	92.3	7.7	82.6	17.4
2. It's appropriate to	a. U.S./Canada	63.1	36.9	44.5	55.5
ban advertising of	b. Western Europe	75.0	25.0	44.4	55.6
products considered	c. Other	76.9	23.1	41.7	58.3
harmful to con-					
sumers.					
3. Many advertise-	a. U.S./Canada	76.9	23.1	16.7	83.3
ments are offensive	b. Western Europe	50.0	50.0	25.0	75.0
because of sexual	c. Other	46.2	53.8	45.9	54.1
appeal.					
4. The use of advertis-	a. U.S/Canada	12.8	87.2	11.1	88.9
ing by professionals	b. Western Europe	53.7	46.3	36.1	63.9
should be prohibited.	c. Other	23.1	76.9	24.9	75.1

Source: Adapted from data originally presented in John Ryans and James Wills, *Consumerism's Impact on Advertising Regulation (Worldwide)* (New York: International Advertising Association, Inc., May 1979). Response size includes 98 consume*rist*s and 78 managers.

— **ILLUSTRATION 9–4** —
Response Groups' Perceptions as to (the Most Effective) Alternative Ways to
Control Advertising Industry (Percentages)

Response Groups	Alternative Ways		
	Increase Government Control	Self-Control	Consumerist Pressure on Industry
Managers	11.7	66.2	22.1
Consumerists	41.1	20.0	38.9

Source: Adapted from data originally presented in John Ryans and James Wills, *Consumerism's Impact on Advertising Regulation (Worldwide)* (New York: International Advertising Association, Inc., May 1979). Response size includes 98 consume*rist*s and 78 managers.

Specifically, this resolution cited the need for member states to consider the importance of regulating advertising to prevent promoting products damaging to human health, safety, and welfare.

At a July 15, 1980, meeting of ECOSOC, the representative of Barbados called for the preparation of model consumer protection law that could then be enacted by developing countries. Considering the general tone of the Group of 77 (developing nations) toward the MNC (or, as the UN prefers, "transnational corporation"), any model law would probably restrict advertising efforts. In addition, other UN bodies, such as the UN Conference on Trade and Development (UNCTAD), has been concerned with consumer protection and restrictive business practices.

In contrast with the developing world, advertising has already been rather heavily restricted by legislative activities in the developed world, especially by the EC and the United States. The consumer protection movement has taken measurable strides as the EC Commission attempts to harmonize the existing consumer protection legislation of the nine members of the EC. *Business America* describes the EC's approach as being a two-track system.[3] One track has focused on specific products and has produced several new laws, such as a foodstuff labeling law. The other track has focused on issues such as consumer credit, product liability, and misleading and unfair advertising. Many of these consumer protection areas directly impact advertising, and the resulting "harmonized" laws often seem to assume the most strident position from the existing member nations' laws. Through participation in a formally established advisory group, the Consumers Consultative Committee, the consumer organizations have played a significant role in EC deliberations.

National Regulation

German advertising legislation has been called the world's "strictest and most specific."[4] Further, the country has added to a healthy legislative list a mandate to respect various voluntary advertising rules or codes. It has been estimated that there are more than fifty central institutions and organizations policing German advertising.

Germany is not alone in this regard, however. In the IAA study mentioned earlier, some fourteen countries were identified by MNC executives as being highly restrictive.[5] In addition to Germany, these included:

---

[3] Ibid., p. 6.

[4] Volker Nickel, "Regulations Battle Creativity in Ads," *Advertising Age/Europe*, Vol. 1, Issue 11 (November 1979), p. 28.

[5] John K. Ryans, Jr., James R. Wills, Jr., and Henry Bell, "International Advertising Regulation: A Transnational View," in *Midwest Marketing Association 1979 Conference Proceedings* (Carbondale, Ill.: Southern Illinois University), p. 37.

United Kingdom   Belgium
France   Argentina
United States   Mexico
Canada   Italy
Australia   Finland
Sweden   Denmark
Austria

The IAA—discussed more fully in the appendix to this chapter—is constantly monitoring the legislation enacted (or proposed) in the various countries, as well as the self-regulatory efforts that are being developed. The following excerpts selected from the June–July 1980 IAA *Intelligence Summary* suggest the day-to-day regulatory changes that affect advertisers:

- Australia: Major drugstore chains have announced a self-regulatory code for advertising pharmaceuticals and over-the-counter drugs.
- Japan: Amendments to the Housing and Real Estate Act will tighten credit terms disclosure and regulate deceptive advertising.
- Egypt: Tobacco advertising has been banned from television sports events for both direct and indirect advertising.
- Panama: Effective January 1981, TV commercials for cigarette and perfume products must be 100 percent locally produced.

These examples run the gamut from direct prohibitions in the case of tobacco advertising on TV sports events in Egypt to Panama's restrictions regarding local content production. A particular concern regarding the latter is Malaysia's recent law *not only* requiring local content but also prescribing quotas for representation of its various ethnic groups in the commercials.

——— Role of Self-Regulation ———

While self-regulation does *not* receive the support of many consumerists, it has been credited with success in several countries. Increasingly, these successes seem to have taken the form of (a) improving advertising quality and (b) reducing the impetus for formal legislative action.

Another recent IAA research report, *Advertising Self-Regulation* by Neelankavil and Stridsberg, has documented the self-regulatory activities in some forty-nine countries.[6] This describes the nature of the self-regulation and the importance it plays in the overall regulatory schema in these countries. (See Illustration 9–5 for the countries included in the research.) Even where self-regulation is employed, however, it has rarely been seen as being adequate to replace legislation.

---

[6] James P. Neelankavil and Albert B. Stridsberg, *Advertising Self-Regulation: A Global Perspective* (New York: Hastings House, 1980), p. 13.

— ILLUSTRATION 9–5 —
Countries With and Without Self-Regulation

Countries with Central Self-Regulatory Bodies	Countries with Some Form of Self-Regulation	Countries with No Self-Regulation
Argentina	Denmark	Colombia
Australia	Ecuador	Cyprus
Austria	Finland	Guatemala
Belgium	Greece	Hong Kong
Brazil	India	Indonesia
Canada	Iran	Liberia
France	Israel	Malta
Germany, Federal Republic of	Korea, Republic of	Pakistan
Ireland (Eire)	Lebanon	Paraguay
Italy	Mexico	Portugal
Japan	New Zealand	Saudi Arabia
Netherlands	Nigeria	Syria
Philippines	Norway	Thailand
Singapore	Sweden	Turkey
South Africa	Venezuela	Zambia
Spain		
Switzerland		
United Kingdom		
United States		
Totals: 19 countries	15 countries	15 countries = 49

Source: Reprinted from James P. Neelankavil and Albert B. Stridsberg, *Advertising Self-Regulation: A Global Perspective.* (New York: Hastings House Publishers, 1980), p. 13. Publication sponsored by the International Advertising Association.

Perhaps self-regulation can best be illustrated by using the United Kingdom as an illustration. The structure employed by the British is a four-tier system designed to implement the *British Code of Advertising Practice.* It is concerned primarily with regulating print advertising, as the British, like most countries, have special commercial broadcast legislation.

Under this system, the entire control mechanism is governed by the Advertising Standards Authority (ASA); at least two thirds of this group must have *no advertising interests.* The ASA monitors the entire control system and investigates complaints. Complaints are initially received from the public and competitors; or they may be the result of internal monitoring.[7]

[7] *The British Code of Advertising Practice,* 6th ed. (London: CAP Committee, April 1979).

The success of this British self-regulatory effort is perhaps best shown by the lack of consumer*ist* efforts for a legislative substitute for the British code.

—— Competitor Actions ——

It was briefly noted in the last section that complaints are frequently initiated by competitors. While not documented, it is frequently felt among advertisers that "they are their own worst enemy."

In an effort to diffuse or totally abort an effective competitor's campaign, a firm may challenge the campaign before the appropriate government or self-regulatory committee. If successful, the advertising campaign is halted; if unsuccessful, some "time may be gained."

—— Implications for the Advertising Manager ——

At the outset, it has been indicated that before any action for the international advertising manager was suggested the nature of the regulatory concern(s) needs to be established. In the past few pages, the current impetus to tightly control advertising practices and the extreme differences in regulatory practices were illustrated. Further, it has been shown that the extent and severity of regulation is likely to increase.

What, then, does the international advertising manager do to cope *not* only with extensive regulatory parameters but with extreme differences in the various national regulations as well?

We suggest that:

1. The advertising manager now knows what types of regulations may exist—and, therefore, what questions to ask when considering a new market.
2. The advertising manager must develop a system for updating his or her existing knowledge of the regulations.
3. The advertising manager needs to direct the efforts of his or her company toward pressing for self-regulation. (This could take the form of supporting the actions of the International Chamber of Commerce, which works to counter prohibitive advertising/marketing legislation.)

Item 2 in particular needs further elaboration. As part of this updating procedure, the international advertising executive can take a three-pronged approach. First, he or she can obtain appropriate source materials such as the IAA's bimonthly *Intelligence Summary* (see Illustration 9–6). Second, the home office manager can require periodic reports from the local advertising manager regarding current legislative or self-regulatory changes in the country. Third, the international advertising agency, the international advertising

— ILLUSTRATION 9-6 —
Intelligence Summary

Intelligence Summary

Published by **INTERNATIONAL ADVERTISING ASSOCIATION**

475 Fifth Ave., New York, N.Y. 10017 • Tel: MU 4-1583 • Cable: INTAVASSOC • Telex 237969 IAA UR

Number 24, October/November 1981

To our readers:

This issue inaugurates arrangement of the information according to topic, type of product and type of media. This should make it easier to read and to refer to for advertiser, agency, and media subscribers.

The former country headings are now incorporated under the major headings.

Henceforth, the major headings will include:

Topics - LEGISLATION/REGULATION - GENERAL, SELF-REGULATION, CONSUMER AFFAIRS, ADVERTISING TO CHILDREN, SEXISM & DECENCY, ASSOCIATIONS, AGENCIES

Products - TOBACCO, ALCOHOLIC BEVERAGES, FOOD, PHARMACEUTICALS, etc.

Media - PRINT, ELECTRONIC, OTHER

There will now be two major parts to each issue. Part I will cover National Developments. Part II will cover International Developments, including European Community, United Nations, the ICC, etc. Each part will contain the new headings, and we will continue the short section on DOCUMENTATION.

The Editors

I. NATIONAL DEVELOPMENTS

LEGISLATION/REGULATION - GENERAL

● Canada - New Copyright Act will be introduced within a year.

● France - Advertising, formerly under Economics Minister, is now under Communications Minister.

● Mexico - Government has prepared first draft of General Law of Social Communication which would control all advertising and all media, stipulating all must have a social mission. Further, cable TV would be provided exclusively by the State.

● Norway - New conservative government will probably begin some advertising deregulation, especially recent law on enforced disclosure.

Source: Reprinted by permission of the International Advertising Association.

manager employs can provide updated material from the field. It should be noted that some countries hold the advertiser and the agency equally liable and subject to similar penalties.

In summary, keeping current on regulatory concerns is not just a means of avoiding legal difficulties, it is essential for strategic planning of your campaign. If, for example, you learn that Panama requires 100 percent local content in its TV commercials, you can do a certain amount of your filming for your pattern campaign in Panama. Thus, part of the commercial shown in other Latin American areas (or even worldwide) might originate in Panama—a distinct cost saving over just making a commercial in Panama and showing it nowhere else.

—— APPENDIX ——

—— WORLDWIDE TRENDS IN ADVERTISING REGULATION ——
by
Sylvan M. Barnet, Jr.

Advertising regulation is becoming a global phenomenon, both nationally and internationally. With the rise of consumerism, special-interest and advocacy groups, heightened awareness and transparency, and the media revolution, problems of regulation are a fact of life with which the advertising community must deal everywhere—particularly in open societies and in market economies.

Those of us in the real world of advertising subscribe to two basic, essential principles. First, if it is legal to sell, it should be legal to advertise. Governments have the sovereign right to control or forbid the manufacture of certain products and to control and forbid their importation from other countries. But, if their merchants and manufacturers have the right to sell products legally, then they should have the right to promote them within the codes of practice that apply to the advertising and promotion industry.

Second, if advertising and promotion in the marketplace must be regulated, the industry feels it is better done by self-regulation rather than through bureaucratic or political interference,

which should be used only as a last resort. Experience has shown that self-regulation is quicker, more flexible, and less costly than government regulation. Equally, experience has shown that government bureaucracy is not as efficient as self-regulatory mechanisms and, despite the bureaucrats' self-righteousness, is no more honest or infallible than administration by other human beings.

One of the problems in today's world is the potential or actual loss of economic freedom that goes hand in hand with the eventual loss of political freedom. So-called liberals and progressives believe that the nation, the individual, and the consumer must be protected by government from the unscrupulous and dishonest businessman. But honest businessmen also want that protection. And what if the businessman is government, as in the case of socialist or mixed economies, and what if the government becomes judge and jury?

The theory behind some of the principles of the so-called New World Information Order of the United Nations (UNESCO) is that the reader or listener should preferably be protected from the advertiser who might prejudice or influence those simon-pure objective editors and journalists. But what if those journalists become the captives of government or political parties through their subsidization? And what if the independent or opposition media become too weak to survive or are banned, as in the case of nonmarket economies and totalitarian states?

What political crimes are being conducted in the name of consumer protection as we approach the fateful year of George Orwell's "Big Brother," 1984? What crimes are being done in the name of protecting national sovereignty from outside airwaves—whether radio, television, or satellite broadcasts—to protect the nation from foreign cultural impurities? Or from unwanted or unneeded goods and services, not within the government's economic development plan and the "national desire" as decreed from "on high"? Or can this also be a ploy to maintain government monopoly over those airwaves?

Is the consumer really an idiot, or is he or she your spouse, as David Ogilvy pointed out? Are we in danger of throwing the baby out with the bathwater if we overregulate or establish a national "nanny" to decide what we, and especially our youth, can see or hear?

What is the sincerity of the United Nations Universal Declaration of Human Rights, which includes the rights to seek and receive information? Does the UN really believe in the free flow of commercial and other information?

These are the problems and questions with which the advertising community is wrestling as a result of the massive changes in the consumer society and the media revolution of the past decade.

Indeed, consumerism has become institutionalized during the 1970s—by governments; by consumerist organizations, of course; but, even more important, by business itself. And this very fact has perhaps made it easier to regulate, to self-regulate, and even to deregulate.

The confrontation that existed in the early 1970s between government, consumerists, and business has been to a not inconsiderable degree replaced by dialogue, cooperation, and even accommodation. It is hoped that this trend will continue into the 1980s, as the *real* problems are identified and as people begin to understand the limitations to obtaining a perfect world.

For tens of centuries, man has sought commercial and economic freedom. Governments have recognized the aspirations of their merchants and have encouraged them to trade as broadly as possible. Certainly, the unscrupulous, the dishonest, and the unfair should be regulated and punished—and this applies to politicians as well. But the large majority of the mercantile world conforms to established codes and rules. The problem is always with a small minority that sullies the efforts of their fellows. The control or policing of this minority is more easily accomplished at the local or national level, within specific cultures and codes of practice.

However, consumerism and regulation have also become internationalized during the 1970s at regional and world levels. This has resulted in such broad efforts as the New World Economic Order and the New World Information Order, the Consumer Protection Program of the Economic and Social Council, the Code of Conduct for Transnational Corporations, the passage of the resolution against marketing of breast milk substitutes and other efforts of the World Health Organization, and the new focus of the International Organization of Consumer Organizations on pharmaceuticals, hazardous chemical products, and on advertising and public relations.

At the European regional level, we see moves to "harmonize" nearly everything—trademarks, credit, product liability codes, warranties, food and pharmaceutical labeling, to name a few. And, we have the Draft Directive on Misleading and Unfair Advertising and the EEC Second Consumer Protection Program. All of this is happening despite differences in national law, practice, and enforcement.

In the media field, there is serious concern about multinational electronic media, and especially satellite broadcasting. And finally, there are codes coming into force on the transmission of transborder data and the protection of individual privacy.

So, we have a cross-current of activities in the national and international regulatory areas, with more and more people becoming involved. And, as Henry VI said, "Beware of the lawyers." And the politicians!

There are numerous types of regulation, such as: *products* (tobacco, alcholic beverages, food, pharmaceuticals, chemicals, cosmetics, feminine hygiene, contraceptives, etc.); *issues* (sex stereotyping, taste/decency, safety, health, ad substantiation, warranties, corrective advertising, antiforeign measures); *techniques* (comparative and co-operative advertising, use of premiums and competitions, use of testimonials and endorsements); *audiences* (advertising directed to children, to the poor and the aged—the so-called vulnerable groups); and on all types of media (preclearance, limitations of commercials, rationing of time, size of billboards, etc.).

The response of the advertising industry has been the adoption of more industry codes and more advertising self-regulation, increasing collaboration with government and consumer organizations, expanded lobbying and public advocacy, development of positions and standardized approaches, development of consumer response mechanisms, policing of mavericks and greater self-discipline, and the education of both the public and employees. Thus, consumer-ism has been institutionalized at the corporate level. And, it should be the purpose of industry and its communicators to show that the most common abuses are not always committed by themselves but also by governments and nonprofit organizations.

The International Advertising Association has been heavily involved in all these industry efforts. It has published monographs on nearly all the major types of advertising regulation in a series called "Forbidden and Severely Restricted Advertising." It is engaged in lobbying efforts that support national organizations. It is gaining a nongovernmental organization status in the United Nations and its agencies; it maintains liaison with the European Economic Commission; it works closely with other organizations, such as the International Chamber of Commerce, the International Federation of the Periodical Press, the International Public Relations Association, and the International Institute of Communications, to name a few.

The IAA also actively promotes self-regulation and has recently helped to write codes for the Philippines and Brazil.

Finally, with the rapid transfer of ideas and the global spread of issues, it behooves the IAA to be knowledgeable about all developments, even before they occur. For this purpose, it maintains a network of Communication and Action Groups within its forty-two national chapters. Much of the information gathered from them forms the basis for the IAA's bimonthly *Intelligence Summary* on national and international advertising issues, regulation, and self-regulation. This forms what is, in effect, an "early-warning system."

The 1980s will undoubtedly see an intensification of all the cross-currents enumerated above. It is clear that the 1980s will see more regulation as well as more self-regulation, a growing and changing consumerist movement, greater information needs and more delivery systems, and increases in public education and public service announcements. And hopefully, it will see a continuation and expansion of honest dialogue and cooperation between various interests as opposed to rigid adversarial confrontation.

The above material was especially prepared for this book by Sylvan M. Barnet, Jr. All rights reserved. Mr. Barnet is Chairman of the Sustaining and Organizational Members Advisory Council of the International Advertising Association, Inc., New York. He is considered one of the leading experts in the area of international advertising regulation.

─── 10 KEY POINTS ───

1. The international advertising manager must *not* assume that the advertising regulatory climate in the various national markets is similar.
2. Consumerist organizations have played an active role in the worldwide "movement" to place greater restraints on advertising.
3. Both the UN and the European Community have taken steps that could lead to even greater regulation of advertising.
4. The international advertising manager needs to be aware that national rules may not only affect the firm's *message* (creative) and *media* (employed) but may also determine where the advertising is *produced*.
5. The international advertising manager needs to develop a system for keeping up to date on the various national advertising laws (enacted and pending).
6. The *Intelligence Summary* published by the International Advertising Association (New York) is an important source of information on worldwide advertising regulation.
7. In virtually every national market there is at least one product that is banned from television (or some other medium).
8. Fourteen countries have been identified as being the most *restrictive* in terms of advertising regulation.
9. The United Kingdom offers a good example of how effective advertising self-regulation can be.
10. The authors recommend that international advertising managers direct the efforts of their companies toward pressing for self-regulation.

10

Managing International Corporate Advertising

— INTRODUCTION —

Corporate advertising is increasingly being employed in markets *outside* the United States, as MNCs seek to establish a common worldwide identity and image for themselves. This chapter focuses on the need for the firm to treat its corporate advertising with the same degree of attention (and importance) that it does its product advertising.

The first ... and perhaps the most important step ... in corporate advertising is the establishment of clear-cut measurable objectives for the corporation's campaign(s). Among the realistic objectives the MNC may wish to achieve in its overseas market(s) is an increase in awareness among target groups or dispelling some myths about its operations or intentions.

Among the topics covered in the chapter are:

- the other types of corporate advertising objectives the MNC may have
- the growth of advocacy advertising
- the recommended steps in international corporate advertising, including some "do's" and "don'ts"
- a discussion of two well-developed international corporate campaigns, one by Digital Equipment Corporation and one by the Henkel Group

In the United States the use of corporate advertising to communicate with various publics has become an increasingly accepted practice of major firms. While the exact figures vary, it has been estimated by respected groups, such as the Association of National Advertisers, that three fourths of all large U.S. corporations employ some form of corporate advertising. Further, a recent U.S. study by Yankelovich, Skelly & White suggests that firms engaged in high corporate advertising expenditures score higher recall than do those doing little or no corporate advertising.

Similarly, it appears that corporate advertising is growing in Europe. However, the base of firms using corporate advertising is much smaller, for example, a *Financial Times* (London) spokesman was quoted as stating that only 34 of the 150 leading British corporations employed such advertising in 1980.[1] While comparable data are unavailable for Europe as a whole, our experience suggests that the total for advertisers on the Continent would be even smaller . . . but on the *increase*.

Historically, of course, many of the more famous international corporate campaigns were sponsored by United States-based firms. IBM and ITT–Europe provide two notable illustrations of such advertising in Europe. For example, IBM initiated an extensive corporate campaign in Western Europe in the late 1970s designed to offset the possible wave of "nationalism" that was becoming apparent. (In 1978 the French Socialist party had announced that, if it were elected to power, IBM and several other corporate giants would in fact be *nationalized*.) IBM's campaign was designed to show that the company was a good citizen with strong local ties and interests—a theme not uncommon for many MNCs.

—— Why the Increase in Corporate Advertising? ——

There are undoubtedly several reasons for the increase in international corporate advertising, just as there are multiple reasons why such advertising is sharply on the rise domestically in the United States. The reasons include:

- the apparent success of many corporate campaigns, such as those of ITT–Europe and IBM
- the increased awareness of the "importance" of corporate advertising;

[1] "Corporate Advertising Gains Acceptance in Europe," *International Advertiser* (March–April 1981), p. 3.

the Yankelovich, Skelly & White research alone has directed considerable attention to corporate advertising
- the recognition that the MNC is "under attack" in developed as well as in developing countries
- the fact that corporate advertising is now recognized as having many *potential* objectives, rather than being seen as simply "image" advertising

Still, the use of international corporate advertising is much debated. As in the past, many top executives perceive corporate advertising as a "waste of communication resources" and prefer to employ *only* product advertising.

Frankly, we find little fault with that view . . . if the firm has no clear-cut, measurable objectives for a corporate campaign. Too often firms just run an occasional advertisement (or campaign) that simply "sounds good," and its broad objective may be to tie its various subsidiaries or product lines together. Then the CEO or managing director of this firm will be one of the first critics of corporate advertising, because it has not been productive. In contrast, it will be our contention here that international corporate advertising requires planning that is equal to (or even greater than) product advertising . . . if for no other reason than that the corporate advertising budget is generally smaller and the target audience is often less receptive.

——— What Is the Range of Objectives? ———

The real potential for international corporate advertising became apparent only after it was recognized that *successful* corporate advertising must be as carefully *targeted* as product advertising. The goals have to be established and explicitly stated. These goals may range from improving the firm's overall awareness level in a given market to taking an *advocacy position* regarding a government policy or the charges of a consumerist group.

Perhaps the true birth of corporate advertising as we know it today was initiated by the image concerns that *all* MNCs began to have in the developing world in the late 1960s and early 1970s. The charges of exploitation, bribery, failure to transfer technology, and even "self-colonization" that were voiced in the UN by developing-country spokespersons needed to be answered, and a number of MNCs accepted this challenge. A 1978 article suggested that many MNCs developed *specific* responses to such charges and carefully targeted them to *specific* publics (most often to government officials in the developing countries).[2] It may have been the specific targeting of this image advertising that led to the corporate advertising of the 1980s.

International corporate advertising may be used by an individual firm, by an

[2] John K. Ryans, Jr., and Victoria Berger, "Use of Advertising to Improve MNC's Overseas Image," *Journal of Advertising*, Vol. 7, No. 3 (Summer 1978), pp. 40–47.

industry grouping, or even by a firm or industry in concert with a host government. However, our primary attention here will be given to the use of international corporate advertising by the *firm*. Recently, the purposes for domestic corporate advertising were classified by S. Prakesh Sethi based on their "tax deductibility." Under this very rational approach, corporate advertising messages ranged from institutional/image goodwill (tax deductible) to idea/issue advertising disguised advocacy (non-tax-deductible). This schema of Sethi highlights the need to distinguish between international corporate advertising that is firm-specific (ITT–Europe's campaign to improve employee morale) and that which is societal-specific (Mobil's direct advocacy campaigns in the United States). Clearly, at this point most international corporate advertising falls into the former category.

With this background, let us look at a number of possible international corporate advertising objectives. Broadly stated, these potential objectives include:

- improving the awareness level of the firm among target group(s), i.e., awareness in general or regarding a particular firm's attribute(s)
- repositioning the firm in relation to its competition among a particular target group(s), either in terms of overall image or regarding the particular firm's attribute(s)
- dispelling a myth or misconception about the firm that is held by a target group(s), i.e., correcting a negative image
- altering the firm's long-run image to the target group(s), i.e., adding new dimensions to the current positive view
- presenting the firm's position on a particular public issue to the target group(s)
- sponsoring a message of social interest, e.g., public service advertising

These objectives, of course, do need some amplification.

Improving Awareness.   A major MNC may be a household name in its "home markets" but relatively unknown elsewhere. (In many instances, the corporate name has much less identity than does its product [or products] brand name.) A firm's "low awareness" may be reflected not only in its sales but often in many other ways also. This latter could include the firm's ability to exercise *leverage* with local employees, distributors, licensees, government officials, or other decision makers (or even its ability to initially access many of these critical publics). Further, the firm may be well known for its ability in one industry but relatively unknown in another phase of its operation. For example, an Exxon may be well known in the energy field but have low awareness as a producer of business machines. Finally, the corporation may have changed its name/identity and thus may need to develop a recognition factor similar to, or greater than, its previous level.

Repositioning the Firm.   A firm may have a generally high level of awareness but still may rank a poor third (or even tenth) in relation to its competition in an industry or with particular influential decision makers. It should be emphasized that the firm may not have a poor image . . . it may have virtually no image. In an article, we noted the importance of a corporation's "corporate authority":

> A short definition of "corporate authority" might be the rank order of share of mind for the names of similar products. While this definition often relates directly to share of market, it is actually much more. For example, it determines what firm carries the most credibility for making product claims or promises in advertising for an industry. Conversely, the low market share brand will have more difficulty with credibility or even in attracting the attention of consumers.[3]

Again, as with lack of awareness, the corporation simply has no strength . . . this time in relation to its competition. It is important to reemphasize that we are not considering only a corporation's market share, although market share may reflect problems for its individual products (or product lines).

An electronics firm may have a specific repositioning objective, such as "improving its *relative* rating as a producer of high-technology electronic equipment among senior-level government officials in Brazil." On the other hand, an appliance producer in the consumer field may wish to "improve its relative rating as a style leader (or as a quality control leader) among appliance retailers in Germany." In either instance, the firm has a specific objective relating to its competitive positioning.

Dispelling Myths or Misconceptions. Few corporations were surrounded by more "image negatives" than ITT–Europe in the early 1970s. The company's image in Europe resulted from the company's alleged involvement in Chilean politics; an antitrust suit controversy in the United States; a highly critical book, *The Sovereign State of ITT;* and the overall anti-MNC view affecting many firms. The company initiated what has been viewed as a highly successful corporate advertising campaign, which directed messages toward particular target markets.

For example, ITT–Europe research indicated that it was faced with morale problems among its own subsidiary personnel in Britain. Directing a campaign with headlines, such as "Who the Devil Does ITT Think It Is?" to this and other comparable critical groups, the company made impressive improvements in its image.[4] (See Chapter 2 for a more extensive discussion of the ITT example.)

It is most important for a corporation to determine if it does have a poor image and what the bases for its negative image are before developing strategies to correct its problems. Then, assuming that the image is untrue or undesirable, it must clearly select the target audiences with whom it wishes to communicate. Altering a negative image is perhaps the most difficult international corporate advertising effort.

[3] Dean M. Peebles and John K. Ryans, Jr., "Using Multinational Advertising Strengths in National Markets," *Advertising & Marketing* (Spring 1980), p. 15.

[4] Nigel Rowe, "Unbiased Ad, PR Best Approach for Multi-Nationals in Europe Markets," *Industrial Marketing* (July 1975), pp. 56, 58–59.

Advocacy Advertising. It has become increasingly "popular" for large corporations in the United States to employ advocacy advertising, that is, to use paid media to present the firm's view on a particular issue. These issues could range from support for a president's inflation policy to a response to critics of the company's profits (or industry profits). It is important to note that in employing such advertising the corporation must be especially sensitive to its *local environment* (culture). Advocating a policy of "equal wages/employment for women," for example, would produce a much different reaction in the Middle East than in the United States. A similar comment could be made regarding virtually any issue and "some market" in the world. According to Sethi, advocacy advertising

> is concerned with the propagation of ideas and the elucidation of controversial social issues of public importance in a matter that supports the position and interests of the sponsor while expressly downgrading the sponsor's opponents and the accuracy of their facts.[5]

The extent to which such advertising is now being employed outside the United States has not been accurately determined as yet. However, in those markets where advocacy advertising would be permitted, it is likely that this will be a vehicle increasingly used by MNCs frustrated by their inability to effectively present their views through normal public relations avenues. It should be noted the rewards are not without risks.

Long-Term Image Advertising. Perhaps the most traditional form of international corporate advertising is *long-term image advertising.* Corporations embarking on this form of corporate advertising typically recognize that they are building "goodwill" and view such advertising as an investment. As part of these long-range efforts, the company may be reestablishing an earlier reputation or seeking to upgrade the way it is now viewed by its target audience(s).

Being viewed as "the industry's leader in research and development" may be a corporation's long-term objective. Rather than "putting out an immediate fire," as in the case of a negative image, the corporation can afford to move more slowly and can carefully monitor (and, if necessary, modify) the program.

Public Service Advertising. The last type of international corporate advertising can be termed "public service advertising." Here the corporation, either individually or working with other corporations and/or the local government, may undertake an informational campaign designed to serve the public's interests. For example, Champion Spark Plug Company has prepared TV commercials on air pollution that have been run in Mexico and the Philippines. These commercials have the governments' support (and encouragement) and have been run as public service advertisements. Champion's identification

[5] S. Prakesh Sethi, "Advocacy Advertising and the Multinational Corporation," *Columbia Journal of World Business* (Fall 1977), p. 33.

(ID) is limited; a short ID at the end of the commercial. Still, by raising the issue of the need to keep an automobile in proper working condition in order to help reduce air pollution, the company at least indirectly benefits from the campaigns.

Two critical questions that arise in terms of this form of advertising are (a) whether such outlays are in the best interests of the firm's shareholders and (b) whether the relevant governmental bodies should be involved in such promotion. The former, of course, is a managerial decision that is often controversial, while the latter recognizes that the governments in most countries, especially developing countries, typically need to be contacted to prevent possible conflict. Further, it is important to remember that a unilateral effort to support some "worthwhile cause" may, in fact, bring a negative or adverse response in some countries, particularly those with highly nationalistic attitudes.

—— STEPS IN INTERNATIONAL CORPORATE —— ADVERTISING MANAGEMENT

With product advertising, it is typically the international marketing and advertising decision makers who are directly involved in the entire planning process. However, with corporate advertising, the impetus often occurs at the top management level or in the public relations division or section. In a widely diversified firm or one with many foreign subsidiaries, it is often the top management (president or managing director) who is in the best position to see that the firm's overall corporate image is not in concert with its individual subsidiary or product(s) images or that the company is "losing ground" to competition or that it needs more effective *leverage* in its *host government* relations.

Regardless of where the initial decision to consider international corporate advertising occurs, however, it is essential to have the full support (and involvement) of top management, as well as the appropriate subsidiary heads who will be affected by the program. This involvement should be encouraged throughout the planning and implementation process. Remember that the company's international corporate advertising more strongly reflects the firm's long-term objectives and policies than does its product advertising. For example, if the theme of an international corporate campaign calls for the company to be "a worldwide R&D leader in its industry," this becomes a long-term commitment that should be in concert with its long-term objectives. Rarely does a product campaign have such a long-term impact on the corporation's overall operations or have such immediate policy implications.

Before deciding on the need for an international corporate campaign, it is recommended that the firm assess its current position with its appropriate publics. And it is further recommended that this assessment take place in *each* country or region where the company currently markets its products or services (or plans to market them). Although sales results may suggest that the corporation has a *low awareness* or a *poor image*, this must be verified with the various target group(s), whether these are potential customers or local influentials such as government officials, academics, or the general business community. This research has the twofold purpose of identifying the nature and extent of the problem and providing comparative data against which campaign results can be measured. Through this research—often in the form of attitude and awareness studies—the corporation often finds that it is not perceived uniformly across the various markets and among the various publics. Such findings indicate the need to establish corporate advertising priorities in terms of markets and among publics. In addition, the research should suggest the appropriate vehicle(s) for reaching the various target groups with whom the corporation needs to *communicate*.

Image/Awareness Research.   As noted in Chapter 7, image/awareness research studies of the type recommended for international corporate advertising can be quite costly. By using one of the many companies that currently conduct *omnibus* studies in Europe today, the firm can obtain some basic data (e.g., its industry ranking) relatively inexpensively. However, the corporation must make certain that the information is obtained from the appropriate target group(s). For example, if the corporation is concerned about how it is viewed by German (or European) retailers or by the general business community, then this is the group that must be *researched*.

—— Seven "Do's" and "Don'ts" ——

In summary, there are certain "do's" and "don'ts" that we suggest to the corporation regarding international corporate advertising. These are:

1. *Don't* give your corporate advertising less attention than you do your product advertising.
2. *Do* involve top management in the planning of your international corporate advertising from the outset.
3. *Do* clearly define your objectives and your target audience(s).
4. *Do* research to determine the attitudes and/or awareness levels of the audience(s) prior to completing your planning.[6]
5. *Don't* assume that the same attitude and/or awareness levels prevail *across* markets.
6. *Do* pretest your campaign theme and creative materials to improve the chance of success.
7. *Do* postresearch—often long-term tracking—to measure the campaign's effectiveness in hitting your objectives.

[6] In addition, develop data on their media habits, bases for attitudes, and other relevant characteristics—through focus groups or personal interviews—if possible.

——— INTERNATIONAL CORPORATE CAMPAIGNS ———

A U.S. industrial company, Digital Equipment Corporation, and a European consumer products company, Henkel KGaA, provide exceptional recent examples of the use of international corporate advertising.[7] While there are slight differences in the planning/implementation approaches followed by these major leaders in their respective industries, each took the fundamental steps that are *essential* for the development of successful international corporate campaigns.

Basically, each of these companies employed a standardized approach to its international corporate advertising, that is, making only the requisite translation/idiomatic changes from market to market or following a standard theme/format.[8] Digital did involve its foreign operations more directly in the campaign planning than did Henkel. It should be emphasized, however, that the reason for the differences in the styles employed (i.e., home office versus *some foreign* inputs) is related more to differences in the firms' organizational structures and to the objectives of the campaigns—not to a fundamental difference in corporate advertising philosophy.

As we review these two international corporate campaigns, we will consider how each corporation approached what we feel to be the essential steps in developing a sound international campaign. By tracing a successful campaign for each firm, we feel that the reader will develop a better understanding of why *each* step is important and how such an approach—modified to fit the firm's objective—can be employed by other business organizations.

——— Digital ———

Digital Equipment Corporation, headquartered in Maynard, Massachusetts, is the world's largest manufacturer of interactive computer systems. And its statistics are impressive. In 1981 the company had total sales of $3,198 million.

Digital is not only a major U.S. industrial firm and an active, experienced

---

[7] The authors wish to acknowledge the cooperation of the following individuals who provided the information for these two examples: Mr. Wolf D. Dittmair, International Marketing Communications Manager, and Mr. David Simler, Corporate Media Manager, Digital Equipment Company, Maynard, Mass.; and Mr. Uwe Hofer, Troost, Campbell-Ewald, Düsseldorf, for Henkel.

[8] The reasons for maintaining such a "sameness" in a regional or "worldwide" campaign, of course, need little elaboration here. These range from the fact that the typical corporate audience(s) for such worldwide campaigns do cross borders themselves, as do the media they read (or view) to the need for the company itself to have a well-defined posture/philosophy in all markets. Further, it is important for the reader to note that we are making a critical distinction between the international corporate campaigns and the occasional local, national campaign. If a firm has a local problem, such as a "bad image" in Chile or Nigeria, this demands *special attention*. Simply including that country in this firm's international corporate campaign is unlikely to produce the desired results.

advertiser; it is strongly committed to foreign markets as well. In fact, roughly 40 percent of its sales are currently overseas.

In 1979–80, Digital's research among four key target audiences suggested that an international corporate campaign would further support its *leadership role*. Let us trace the firm's activities, beginning with the preresearch and continuing through the campaign itself. Finally, we shall consider its results to date.

Research.   Initially, Digital conducted attitude and awareness research among target audiences in the United States, Canada, and Europe in December 1979 and January 1980. The technique employed for most of the research, including middle and top managers in both commercial and nonprofit organizations (universities, hospitals, and government agencies), was focus groups, while personal interviews were used with the top managers in large European corporations. Though nonprojective, this initial phase of the research suggested to Digital how these critical decision makers viewed the company in relation to other computer vendors and what issues were important to them.

Planning/Creative.   During the spring (March–April 1980), the strategy for the corporate campaign was developed. As shown in Illustration 10–1, the company had two specific objectives for the campaign. In this phase of the campaign's development, the corporation's advertising agency (Benton & Bowles, Inc.) was involved in the interpretation of the research and its subsequent creative execution. Further, overseas subsidiary representatives of Digital and top management were consulted in the concept development for the campaign. The resulting concept (and particularly the tag line) were then tested (July 1980) in personal interviews, that is, split testing of the execution was employed, and the possibilities of any latent problems were probed.

First Benchmark Data.   After the concept was selected and approved and while the final preparations for the campaign were completed (September–October 1980), Digital conducted benchmark research in Europe, the United States, and Canada. In other words, Digital obtained projectionable attitude and awareness data to use as a *base point* against which future results could be measured in order to determine the campaign's effectiveness.[9] (The technique employed in the benchmark research was the telephone interview.)

Second Benchmark Data.   The international corporate campaign was initiated in the early fall of 1980. In September 1981 a second wave of benchmark data collection occurred. Again, telephone interviews were conducted among the target audiences in selected European countries where the campaign had

---

[9] By collecting its base point data just prior to the initiation of the campaign, Digital was able to eliminate the effect of any changes in perceptions that might have occurred between December 1979 and October 1980.

been (and continued to be) run. This research provided comparative data against which the earlier attitude/awareness benchmark results were compared. In addition, a minor concept study was completed to determine the continued viability of certain aspects of the campaign.

These results indicated that the campaign was producing the desired results, that is, meeting the firm's objectives with the target audiences. And the campaign was continued.

The Campaign. Illustrations 10–2 and 10–3 present first a sample of the English version of the campaign and then the same advertisement in one other language. All carry the central campaign theme: "We Change the Way the World Thinks." To reach Digital's target audiences, the advertisements appeared in leading business magazines and business dailies in the selected local European markets, as well as in the United States and Canada (Illustration 10–1). In addition, Pan-European publications were employed.

— ILLUSTRATION 10–1 —
International Corporate Overview of the Digital Campaign

Objectives:

1. Generate awareness and reassurance of Digital as a global leader in the computer industry.
2. Reinforce Digital's status as a technological innovator with a special interest in the practical application of computer technology.

Primary Target Audence:

Top and middle management in:

- large companies
- universities
- health-care organizations
- government agencies

Secondary Target Audience:

- heads of smaller companies
- current and potential employees

Theme:

"We Change the Way the World Thinks"

Campaign Coverage (Countries):

England	France
Netherlands	Spain
Sweden	Denmark
Austria	Canada
Germany	Italy
Switzerland	Belgium
Finland	Norway
Ireland	United States

Media:

- leading local business magazines and business dailies
- Pan-European publications (select) (a total of roughly 50 publications)

— ILLUSTRATION 10-2 —
English Language Version of the Digital Equipment Corporation
International Corporate Campaign

Digital's are changing world thinks.

When we introduced the Mini-computer, over 20 years ago, we immediately established ourselves as industry pioneers. For the first time, computers were taken out of the computer room and made available to people who were not necessarily computer experts. It was a major change, the first of many we've made since then.

Over the years, we've made computers smaller yet more powerful, less expensive yet more reliable, more versatile yet easier to use. We've specialised in systems that

In Brisbane, Australia, the Courier-Mail uses Digital's computers to produce one of the world's largest newspaper classified advertising sections more quickly, accurately, and economically than ever before.

put information exactly where it's needed, in the hands of the people who actually use it in their work.

In the United States, Boeing Aerospace engineers, exchange data instantly thanks to Digital's state-of-the-art computer networking technology.

These changes have allowed us to bring computer technology to whole new fields, changing them in turn.

Now, with over 55,000 people in over 40 countries, with over $2 Billion in annual sales, we're one of the world's biggest, most respected computer companies. And we'd like to share our experience with you.

We manufacture one of the broadest lines of proven equipment in the industry, so we can offer you a system that's as large as you need,

computers the way the

but no larger. When you need more capacity, the extensive compatibility of our systems, lets you add it on gradually, without sacrificing your original investment.

As for follow-through support, Digital is second to none. We have over 14,000 service people world-wide, devoted only to maintaining your equipment, training your people and keeping your system running smoothly for as long as you use it.

So if you want the technology, the expertise, and the follow-through capabilities of a leader in the industry, talk to us.

In Switzerland, millions of motorists can now cross under the Alps through the new 17KM St. Gotthard tunnel with their safety ensured by a control system using Digital computers.

Digital Equipment Co. Limited,
Digital House,
252-256 Kings Road,
Reading RG1 4H4.

digital
We change the way the world thinks.

In Milan, Italy, Digital brought computers right to the floor of the Alfa Romeo factory, to perform extensive dynamic testing on every engine produced.

Source: The authors wish to acknowledge the cooperation of Mr. Wolf D. Dittmair, International Communications Manager, and Mr. David Simler, Corporate Media Manager, Digital Equipment Company, Maynard, Massachusetts.

Los ordenadores Digital están cambiando la forma de pensar del mundo.

Cuando hace más de 20 años Digital fabricó el primer miniordenador, dimos el primer paso como pioneros de la Informática Interactiva. Por primera vez, los ordenadores salieron de su sala de cristal y quedaron al alcance de gente que no era necesariamente experta. Fue un gran cambio, el primero de los muchos que hemos aportado desde entonces.

A través de los años, hemos construido los ordenadores más pequeños pero más potentes, menos caros aunque más fiables, más versátiles pero también más fáciles de usar. Estamos especializados en sistemas que llevan la información exactamente allí donde se necesita, hasta las personas que la precisan para realizar su trabajo.

Estos cambios nos han permitido llevar la informática a nuevas áreas, contribuyendo a la transformación de éstas.

En los Estados Unidos, los Ingenieros Aeronáuticos, intercambian datos instantáneamente gracias a la tecnología de los ordenadores de vanguardia de Digital.

Hoy, con más de 57.000 personas trabajando en 40 países, con más de 2.300 millones de dólares de ventas anuales y con la experiencia de más de 250.000 ordenadores instalados, somos una de las mayores y más prestigiosas empresas del mundo, y nos gustaría compartir nuestra experiencia con Vd.

Fabricamos la más extensa gama de ordenadores de la Industria, por lo tanto podemos ofrecerle un sistema de informática tan grande como Vd. necesite, pero no mayor. Cuando precise más capacidad, la gran compatibilidad de nuestros sistemas le permitirá expandirla sin sacrificar la inversión inicial.

En Suiza, millones de conductores pueden pasar ahora a través de los Alpes por el nuevo túnel de San Gotardo, de 17 Km. de longitud. Un ordenador Digital controla todos los parámetros de seguridad para la circulación y las personas.

Una vez instalado su equipo, una excelente organización de más de 14.000 personas en todo el mundo estará dedicada a su mantenimiento, entrenando a su personal y cuidando de que todo el sistema funcione a la perfección durante el tiempo que Vd. lo requiera.

Así pues, si Vd. necesita la tecnología, la experiencia, el apoyo y la garantía de un líder en Informática, llámenos.

En Italia, Digital ha instalado ordenadores en las naves de la factoría Alfa Romeo, para realizar controles de calidad dinámicos de cada motor fabricado.

Digital Equipment Corporation, S. A.

Agustín de Foxá, 27. Madrid-16. Tel. 733 19 00.
G. Vía Carlos III, 136. Barcelona-34. Tel. 204 79 00.

digital

Cambiamos la forma de pensar del mundo.

Source: The authors wish to acknowledge the cooperation of Mr. Wolf D. Dittmair, International Communications Manager, and Mr. David Simler, Corporate Media Manager, Digital Equipment Company, Maynard, Massachusetts.

——— Henkel KGaA ———

The Henkel Group, headquartered in Düsseldorf, West Germany, is one of the world's leading chemical companies and ranks 215th in *Fortune*'s Foreign 500.[10] This family-owned company's product line ranges from laundry and cosmetics products to adhesives and industrial cleaners.

Currently, Henkel has roughly 100 subsidiaries in some 40 countries and does business in more than 160 countries.

As noted earlier in connection with the *Fa* example (Chapter 3), Henkel has long practiced a standardized approach in its advertising.

In 1980, Henkel achieved 58 percent of its sales in foreign markets and adapted its advertising policy to the changed circumstances. Research findings indicated an incongruence between the way management and the public *perceived* the company, or, rather, a difference in its *desired* versus its *real* corporate image. Clearly, the company was *not* viewed negatively; rather, it was either understated in importance (West Germany) or had a low overall awareness (foreign markets). Henkel wanted to be seen as a specialist in applied chemistry with more than 8,000 products, as an international firm and a "family" company.

Research. Like many leading firms, Henkel has been conducting regular corporate image research. It was through such image analysis that Henkel became aware of its problem. The company was especially concerned that it have both a high awareness and a positive image among key decision makers in its various markets. Outside Europe, it was particularly concerned with improving its awareness and establishing a clear-cut, positive image in the United States, Mexico, and Brazil. (These findings provided the benchmarks for the later comparative analyses.)

To achieve its communications objective(s) with its target audiences (Illustration 10-4), Henkel and its advertising agency (Troost, Campbell-Ewald Gmbh) developed two concepts for pretesting—one presenting the company's achievements (direct) and the other utilizing relatives or friends of company employees to provide information about the company (indirect). The pretest established that the indirect approach best achieved the company's overall image objectives, including the "family" orientation it sought to establish.

Central Theme. The next step was to develop a series of advertisements to be employed in the campaign based on the pretest findings. (Owing to the need to reach a carefully targeted audience on a regular basis and to minimize *wastage*, Henkel chose to use only print media.) The resulting series of sixteen different advertisements (eight developed in 1980 and eight additional ones in 1981) all had the same central characteristics:

[10] *Fortune* Vol. 104, No. 3 (August 10, 1981), p. 211.

— ILLUSTRATION 10-4 —
International Corporate Overview of the Henkel KGaA Campaign

Objectives:

1. Generate increased awareness of Henkel, especially as an international company.
2. Increase positive image as a specialist in applied chemistry among target audiences.
3. Eliminate image of Henkel as a manufacturer of *only* laundry products.
4. Emphasize Henkel as "a family enterprise" with an international character (and a concern for society).

Target Audiences:

Decision makers and opinion leaders in:

- business and financial communities
- business journalism field
- business partner companies
- personnel field
- fields of economics, research, politics, and culture, and among its own employee leadership

Theme:

Campaign employs a standardized series that depicts an authentic member of an employee's family in one of its subsidiaries, who describes some aspect of Henkel's activities.

Campaign Coverage:

Western Europe   Latin America
United States

Media:

- *Fortune* (worldwide)
- local and regional business publications in key market areas, including France, Italy, the United Kingdom, Belgium, the United States, the Netherlands, Brazil, and Mexico
- West German business publications

Source: The authors wish to acknowledge the cooperation of Mr. Uwe Hofer, Troost, Campbell-Ewald, Düsseldorf, for the Henkel materials.

- the notation that it was part of a series
- a picture showing the spokesperson and a caption line indicating the individual's relationship to a Henkel employee
- a headline that captures the reader's attention and is relevant to the "story"
- a story that deals with day-to-day Henkel activities in a given country and that, taken with the other advertisements in the series, suggests the comprehensive, worldwide character of the company
- a block tying the local company (featured in the advertisement) with a description of the overall size and product range of the group
- the company logo (printed in red) and the slogan "Chemistry working for you"

Media/Strategy. The initial campaign in 1980 called for *Fortune* magazine to be used worldwide and other business/news publications to be utilized regionally. Roughly one third of the company's budget was spent in the United States (exclusive of *Fortune*'s share) and another major share in West Germany, which still is Henkel's leading market. In Europe, the European editions of *Newsweek* and *Time*, along with selected German publications, were employed. The language employed was primarily English (or German), and the same eight advertisements were used.

For 1981 the initial campaign results suggested a modification in media strategy. While keeping the basic standardized theme (and specific stories) described above, the company found that it could better target various key national markets through the use of indigenous publications and translated advertisements. Again, *Fortune* was used worldwide, while leading local business publications (rather than news publications) were used in France, Italy, Spain, the United Kingdom, Belgium, the Netherlands, the United States, Mexico, and Brazil. (The appropriate national language was employed in each of these *specific* countries). Flemish and English examples of the campaign are provided in Illustrations 10–5 and 10–6, respectively.

Results.   At the time of publication, no additional benchmark results are available to fully assess the 1981 campaign. However, the company has received sufficient feedback from the target market through various measures to suggest that it has been an unqualified success. These include inquiries for more information from opinion leaders, and a pretest and a subsequent posttest conducted among *Fortune* readers. The latter indicated sharp increases in corporate image/awareness and product knowledge.

——— The Two Campaigns: An Assessment ———

Critics of the centralized approach to advertising planning/strategy and the use of standardized advertising generally highlight the lack of local sensitivity found in such advertising. Perhaps the two cases described in this chapter best illustrate just how much sensitivity can be provided while using *centralization* and *standardization*.

As the reader will note, each of the companies *first* recognized its need for a corporate campaign as a result of ongoing image/awareness research. This research highlighted these needs and suggested some bases for their problems. Next, each company recognized the importance of having the same corporate image in each market (or worldwide) . . . a major multinational is simply deluding itself if it feels it can be viewed as a small national firm in the various markets where it operates. Corporate advertising in particular lends itself to a "one-face" approach.

Then, the two companies pretested the basic theme or concept of their corporate campaign. This approach again allows for the identification of localized problems that may be corrected prior to the actual launching of the campaign. (And Digital heavily involved its overseas personnel in the initial phases of the campaign.) Further, since an image campaign is often longer

— ILLUSTRATION 10–5 —
Flemish version of the Henkel Corporate Campaign

Een chemie-onderneming vanuit een ander perspectief. Serie 7

Loredana Naso over haar vader Alfredo, mecanicien bij Henkel Italiana.

„Omdat mijn vader bij Henkel kwam, konden wij in ons vaderland blijven."

„Wij Italianen houden boven alles van twee dingen: onze familie èn ons vaderland. Dat wij vandaag de dag als gezin bij elkaar kunnen leven en dat hier in ons vaderland, beschouwen wij als een heel bijzonder geluk.

Het eerste bedrijf waar mijn vader goed werk had, werd op een dag naar het noorden verplaatst. Het tweede werd gesloten.

Twee jaar was mijn vader zonder werk en zonder hoop. Hij stond op het punt om in Turijn of Milaan iets te gaan zoeken.

Toen ontdekte hij in de „Messaggero' de advertentie van een chemie-onderneming – Henkel Italiana. Zij zochten een mecanicien.

Deze keer hadden wij geluk. Mijn vader kreeg de baan. Hij werkt in de centrale werkplaats. Allen waarderen hem als een vindingrijk knutselaar. Hij heeft een goed èn zeker inkomen.

Op die manier konden mijn ouders mij naar vakkursussen voor boekhouding en comptabiliteit sturen, mijn broer zelfs naar de universiteit in Rome. Hij studeert daar elektronica en zal binnenkort ingenieur zijn. Wij hopen allemaal dat hij dan net zoveel geluk heeft als mijn vader en een even goede baan vindt."

Mijn vader Alfredo

Henkel Italiana S.p.A., Milaan, met produktiebedrijven in Ferentino en Lomazzo, is één van de rond 100 firma's van de Henkel-groep in meer dan 40 landen. Wereldomzet 1980 = meer dan 7,6 miljard DM. 33.000 medewerkers. Hoofdkantoor van de Henkel-groep: Düsseldorf, Bondsrepubliek Duitsland. Produktdivisies o.a.: was- en reinigingsmiddelen, cosmetica, kleefstoffen, industriereinigingsmiddelen, vetchemische produkten, textiel- en leerveredelingsmiddelen. In totaal 8.000 produkten op alle levensgebieden.

Chemie, die van nut is.

Source: The authors wish to acknowledge the cooperation of Mr. Uwe Hofer, Troost, Campbell-Ewald, Düsseldorf, for the Henkel materials.

— ILLUSTRATION 10–6 —
English version of the Henkel Corporate Campaign

Another view of a chemical company. Sequence 12

Will Rodzewich, student, about his father, chemist with Henkel's Amchem Products, Inc., Ambler

"I try to be like dad at Henkel: always on the ball."

"A winner sees an answer for every problem, a looser sees a problem in every answer – that's what my football coach always told us. According to that, dad is a winner type.
As a chemist in research and development with Amchem Products, a Henkel company, he has to face a lot of new customer problems in the automobile and other industries. In general terms, the problems are how to prepare metals for car bodies, containers or cans to inhibit corrosion and to give maximum quality to the consumer.
What kind of problem it may be, dad has an answer. He is sent to the customers to find the right solutions and to complete them. That's why

dad is travelling so much – within the U.S.A. and to foreign countries as well. He has been to many other companies from Pennsylvania to Japan. One of them was a Henkel company in Germany which had taken licenses of dad's Amchem more than twenty-five years ago. When Henkel acquired Amchem in 1979, dad said: that will make a good union. I think he was right. Since then his company has expanded and so did his responsibilities.

I've tried to be a winner in football. And so I'll try as a mechanical engineer."

Edward, my dad

Amchem Products, Inc., Ambler, Pennsylvania (U.S.A.), is one of more than 100 companies of the Henkel Group, situated in more than 40 countries. Worldwide sales 1980 = 7.6 billion DM. 33,000 employees. Headquarters Dusseldorf, Federal Republic of Germany. Product range includes laundry products, household cleaners, cosmetics, adhesives, industrial cleaners, oleochemicals, auxiliary products for textile and leather industries. Over 8,000 products for all walks of life.

Henkel

Chemistry working for you.

Source: The authors wish to acknowledge the cooperation of Mr. Uwe Hofer, Troost, Campbell-Ewald, Düsseldorf, for the Henkel materials.

term in its orientation, the firm needs to be prepared to make any necessary modifications that may seem appropriate as the campaign progresses. Digital, for example, did a second benchmark study that indicated the campaign was producing the desired results, while certain Henkel feedback information suggested that some media modifications were necessary in the second year of the campaign (1981) in order to more closely target their market. Such *flexibility* should be inherent in the use of central planning/strategy and standardized advertising.

Finally, both campaigns illustrated here are strong advocates of the use of *control procedures* (developing measures for determining whether or not the campaign achieves its objectives). While some may view these control procedures as merely an added cost, they should be built in as a basic part of any campaign to ensure that the firm's objectives are being achieved.

Corporate advertising may simply not be practical for all firms. However, even firms with a limited budget or those that employ only product advertising need to be aware that *any advertising they do (or that their subsidiaries do) reflects on the company's image*. Thus, any advertiser is in effect doing some "image advertising" even if it is not a well-conceived corporate plan. Let us suggest a little test. If you are an international advertising manager in a company that allows its overseas subsidiaries, distributors, sales office, and so on, free rein in their advertising, obtain some recent sample copies of the advertising employing your company name from three or four adjacent markets. For example, obtain some copies from the Netherlands, Belgium, and Germany or from France, Italy, and Austria. Then array this advertising side by side and think of yourself as a businessperson traveling between these countries. Would such a person have a single, clear image of your company and its products? For many companies the answer is *no*, and yet business people do travel.

Undoubtedly, overseas corporate advertising will increase in the future. Some of it will continue to be directed toward achieving awareness, better image, and the overall desired corporate identity, including its family of products or services. Other corporate advertising will likely take on a greater advocacy role as companies see advertising as the best means of communicating a position on a current issue. In any event, we want to again stress the need for giving the same (or even greater) attention to the planning directed toward such advertising that is given to product or service advertising.

—— 10 KEY POINTS ——

1. The MNC must give the same detailed attention to its international *corporate* campaigns that it does to its *product* campaigns.

2. MNCs are increasingly becoming aware of the need for (and value of) a single worldwide image and level of awareness.

3. The use of advertising research to provide a base point for future *effectiveness* comparisons is an important element of corporate advertising.

4. The MNC needs to establish clear-cut measurable objectives for its corporate campaign(s).

5. These corporate advertising objectives must be specified in terms of the particular target audience(s), whether customers or a wide range of national influentials.

6. The use of advocacy advertising and public service advertising by MNCs is increasing worldwide.

7. Top management should be actively involved in the planning of the MNC's international corporate advertising from the *very beginning.*

8. The MNC should *never* assume that it has the same level of awareness and attitude levels in various markets; each national market may vary significantly.

9. Digital Equipment Company and the Henkel Group cases demonstrate how research plays an essential role in the corporate campaign.

10. Every international advertiser must be aware that *any* advertising the advertiser does reflects on the company's image . . . regardless of whether or not it is a corporate campaign.

11

Managing Industrial Advertising

— INTRODUCTION —

We recognize that the problems of industrial and consumer goods marketers are often *quite different*. This is especially true in regard to international advertising. Naturally, the two groups differ in product *usage* and buyer *characteristics*. In addition, the consumer goods producer normally has a much larger *advertising budget*.

While we stressed the many advantages of centralized advertising decision making in earlier chapters, it is the industrial marketer who is especially well suited to employ this *strategy*. Generally, culture per se should be of limited concern to the industrial marketer; it is the environment in which the product is used that may pose some concerns. For example, the production line in a plant in Pakistan may be quite unlike one in Peoria.

In this chapter the following topics are considered in some detail:

- basic advertising "traps"
- priorities for the advertising function
- advertising campaign strategy analysis
- trends in the international business press
- industrial advertising agency alternatives

Of special interest to many international industrial advertising and marketing managers will be the examples presented at the end of the chapter in the section, "Some Company 'Cases.'"

Are the international problems of industrial and consumer goods advertisers so different? We feel that the answer to this question is *yes*. And, in earlier chapters, we *have* cited several industrial marketing examples and pointed to a few key consumer/industrial market differences. However, the very nature of the markets differs so greatly that it would be unwise to suggest or imply that "advertising is advertising"—that, for example, the consumer goods purchaser and the industrial buyer in Venezuela are "all the same."

In fact, we see a much greater *commonality* between a machine tool industrial buyer in Venezuela and one in Sweden than would ever be present for a consumer product. This strongly suggests a greater opportunity for the industrial advertiser to standardize a campaign worldwide. On the other hand, the media possibilities for delivering this standardized message may be much more limited for the industrial marketer than for the consumer goods producer.

In this chapter we shall review much of the earlier material, placing it in an industrial context. The importance of culture, the approach to organization, and the role of advertising agencies all need to be considered in terms of the industrial advertiser's *needs*.

Recognizing Overseas Opportunities

U.S. industrial marketers are becoming increasingly interested and involved in overseas markets. Let us look at two industries that reflect this change. Machinery exports increased from $36 billion to $46 billion between 1979 and 1981, while overseas capital investment by U.S. firms in the primary and fabricated metals industry *tripled* during the same period. With this increased attention to foreign industrial opportunities has come the expected need to "know more about international industrial advertising."

Naturally, all the growth has not resulted from firms that are new to overseas business. There are many MNCs and other corporations that have extensive knowledge of overseas international marketing and advertising practices and whose efforts are increasing. Still, the newer firms (often smaller firms) do account for much of this activity, as well as for the demand for more marketing and advertising information. Their needs will receive much of our attention.

SOME BASIC ADVERTISING "TRAPS"

Possibly no area of marketing has received less imaginative attention than that of international industrial marketing. The traditional domestic assumption has been that the industrial buyer is the personification of the "economic man," yet overseas the same group often see the same buyer as especially subject to the influence of the environment. This is just one of the inconsistencies and principles that we will challenge. Therefore, many of our views here may seem a bit heretical and may even have implications for the domestic industrial market.

While it is difficult to generalize about something so varied as industrial products/markets, we feel that there are many *traps* that may occasionally catch even the experienced international industrial advertising or marketing manager. These industrial advertiser *traps* are:

1. Focusing on market/country *differences* rather than on *similarities*. (Cultural concerns should be minimized.)
2. Segmenting by *country* rather than by *buyer categories*. (Fabricated steel and electrical goods purchasers differ more in product needs/appeals than in geographic location.)
3. Assuming that the overseas buyer relies most heavily on local media for information. (Some United States-based business publications are the standard information sources worldwide.)
4. Employing separate advertising agencies for each local market. (Again, this is an overreaction to cultural concerns.)
5. Failing to effectively utilize the overseas clout the industrial advertiser has. (This refers to the clout it has achieved through its domestic or third-country reputation in *either* the industrial *or* the consumer field.)
6. Deciding that its limited foreign budget makes it necessary to "cut corners" in media selection and to eliminate any form of advertising research. (There are many low-cost techniques that can provide useful data.)

There are, in fact, so many traps—myths and unfounded principles—surrounding international industrial advertising and marketing that the newer industrial advertising manager almost needs to be preconditioned to question *anything*. An appropriate "why" will often put to rest the unsubstantiated admonition: "You never do _____ in _____."

To further avoid the *traps*, we suggest keeping in mind that one of the industrial advertiser's primary objectives is to increase the *proportion* of the available budget that "is actually spent on effectively communicating with the target audience." Any unnecessary duplication of production costs, creative planning, and the like reduces the proportion of the total dollars, pesos, or lira that is available for such *target audience communication*. Another useful question to ask, therefore, is: "Could these funds be better directed to purchasing additional business publication space, direct mail, or whatever medium that is appropriate?" Similarly, expenditures designed to better identify, or more effectively communicate with, that target audience are valid.

——— Multimarket Creative Development ———

Simply defined, "industrial advertising" refers to advertising in support of the sale of products/services used by industry/business, such as tools, machinery, chemicals, materials for manufacture, subassembly components, bank services to business, and marine insurance. By this definition, the creative work involved in preparing the international advertising is generally less complex than it is in advertising consumer products, and it is finding the medium for delivering the message that becomes far more difficult.

Creative Development. When we say that the creative development is less complex we refer, of course, only to the transition from the U.S. domestic market to many world markets. Most industrial advertising is inherently intricate. For most items advertised there are many different types of customers, and *each* of these target markets sees the same product in a different light (i.e., for a different use/need). Thus, internationally, as domestically, industrial advertisers must avoid the *trap* of failing to *target effectively.*

Conceivably, one ad prepared for a brand of beer or face soap could appropriately appear in any publication read by a mass consuming audience. However, it might require ten different ads to reach the prospective customers for a transparent packaging film. The makers of textiles, toys, candy, picture books, hand tools, soap powder, and a grocer's self-service meatpacking all have different requirements, and problems to be solved, with this same packaging film. The people creating this advertising must be able to project themselves into many different industry problems to develop advertising that will communicate to each type of customer meaningfully.

Once this careful targeting is completed and the "ten different ads for transparent packaging film" are prepared, however, the same ads—with appropriate translations—can often be employed overseas. It is only when the same type of buyer has different use(s) for the product that the same advertisement would be inappropriate.

Those who advocate modifying all advertising to respond to *cultural concerns* will naturally disagree with us. We do, however, set certain conditions for such *standardization.* First, the use of the same advertising for multiple markets should be a predetermined strategy . . . not an afterthought. This requires the avoidance of *national* references, such as "in the good old USA," and suggests getting some inputs, if possible, from your overseas subsidiary, overseas sales office, or even an export management firm if that is how you market overseas.

Second, if such an assignment specifies that these ads are to be translated into different languages for overseas publications, a creative caution would be to avoid clever, unusual English in writing the ads. This situation would also require that the selected illustration be perceived as universal . . . or one that portrays advanced technology with which worldwide customers can all identify.

THE INDUSTRIAL ADVERTISER AND THE ——— QUESTION OF INTERNATIONAL CULTURAL DIFFERENCES

Basically, we would suggest that the industrial marketer who takes products overseas has more, and more serious, unrecognized problems to contend with than cultural differences. The most serious problems are those created by a *lack of sufficient funds to do the thorough job.*

Cultural differences are minimal for most industrial advertisers. Products are seldom promoted with emotional or other psychological appeals. The product use or user will seldom associate such purchase decisions with anything social, political, or religious. However, there are environmental differences between the various national markets that can go unattended owing to the lack of funds to travel for investigation and to prepare a sufficient number of different advertisements to perform the thorough and precise target communicating necessary for success.

Lack of Available Money.   Almost by definition, industrial advertising means a lower advertising budget. This axiom has little correlation to the size of the company or the products' profit margins. Business practices associate most industrial products primarily with personal selling (which it is); low-cost publication space (compared with consumer magazines); and inexpensive direct mail (which it is not). This fails to recognize a high-cost requirement for advertising production (many more ads usually required); *plus,* for the international industrial advertiser, traveling personnel to study the intricacies of product use environments and advertising environments (particularly in finding efficient media for communicating to target audiences).

The Offshore Fog.   In seminars conducted by the authors, it is not unusual to encounter people with several years' experience in international industrial advertising who have had limited (or no) travel abroad. They are struggling with what they refer to as "cultural differences"—trying to arrange for illustrations that show their machine tool lathe or electrical transmission systems in separate atmospheres for Germany, England, and Italy. At the same time, they are not aware of environmental technicalities, such as the fact that in Denmark it is illegal for secretaries to use the three-legged typing chairs that are so common in the United States.

The end use of production is often not properly addressed in international industrial advertising—end use in terms of being appropriate to media and audience—in order for customers to project themselves as potential users. This, of course, requires several ads for the same product . . . how the same materials handling equipment looks operating in an appliance factory, a bakery, or a soft drink bottling firm . . . advertising that is appropriate to the journal and its audience.

The ad that appeared in the United States simply may not communicate with the intended projected image. This signifies, not cultural differences, but environmental differences. By recognizing at the outset that an advertisement or campaign is to be employed in multiple markets, the advertising manager can select illustrations that suggest *no particular* national environment. While this simple principle seems to be just good common sense, it is surprising how often it is violated in practice.

The availability of appropriate and efficient media is probably the thickest fog of all. This subject will be discussed in detail later in the chapter.

——— INDUSTRIAL MARKET COMMUNICATIONS ———

Industrial product marketers often look at market communications with a sense of frustration at finding ways of reaching their customers with an effective selling message. The primary reason for seeing more obstacles than opportunities appears to be that industrial advertisers (a) can seldom use the mass media effectively and (b) often define their target audience much too narrowly to find any type of medium that appears to be efficient. The manufacturer of equipment, or subassemblies, used only on helicopters can count his or her customers on the fingers of one hand. If this same manufacturer can project a target to suggest that his or her product principle can be adopted for use on other critical mechanical equipment, advertising could be used to open the way to many new types of customers.

——— PRIORITIES FOR THE ADVERTISING FUNCTION ———

As opposed to the advertiser of consumer goods, the industrial advertiser can most systematically segment the advertising target audience—placing each target in priority order and finding that the highest-priority targets are the least expensive to reach . . . peripheral expansion becomes increasingly more expensive. This places the small industrial advertiser on a par with his or her competitors *vis-à-vis* the consumer products advertiser who must compete for mass consumer awareness.

——— Taking One Step at a Time ———

An industrial advertiser can expand market communications as he or she desires to expand his or her business (see Illustration 11–1).

1. *Manufacturers' Representatives — Selling Agents — Distributors*
    Whatever form the basic product distribution takes, the industrial marketer must first provide basic selling aid communications. This

— ILLUSTRATION 11-1 —
Taking One Step at a Time

Industrial Market Communications

Sales Representatives, Agents, Distributors

START: Product Specifications and Data, Catalogs— Sales Support

Active Customers

ADD: Continuous Communications—Direct Mail

Known Potential Customers

ADD: Direct Mail—Trade Journals—Product Demonstrations

Unknown Potential Customers

ADD: Trade Journals—Direct Mail—Trade Fairs

General Corporate Awareness

ADD: Public Relations Events—Publicity Releases— Permanent Exhibits involves product specification and data literature, catalogs, product testing, and demonstrated performance information—everything the sales functions need to present a product to a potential customer. This done, there should be added—

2. *Active Customers*

Before looking for new customers, the next priority should be the care and maintenance of existing customers. A company's communications should constantly reinforce the customer's good judgment in choosing the *right product*. Customers should constantly be reminded of the product's quality and performance, and sometimes it helps to reinforce their judgment by letting them know about other important users of the same product. In other words, even purchasing agents have some cognitive dissonance.

It is usually most practical to use direct mail advertising for this type of communication. To attract new customers, the first action can be to *add*—

3. *Known Potential Customers*

If every salesperson sells your product to every known potential customer, you have both remarkable salespersons and a remarkable product. It is more practical to think of a good sales operation as having a well-defined list of potential customers that are categorized to describe their type of business and potential volume as potential customers. Infrequent customers should also be included in this category.

This kind of information is valuable input to an industrial communications program. The quality and volume of this information will require analyses by communications specialists to determine how best to reach and influence this potential business.

The content of this information and the type of product will aid greatly in determining the selling strategy and the choice of media.

a. If a product would have such general use as filing cabinets or janitor supplies, the customer category would be less critical than it would be in the case of, say, chemical compounding ingredients or hydraulic pumps.

b. Almost any product *can be* offered as a quality-produced *commodity* offered to potential customers in such a way as to allow them to determine if and how it might be used. Or a product *can be* offered as the *solution* to known customer problems.

c. Regardless of the size of the initial potential customer-list, it will be the size of each classified customer group that will determine the communications method. Essentially, this refers to specifically how the advertiser must address each group.

From the above discussion, one could be led to the conclusion that direct mail advertising is the only media solution. However, this should depend on the size of the resulting audience(s), and how critical it is to target a very narrow group. One should be constantly aware that direct mail advertising is by far the most expensive type of advertising per customer contact—and that trade publications are then available that can be used as a form of direct mail to contact a larger audience at less cost.

The ability to use trade publications as direct mail will depend, of course, on whether or not there is a publication that *generally* reaches your target audience in the country where you wish to advertise. The rest is only a matter of executing your presentation designed with the same details as would be offered in direct mail and to use special response devices such as coupons or return postcards. To this action, and to further expand business opportunity, one can *add*—

4.   *Unknown Potential Customers*

In many ways, the analytical process is reversed from the considerations given to campaigning from a list of known potential customers. Instead of looking for media to reach known customers, one is looking at media that are most apt to contain customers—the media are to be categorized, and doing this poses a greater problem as one considers the lesser industrially developed international markets where trade publications are also not well developed.

Looking toward the alternatives to finding media efficiency for finding unknown customers, one might consider the following:

a. Use of both the vertical and the horizontal trade press is of course the optimum situation for the industrial advertiser in any market. This subject will be detailed later in the chapter.

b. A general industries trade press will often be available in lesser developed countries, usually in the form of a business management/finance category and possibly a general industries/manufacturing journal. One can expect to find specialized journals for the industries that dominate trade for a particular country (e.g., mining, petroleum, rubber).

c. Regional or international trade journals are continuing to become of greater importance, particularly in the Middle East markets and markets in Southeast Asia and Central Africa. They also are found in Latin America; however, many countries on the South American continent are also developing a rather sophisticated selection of local trade journals. The use of regional journals will, of course, depend upon how well existing journals cover the advertiser's target market and how narrow a target market is demanded by the advertiser.

The major international journals, particularly in the areas of executive management and highly technical subjects, often represent greater authority to customers in developing markets than do local publications—language becomes an obstacle for consideration for reaching large audiences.

   d. General circulation newspapers might look strange on a media schedule for advertising corrugated shipping cartons or automatic spot welding equipment—but in what country? Advertising is meant to communicate a message. There are markets where there is no alternative—and where the newspaper reaches *everyone who reads*. The advertisement itself segments the market by addressing itself to the target audience. If no other media also reach such an audience, potential customers are likely to appreciate the information and will respond.

   e. Direct mail can also play a role in finding unknown potential customers. It is only a matter of finding a target mailing list . . . by:

- purchasing a list from mailing services
- buying the use of publications' circulation lists
- using association membership lists
- obtaining government industry classification registrations
- creating a list from the classified section of many telephone directories

To an international advertiser, direct mail can mean a mass mailing in the thousands in one market and five individually typed letters in another market, but they all need the expertise and experience of a professional communicator if one is serious about the professional development of a strong future market.

   f. Trade fairs can also help discover unknown market potential. This time the tables are turned on potential customers. The advertiser stands in one place and lets the customer find him or her.

An international marketer is logically going to think in terms of his or her own experience when looking to sell a product in overseas markets. The local market developer cannot always be aware of all of the potentialities for many products because new product ideas and advancements in manufacturing processes cause change. The trade fair is unique because customers emerge from unimagined sources.

The manufacturer of air compressors did not know that a pottery maker uses compressors.

A surgical supply manufacturer is discovered that needs heat-treating equipment.

A furniture manufacturer wants to buy a system of conveyors.

A mining firm is looking for communications equipment.

Sometimes the trade fair experience leads only to miscellaneous, onetime orders; sometimes it discovers whole new industry applications for industrial products. And, sometimes, it is the only way to expose a product to government buyers who are the local nation's biggest buyers.

Beyond the direct search for unknown customers is the broader goal of letting a public know that a firm exists by *adding*—

5. *A General Corporate Awareness Campaign*

Many companies can expand their business only if a public (or industry public) is aware that a company does exist and is aware of what they offer.

Since the target market is not well defined, it is difficult to organize a selling proposition. Therefore, the communicator must talk about his or her company, how the products are made, what the products will do, and problems the product can solve. This can, of course, be done by advertising in publications; however, it might achieve greater reader interest and creditability if done via publicity releases. (In some markets these are not free.)

An international industrial corporation *can* advertise and make itself known in any country in the world. Some countries are more difficult than others. The international industrial companies that encounter the most problems are those that expect their local sales representatives to solve all the problems of market communications instead of providing a professional communicator—the home office does not provide sufficient support in direction, materials, expert counsel, and money.

—— ADVERTISING CAMPAIGN STRATEGY ANALYSIS— —— INDUSTRIAL ADVERTISING

—— The Vertical-Horizontal Analysis ——

The vertical-and-horizontal analysis was probably conceived for campaign strategy planning because it accommodates the structure of industrial and business trade publications: horizontal plotting to correlate with publications circulated to various types of specialized industry and vertical plotting to correlate with occupational functions that exist across many industries. If one is considering a media strategy in the United States or another country where there exists a sufficient media menu to accommodate the result of such a planning approach, this method of analysis remains appropriate. In addition, this same analytical approach can be most effective for approaching market communications strategy in any country, forgetting the availability of media at the outset.

—— Sales History Analysis ——

Horizontal. For international companies with a sales experience record in the country being considered for industrial advertising, their own record of past sales is the best place to start the analysis of the horizontal (industry) classification. Where did the business come from? From sales documents, classify the types of industry specialization that have constituted past business. This can be done by using a system of classification that is used by a host country government, or by an industrial community that may later aid in media (or mailing list) planning; or one may need to establish an ad hoc classification. Once this organization has been qualified by group classification, it should then be quantified by importance of volume of business received—and then possibly requantified according to priority of business potential, if sufficient additional information is available.

Vertical. Now that it has been established *where* the business is, we must next establish *who* is to be contacted in order to acquire the business. Again, from existing sales documents and correspondece, and by interviewing field sales personnel, the titles of the persons (and personal names for direct mail advertising) in each industry category who are most influential in making purchase decisions for your kind of product, materials, or service should be ascertained. Plotting these functional occupation categories can open communications from a professional direction (as opposed to an industry classification).

In looking at occupational categories, caution is advised regarding the "purchasing agent." This functional title will appear on almost all purchase orders. Salespersons for many products will indicate that they spend little time with the purchasing agent. It is usually true that except for generic supplies, fuel, and replacing standard office equipment, the purchasing agent arranges for the purchase but does not make the all-important specification for the item to be purchased.

Nevertheless, this function cannot be ignored in a well-structured industrial communications strategy. At times the purchasing agent can be influential during internal considerations regarding specifications—and the supplying salespersons may not be aware of that fact. The purchasing agent can also work against a certain supplier who chooses to ignore his or her function—and show preference for a supplier who has kept him or her informed about the company's products/services.

—— INITIAL ENTRY INTO FOREIGN MARKET ——

Although the information input will not be as specific, and possibly not as accurate, as information taken from a company's own sales record, it is possible to prepare a similar analysis (horizontal and vertical) using a combination of sources. For the horizontal analysis one should turn to government and/or industry association statistics and general information. If the company did a market feasibility, or industry potential study prior to foreign market entry, this would be a natural source as well.

From a vertical standpoint, one can only consider buyer experiences taken from other, "similar" markets as a starter. The complete analysis will be more valuable when actual sales experience can be introduced.

To demonstrate this horizontal-vertical analysis, let us use a hypothetical example . . . a firm we will call Imperial Gear Design Ltd. And let us assume that this hypothetical British firm wishes to promote its primary product, a power transmission reduction gear assembly.

From its analysis (Illustration 11–2) one can see that business for reduction gears has come from thirteen industry classifications that use these subassemblies in machines they manufacture. Imperial's best sources of business in country "A" have been manufacturers of textile- and papermaking machinery; however, mining machinery manufacturers are the biggest potential source.

If, in the country being considered, there are trade journals for those three industries, they would represent the top priority for a horizontal campaign. It might be necessary, however, to use one general technical industries journal, and still attempt to target your message to the specific concerns of all three industries.

For vertical consideration we elect two priorities: design engineer and operating management. Both types of publications (if they exist) would reach not only the priority industries but also the right functional occupation in all industries for potential business. Again, substitutes may be necessary. Possibly there is at least one business/financial publication that reaches management. If there is no indigenous design engineer's journal, perhaps investigation would reveal one or two such publications coming from other countries that are regularly read by design engineers of the country in question. This is an occupation that thrives on information. Design engineers do read something—find out what it is.

Direct mail advertising (designated by the solid blocks in Illustration 11–2) is, of course, the more precisely targeted audience. Targets are selected based on a highest purchase influence prioritizing of potential recipients. The purchasing agent is not that much of a specific target to be communicated to specifically for many products. He or she will usually be added to other targeted mailing lists (e.g., would send him or her a carbon copy of a letter directed to the design engineer).

Occasionally a buyer's influence will appear out of the pattern, as we suggest in Illustration 11–2, "plant manager" in the mining machinery industry. When plant managers can be discovered through investigative analysis, they will sometimes represent the little gems that make the difference between a good and a great industrial market communications program.

——— OPERATIONALIZING INTERNATIONAL ———
INDUSTRIAL ADVERTISING

It is not essential to focus on some of the operational differences that face the industrial advertiser overseas. Decisions must be made and policies developed regarding media selection/evaluation, the employment of an adver-

— ILLUSTRATION 11-2 —
Horizontal-Vertical Analysis of Imperial Gear Design Ltd.

IMPERIAL GEAR DESIGN, LTD.

PRODUCT:
POWER TRANSMISSION REDUCTION GEAR ASSEMBLY

MANUFACTURERS OF MACHINERY FOR:	PRESENT BUSINESS VOLUME	MARKET POTENTIAL	EXECUTIVE MANAGEMENT (7)	OPERATIONS MANAGEMENT (2)	SALES MANAGEMENT (8)	PLANT MANAGEMENT (4)	PLANT SUPERINTENDENT (5)	DESIGN ENGINEERING (1)	MAINTENANCE ENGINEERING (6)	PURCHASING AGENT (3)
CONSTRUCTION		4								
MINING	5	1				■		■		■
OIL FIELD	6	5								
ELEVATORS										
CONVEYORS	4									
HOISTS & CRANES										
METAL WORKING		6								
ROLLING MILLS	3							■		■
FOOD PROCESSING										
TEXTILES	1	2						■		■
WOODWORKING										
PAPERMAKING	2	3						■		■
PRINTING										

Purchase Influence Priority shown in column headers: 7 2 8 4 5 1 6 3 tising agency, the degree of local subsidiary or sales force involvement (if the firm has overseas subsidiaries and/or sales forces), and any advertising research that is to be conducted. Also, budgets must be established, but the approaches to industrial advertising budgeting overseas are not greatly different from those employed domestically. (Unfortunately, these usually are a predetermined percentage of forecast sales or an arbitrary absolute amount, rather than based on a careful analysis of the funds needed to reach particular buyer groups in each market.)

Media.   While the message for most industrial advertising is basically technical and the information required by most overseas markets is primarily the same, one cannot always expect to find the same types of industrial media from one market to the next.

In the U.S. market we are accustomed to organizing a media mix from among (a) business journals, (b) trade journals (vertical and horizontal), and (c) direct mail. We are accustomed to having available reliable circulation data such as Business Publication Audit of Circulation and efficiently cross-referenced mailing lists for sale. Outside of Europe one could probably count on the fingers of one hand the number of overseas markets that could offer the industrial advertiser such a menu from which to choose. It should also be noted that in many instances where these classifications of media are available, the reliability of the circulation data and the quality of the journal can be extremely questionable. This has led many industrial advertisers to rely most heavily on foreign editions of U.S. publications (or on the U.S. editions if they have wide overseas coverage for the particular target group).

Let us consider some of the foreign markets in terms of media availability . . . first Europe. It would be an almost impossible task to assemble sufficient information to discuss this subject by examining individual national markets.

To generalize, one can say that in most European markets one can consider media generally comparable to the U.S. media insofar as local business and trade journals are concerned. In fact, in the field of highly technical journals some of the European publications would rate from excellent to outstanding. Proper guidance in making the most efficient selection is the most important consideration. *Standard Rate & Data* has editions for eight countries, including France, Britain, Germany, Switzerland, Italy, and Mexico. As in the United States, this is an extremely valuable tool for the advertiser.

The local subsidiary or sales manager can often be an important source of trade journal or business publication advice. The critical question, of course, is what the reliable information source used by your customers or prospective customers is. Your representative(s) should have some suggestions. If the firm relies on this approach, however, it is advisable to ask it to send you copies of these publications/journals. Much can be learned about the readers from looking at the level of the articles and at the other advertisers.

Direct Mail.   Direct mail can offer a few more problems than one will experience in the U.S. market. The broker of organized, carefully classified and cross-referenced, guaranteed lists is not available in every country. Publications do not, as a general practice, sell the services of their mailing lists—and when they do, costs are very high. In several countries it is considered an invasion of privacy—and therefore illegal—to sell (or otherwise make available) lists of addresses with personal names. This "selling of lists," of course, is a frequent practice of associations, publications, credit unions, and so on in the United States and is an important source for most direct mail houses.

In a few countries well-organized lists are available with personal names and business titles in selected industrial classifications. However, there are a greater number of categorized lists available without personal names.

The advertiser who assumes an appropriate business title to put with a business address takes a risk unless he or she has local expert guidance. When selecting an appropriate U.S. business title for a foreign language translation, one might miss the target by several degrees. (One company offering extensive direct mail service is V M/B, Inc., Amsterdam and Houston, a subsidiary of Ogilvy & Mather.) In general, European business titles are one to two levels higher than for similar positions in the United States, that is, U.S. "manager" = European "director," U.S. "director" = European "administrator," U.S. "president" = European "director general" (examples from French-speaking countries). Plus, there is the added consideration that in European companies in many industries the industrial buying decisions are made at a higher business level.

The Mailing List without a Name—without a Title. It happens in the United States, but it is more apt to happen in Europe—secretaries are instructed to discard mail that does not include their boss's personal name. What about expensive direct mail with only the company name and address? "The office mailboy takes charge of your advertising campaign." If it looks like advertising, he is very apt to deliver your four-page, four-color, illustrated, diagramed mailing piece for a fifth stage, acid resistant, computerized, fail/safe controls valve to the company's advertising department. It cannot use one . . . so it puts your $1.86 investment in the wastebasket.

The fight for winning the industrial direct mail battle for U.S. companies mailing communications materials to potential European customers is won every day, but not without considerable assistance and not without individual consideration of each country.

There do exist today, in the United States, direct mail specialists that are going "international" . . . meaning that they have associated themselves with European (or South American or Japanese) direct mail organizations. They can, for certain industries, in certain countries, organize and implement effective direct mail campaigns without difficulty.

For other industries, and in other countries, they may have sufficient expertise, overseas experience, and contacts so that they can organize additional direct mail campaigns if they are authorized to do a bit of traveling on your behalf. A good specialist, for example, can tell you whether to print your brochures/letters in the United States or overseas (and where overseas) and can further suggest which country offers the lowest-priced mailing base. (Remember, postage differences alone can dramatically affect your costs—and also that mailing rates can be negotiated.) It is possible that such a service could also handle publication evaluation and advertising placement.

—— Countries Outside Europe ——

One would need to say that there exist markets that are highly sophisticated in industrial advertising—Mexico, Brazil, Australia, New Zealand, Japan, South Africa, to name a few that would relate to the subject as discussed for European countries. Beyond this, the lack of reliable advertising assistance for the international industrial advertiser becomes more apparent. And, without onsite experienced advertising expertise or media consultants, it may not be a viable consideration to make media investment judgments from a distant home office. Still, in many countries, you are left with merely advertising in the overseas editions of U.S. business publications or with finding the expertise in the United States to provide you with guidance. Fortunately, there have been special media service organizations that have developed in the United States, primarily to help the firm with the smaller budget to advertise in some of these markets. (These will be discussed in a later section.)

—— Trends in the International Business Press ——

Madison Avenue recently stated that "the fastest growing segment of the business press . . . is international publishing."[1] This movement by American publishers includes everything from licensing agreements to international editions to joint ventures and even *purely* international magazines with *no* U.S. circulation. McGraw-Hill alone is investing $900,000 in special Chinese editions of *Chemical Engineering, Engineering News-Record, Coal Age,* and *33 Metal Producing*. Still, in mid-1980, international revenue accounted for only 11 percent of McGraw-Hill Publications' total revenue.[2]

And so it is with much of the international business press. Large Western national publishers may acquire existing journals and/or produce "new" overseas publications practically overnight, depending on the trends in the international business news.

In the late 1950s publishers were rushing out trade and business publications directed to Southeast Asia. They used every conceivable kind of mailing

[1] Joan Zazzaro, "General Trends in Business Publishing," *Madison Avenue,* Vol. 22, No. 7 (July 1980), p. 73.

[2] "McGraw-Hill Cautiously Measures Markets Abroad," *International Advertiser* (July–August 1980), p. 26.

list for distribution—mostly the roster of government officials and members of industrial and marketing associations. These were directed to Japan, Taiwan, Singapore, South Korea—areas of current industrial expansion. In the 1960s the same movement took place in response to aid for development of the Central American and newer African countries. About the same time there was also publishers' interest in Israel. In the early 1970s every publisher had a journal for the Arabic countries, and they started discontinuing their efforts in previously "hot" business areas.

"Normalization of relations with China," together with war and resulting economic instability in the Arab bloc plus general instability in Central America, have caused publishers to again swing their investment to the Far East—with emphasis on China. All of this can be said to represent outstanding publishing efficiencies and a real service to international industrial advertisers. However, there are also certain cautions to be considered:

1. Modern graphic arts technology in the hands of experienced publishers can produce a very respectable product in a very short time, often faster than publishers develop an understanding of the various foreign business communities. One sometimes feels that the advertiser is a far more important customer than the real customer of the publisher, i.e., the target reader of the publication. Producing a viable journal, by Western standards and interests, is not difficult. Knowing how to effectively communicate in lesser developed countries—and reaching the right people—is another matter. Therefore, one should exercise caution when investing in attractive *new* journals that offer large circulations early in their existence. Look first at the journals that have a long tradition of reader service, even those that might appear to be less sophisticated. Your prospective buyers may have a bit more comfortable confidence in them . . . unless, of course, they carry the acceptance of a McGraw-Hill, a Crain, or a Johnston.

2. One often encounters business and trade journals that, while published in and for a domestic circulation such as is found in the United States or Germany, do have a long tradition of acceptance and are recognized for their authority by a substantial foreign circulation. It is usually considered necessary to use journals printed in local languages. Yet, serious technical people of many nationalities are often accustomed to using English-, French-, and German-language references to stay current with advanced technology. It may well be that, for some industrial advertisers, the U.S. publications to which they are accustomed provide sufficient customers overseas as well. An in-depth look at their circulation would provide you with the information you need to assess the extent of such publications' overseas coverage. You may simply need to include in your advertising an overseas address or an information request form/card to an overseas maildrop in order to establish inquiries.

3. An offshoot of the use of a U.S. business or trade publication is the foreign regional editions of many of these same respected publications. There is a seemingly endless group of these publications, which include: *Advertising Age's Focus* (Europe), *Business Week Europe, Business Week Asia,* and the *Asian Wall Street Journal.*

   These publications provide a "middle-of-the-road" position for the firms that prefer to have a degree of localization but have greater confidence in U.S. publications. (This confidence may be related to rates, circulation data, or content.) Other firms use some local (national) publications in high-potential markets and then supplement them with these U.S. (or another Western country) overseas special editions. Obviously, this latter approach produces a degree of redundancy. On the other hand, it provides the advertiser with a voice in a number of smaller country markets that are not large enough to support a separate local budget.

4. A number of Pan-European industrial publications offer an additional outlet in some industries. A few are published by the European subsidiaries of U.S. publishers. (An example would be *World Mining,* published by Miller Freeman.) Others, such as *International Equipment News,* are published by European firms that are specializing in Pan-European publishing. An important consideration in these publications is the opportunity to reach the total European market at a *lower cost.*

5. Industrial firms desiring a broader-based business audience, rather than a specialized trade target group, have the alternative of using a business/economics-oriented publication designed for particular geographic or language audiences. These would include *L'Expansion* (France and French language), the *Economist* (British and English language) and *Maclean's* (Canada). While designed somewhat more as a news magazine, *Vision* (Latin America, Portuguese- and Spanish-speaking countries) appears to offer somewhat similar opportunities to reach general business readers in South America.

6. There exist today a number of publications with titles and descriptions to indicate that they are sponsored or approved by the United Nations. They may have some "UN connection," such as being published by a member delegation (or individuals who are members of a national delegation). One should be very cautious about using this type of print medium. While a few may indeed offer the advertiser a solid investment opportunity, too many do not. To select just one such publication appears to automatically invite overwhelming solicitation from them all—the more aggressive of which will not stop short of a form of "high pressure tactics"—i.e., "You advertised in Country A's publication and not ours, so we won't permit the sales of your products in our country."

7. A final alternative business or trade publication is suggested by Champion Spark Plug Company's *Motor Mail,* which is now pub-

lished in thirteen separate editions. This quarterly publication, containing automotive news and some Champion advertising, is sent to a carefully developed list of Champion dealers, customers, etc., in Europe and other markets. As shown in Illustration 11–3, all editions have the same basic format but are published in the appropriate language.

A typical edition might contain an article on motorbike engines and a look at the car of the 1990s. These same articles appear in the German, Norwegian (etc.) language issues, along with one or two "local" articles. Advertising per se is kept to a minimum, but the Champion logo and the topics covered provide a strong communications link between the company and its target groups.

—— THE TRADE FAIRS ——

With a few notable exceptions, such as the 1981 CONEXPO trade show in Houston, trade shows seem to have become a lesser medium for exposing industrial products to U.S. customers. (And CONEXPO might better be classified as an international event staged in the United States.) Yet, they are becoming of increasingly greater importance in other developed and less developed countries. This has been especially true for lesser developed countries' buyers and representatives who seek products in the Western world and find the trade fair to be an excellent place to do "comparative shopping."

Similarly, trade fairs play an important marketing role in China and Eastern Europe. To these customers, there are the obvious motives of learning about new technologies and about more efficient tools and materials. Western national industrial marketers are finding the trade fair their best, and sometimes only, opportunity to exhibit and demonstrate their products to the emerging world. In 1980 the United States sponsored a trade fair in China. It was the first opportunity many U.S. manufacturers had to contact this emerging market since before World War II, and a large delegation of U.S. firms was represented.

It is important to consider who, in a national market, is a perspective customer. If government controls almost all industry, then government becomes the only customer for many industrial marketers. Trade fairs in the sophisticated free markets will draw this kind of potential customer. While inviting these customers to your "own trade fair"—that is, an expense-paid trip to your factory to see a demonstration—could be more effective, this often is not the preference of the government. Although too often trade fairs in countries with government-controlled industry are sponsored by that government for oblique propaganda purposes, participation in these fairs may be a condition of entry into the market.

Western Europe, on the other hand, represents a developed and open marketplace where trade fairs and exhibitions still provide an important

— ILLUSTRATION 11-3 —
Champion Spark Plug's Trade Journal
Mailed in nine languages to just under 400,000 automotive trade
prospects around the world

avenue for contacting prospective industrial purchasers. In 1981 there were roughly 800 trade fairs and exhibits. Most of these are so highly specialized, however, that the industrial firm—unless it is quite diversified—will probably need to be concerned with only two or three of them. The history of trade fairs in Europe dates back to 710 A.D. in St. Denis, near Paris, so it should not be surprising that, to many industrial purchasers, using this medium as a source of communication is a "way of life." Perhaps the best-known general fairs are held in Hanover, Milan, and Paris.

Choosing the appropriate trade fair for your product display(s) is naturally a critical decision. Typically, information may be obtained from the U.S. Department of Commerce (or U.S. Department of Agriculture for food-related products) as well as from the firm's own trade association, which will provide assistance in regard to this decision making. In addition, a number of agencies specializing in trade fairs have developed. These not only provide selection and preparation assistance but also help in your posttrade fair performance evaluations.

The article in the appendix to this chapter contains a rather extensive discussion of the use of overseas advertising research by the industrial advertiser. Some suggestions for "inexpensive" research activities are offered. Among these are recommendations for using the trade fair to provide important advertising/marketing information.

—— INDUSTRIAL ADVERTISING AGENCIES ——

Most major U.S. advertising agencies have specialists to handle overseas media planning and buying for their clients, as well as a full range of other services (creative to administrative). These agencies often have predominantly consumer goods clients, who have "some" industrial needs, as well as a few MNC industrial accounts.

Current data support this conclusion. Among the thirty-seven U.S. agencies with over $15 million gross income in 1980, only twelve reported no overseas business. Most of these twenty-five large agencies with overseas billings are primarily consumer goods agencies, however. In fact, a careful review of their media placement suggests that just three of the twenty-five agencies had 10 percent or more of their billings from industrial accounts.[3]

A number of large U.S. agencies have recently begun to acquire smaller industrial agencies to provide themselves with an *industrial advertising "division."* This allows them to serve the domestic and overseas industrial needs of their primarily consumer goods accounts. (Ogilvy & Mather provides just one such example.)

The typical industrial marketer's alternatives regarding the selection decision of its advertising agency(ies) for its overseas advertising are as follows:

[3] *Advertising Age*, Vol. 52 (March 18, 1981), pp. 1–116.

- employing a medium to large United States-based agency—often the one handling its U.S. industrial advertising—with overseas branches (network) or subsidiaries
- employing a small to medium *United States-based agency* with no/few equity arrangements overseas but that is a member of an affiliated group that has worldwide representation (the agencies typically exchange account services; e.g., I handle your U.S. space purchases, you handle mine in Auckland)
- employing a series of foreign agencies in key overseas locales (and handle the remainder, as in the next item)
- employing a smaller, United States-based agency that handles your foreign advertising, including media placement, etc., from the States
- employing your own in-house advertising department to do the bulk of your foreign advertising; perhaps using specialists for occasional services such as direct mail

Regardless of the method selected, several of the earlier points made regarding coordinating your program must be remembered.

Let us suggest a few criteria to keep in mind when you make your agency decision:

1. Select an agency (or agencies) that will give you coverage in your markets *and* that will provide enough clout with its overseas "connections" to ensure that your needs will receive *attention*.
2. Select an agency (or agencies) that will consider your *account* to be important. Often a smaller client may receive only *minimal attention* if there are many larger accounts in the agency.
3. Select an agency (or agencies) with an understanding and appreciation of industrial markets/advertising. Direct experience is a real *plus*.
4. Select an agency (or agencies) that recognizes the *positive* implications of a standardized approach to industrial advertising.

Finally, recognize that an in-house department, coupled with the use of media specialists, may offer the smaller advertiser the most viable alternative if the advertiser finds that the above criteria are not being met by the available alternatives.

Finding an Agency.   What if the industrial advertiser wants to employ an advertising agency for a specific foreign market but does not know where to begin looking? One alternative in simply identifying "available" agencies is to use the services of the Department of Commerce (DOC). The DOC has a publication that provides some basic information on the agencies in each country. The company can then contact a select number of these agencies and ask them to provide a client list, samples of their work, and so on. As an initial screening, it is recommended that only agencies that currently represent MNC, especially U.S., clients be selected for further consideration. For more qualitative information, the advertiser can then telephone one or more of the agency's major industrial clients to determine the extent to which they have been satisfied by the agency's performance. Finally, before asking for an "agency presentation," it is useful to visit at first hand those agencies that remain under consideration. While these steps are quite similar to those recommended for a consumer products firm, a particular concern is these agencies' experience with industrial advertisers. (For more information, see article at the end of chapter 6.)

As suggested earlier, some international industrial advertising managers have found that employing the same advertising agency that is used by the company's consumer goods division(s) is a viable alternative. In fact, it is possible that your industrial advertising campaign—publication and direct mail—could be considered part of the firm's total corporate account and handled on a reasonably affordable basis. The local agency used for your firm's consumer products group(s) might well have all the facilities at hand to do a most effective job for you and, if it is part of a larger network, may provide you with a central agency headquarters for overall control at the same time. However, a note of caution is in order: Most industrial advertising campaigns are seen by "consumer goods" agencies as low-budget, high-service accounts. It would be unusual for an industrial advertiser to be able to employ a highly qualified "consumer" agency without having to pay an excessive service fee or negotiate on the basis of the consumer account business they are receiving.

Finally, useful information can be obtained from advertising trade associations. The industrial advertiser can seek advice from the International Advertising Association for recommendations on local industrial agencies in the countries of your concern. After making the contact, the same screening process suggested above for those names obtained from the Department of Commerce publications is recommended.

—— Special Service Groups ——

Fortunately, a number of service groups/agencies have developed to meet the growing special service needs of the international industrial advertiser, especially the smaller advertiser—for example, smaller industrial accounts with limited budgets that may have particular problems, say, in media selection or scheduling. This has led to the development of the service firm that will handle the smaller accounts.

One such overseas media firm is Michael Jarvis & Associates, Inc. (MJA), part of Euro Center Communications, Inc. (New York). The latter is a full-service communications group. MJA numbers among its accounts not only industrial advertisers but also many U.S. advertising agencies, which have few overseas industrial media needs, so that it would be inefficient for them to have such specialists "in-house." MJA offers its clients such services as media planning and research, media buying, and coordination and translation. It is particularly worth noting that the firm handles accounts even in the $25,000 range.

—— Some Company "Cases" ——

One of the biggest concerns of most overseas industrial advertisers is that there are few bases on which to compare their overseas advertising approach, that is, policies, procedures, and plans. Except for the occasional article in an industrial journal describing a "success story," they really are left with only consumer good "comparables." There are some excellent cases, however, that suggest that no single way is best.

Illustration 11–4 presents examples of how six U.S. industrial firms are approaching their overseas markets via advertising. (Senior advertising executives from each of these companies recently attended a seminar conducted by one of the coauthors and agreed to share this information about their companies.) Naturally, their advertising budgets vary widely, as do their organization structures, but none has a budget comparable to that of a consumer products firm. (See also Illustrations 11–5, 11–6, and 11–7 for additional materials related to three of these firms.) What is important here is not that any given approach is preferable but that these firms do suggest a variety of ways to handle overseas industrial advertising. Again, permit us to say that it is the nature of the firm's target market and its objectives that should be the basis for all industrial advertising decisions, as it is with consumer advertising.

— ILLUSTRATION 11-4 —
U.S. Industrial Firms' Approaches to Overseas Markets via Advertising

Name of Co.	Principal Products	Foreign Subsidiaries (# if more than 1)	Foreign Sales Offices	Target Markets
Manville Corporation	Building insulation General construction products Filtration materials Industrial/commercial insulations Minerals Pipe Roofing products Sealing components	Argentina Australia Belgium (2) Brazil France Italy Mexico Singapore U.K. West Germany	Japan Lebanon Saudi Arabia West Germany	Construction: Engineers Architects Contractors Industrial: Engineers End users Filtration: End users
Gates Rubber	Automotive V-belts & hose Hydraulic hose & couplings Industrial V-belts & hose	Belgium Brazil Canada Mexico S. Africa Venezuela	Principal Cities Worldwide	Automotive Construction Fleets General industry Mining Petroleum
MSA Int'l.	Safety products for industry	Australia Brazil Canada Chile France India Italy Japan Mexico Netherlands Peru Scotland Singapore South Africa Spain West Germany	80 Repre- sentatives	All industrial sectors

— **ILLUSTRATION 11–4 (continued)** —

Overseas Distribution Approach	Ad Agency	Overseas Advertising Approach	Media	Advertising Research
Distributors' own salesforce Other representatives (dependent upon product, region)	Broyles, Allebaugh, & Davis (Denver)	Two approaches: 1. Prepared in U.S. Translated from English after approval, produced in U.S. for distribution (Europe, Japan & some Latin American subsidiaries). 2. Headquarters develops guidelines and approves creative (all other markets).	Trade publications Catalogs Literature Trade Shows	Minimal pretest (distribution preview) Posttest inquiry some benchmark (user, U.S.)
Distributors' own salesforce	Broyles, Allebaugh, & Davis (Denver)	Two Approaches: 1. Affiliate ad managers responsible for all promotional literature, catalogs, programs. They are also responsible for trade ads on a limited basis. 2. Headquarters administers worldwide trade magazine campaign.	Trade publications Catalogs Promotional literature	None
Subsidiaries' own salesforce Sales representatives	KM&G	Two Approaches: 1. Headquarters handles for Latin America, Southeast Asia, Middle East. 2. Subsidiaries administer own programs.	Trade publications	Media studies only

(continued on page 258)

— ILLUSTRATION 11-4 (continued) —

Name of Co.	Principal Products	Foreign Subsidiaries (# if more than 1)	Foreign Sales Offices	Target Markets
Steiger Tractor Inc.	High H.P. 4-wheel drive agricultural tractors	Australia	—	Large farmers
Symons Corporation	Modular and custom forms for concrete construction; underground construction support equipment	—	—.	Construction Mining
Hydril	Supplier to oil industry for exploration and production endeavors	Britain	Britain Canada Greece Mexico Scotland Singapore	Oil exploration Production end users

— ILLUSTRATION 11–4 (continued) —

Overseas Distribution Approach	Ad Agency	Overseas Advertising Approach	Media	Advertising Research
Independent dealers, usually one per country, often with multiple outlets	Davis Harrison Advertising (Chicago)	International agriculturally oriented print media coupled with cooperative support of dealer efforts in local advertising, trade shows, and demonstrations.	Trade publications Trade shows	Informal. Base upon input from sales staff and response from dealers, farmers, and staff
Own sales people in overseas offices with support from domestic.	In-house	In-house agency produces and translates for overseas markets.	Trade publications Catalogs Brochures Audio-visual Trade shows Articles Technical papers Personal contact	Ongoing basis

— ILLUSTRATION 11–5 —
English Version of Steiger Tractor Advertisement

10,000 STEIGER TRACTORS ARE WORKING FOR THE WORLD'S MOST SUCCESSFUL FARMERS.

Steiger 4-wheel-drive tractors farm more land with less labor in less time than any other type of farm tractor.

Steiger tractors increase one-man productivity to a level which is impossible to achieve with 2-wheel-drive tractors.

Farmers with Steiger tractors can increase the acreage they are able to farm. They save on labor and fuel costs. They are able to improve yields by getting their fields tilled and their crops planted quickly. And Steigers are capable of dozing and pulling scrapers in order to improve the land.

Steiger is the originator of big 4WD tractors for farming. It offers the longest line of individual models. The company operates from a new and modern factory which is the only one of its size and kind built specifically for manufacturing 4WD tractors

The reason for Steiger's excellent service record can be found in the tractors themselves. From front to rear, each is built for heavy pulling. Within its ½-inch plate steel frame are carefully matched driveline components. The power train is engineered with more than enough strength to handle the power and torque developed by the big Caterpillar or Cummins engines.

Under load, weight is distributed evenly, front and rear. This balance gives maximum all-around traction, less slippage and more drawbar pull. Steiger's low, stable frame oscillation keeps all 4 wheels firmly on the ground when you're working rough, rolling land or crossing ditches.

Steiger cabs are comfortable, quiet and functional. All controls are located within easy, natural reach. They are engineered so that an operator can quickly develop the driving skills needed for efficient pulling of wide implements at rapid speeds.

Steiger tractors are designed with particular emphasis on easy maintenance. Whatever needs attention, whether it is routine service or replacement of a major component, the problem is easy to get at and to fix.

Ten different Steiger models are available from 225 to 470 engine horse power (180 to 387 drawbar horsepower). You have your choice of Caterpillar or Cummins diesel engines and automatic, power-shift or 20-speed straight-gear transmissions.

All are built to give you the most tractor available in farming today.

STEIGER®
3101 1st AVE. N., FARGO, NORTH DAKOTA 58108
701-293-4400   800-437-4672

POWER FOR THE LONG PULL.

— ILLUSTRATION 11–6 —
Spanish Translation of Illustration 11–5.
Note that the advertisement is a literal translation.

10,000 TRACTORES STEIGER TRABAJAN
PARA LOS AGRICULTORES MAS EXITOSOS DEL MUNDO

Los tractores agrícolas de Steiger de transmisión en cuatro ruedas labran más terreno con menos mano de obra y en menos tiempo que cualquier otra clase de tractor agrícola.

Los tractores Steiger aumentan la productividad por hombre a un nivel imposible de alcanzar con tractores de transmisión en dos ruedas.

Los agricultores que disponen de tractores Steiger pueden aumentar la superficie cultivada. Ahorran en mano de obra y combustible. Hacen crecer los rendimientos al labrar sus tierras y plantar sus cultivos más rápidamente. Además, los tractores Steiger pueden llevar cuchillas o arrastrar traíllas para mejorar los terrenos.

Steiger es el creador de los tractores agrícolas grandes de cuatro ruedas motrices. Ofrece el surtido más grande de modelos. La compañía trabaja en una nueva y moderna fábrica, única en su tamaño y tipo, construida especialmente para la fabricación de tractores de transmisión en cuatro ruedas.

La razón del excelente récord de servicio de los tractores Steiger se encuentra en los mismos tractores. De cabo a rabo, cada uno se construye para grandes fuerzas de tracción. En su chasis de acero de 12 mm de espesor van los componentes de la transmisión perfectamente adaptados uno con otro. El tren de potencia está diseñado con resistencia más que suficiente para recibir la potencia y torsión desarrolladas por un gran motor Caterpillar o Cummins.

Bajo carga de funcionamiento, el peso se distribuye uniformemente adelante y atrás. Este equilibrio permite la máxima tracción del conjunto, menos deslizamiento y mas tracción en

la barra de tiro. La oscilación del chasis de los tractores Steiger es baja y estable, y mantiene las cuatro ruedas firmemente apoyadas sobre el suelo al trabajar en terrenos difíciles y ondulados o al cruzar zanjas.

Las cabinas Steiger son cómodas, silenciosas y funcionales. Todos los controles están ubicados al fácil alcance de la mano. Están diseñados de modo que el tractorista pueda aprender rápidamente a arrastrar implementos anchos a velocidad rápida.

Los tractores Steiger se fabrican dando especial atención a la facilidad de mantenimiento. Sea cual fuere el problema, ya sea servicios de rutina o reemplazo de componentes principales, la reparación es de fácil acceso y ejecución.

Hay disponibles diez modelos de tractores Steiger con potencias de 225 a 470 CdeF al motor (180 a 387 CdeF en la barra de tiro). Usted puede elegir entre motor diesel Caterpillar o Cummins y transmisión automática, servotransmisión o transmisión de engranajes de 20 velocidades.

Todos construidos para darle más tractor agrícola por su dinero.

STEIGER
3101 1st Ave. N. Fargo North Dakota 58108 E.U.A.
Telefono 701 293-4400 Telex 910 673-8340

POTENTE TRACCIÓN
DE GRANDES ALCANCES.

— **ILLUSTRATION 11–7** —
**Examples of Hydril "Tubular Products" Catalogs.
These catalogs all are 52 pages in length and differ *only*
in terms of language translation.**

—— APPENDIX ——

—— INTERNATIONAL MEDIA RESEARCH ——
A PANDORA'S BOX
OF PROBLEMS AND FRUSTRATIONS
by
John K. Ryans, Jr.

Advertising research on international publications can be a "Pandora's Box" of problems and frustrations for U.S. international industrial marketers.

Even savvy marketers usually don't know what types of research techniques are most often employed to evaluate international business publications. This points to general frustration about foreign advertising. As one manager stated, "One of the major problems in international advertising is the lack of information and (the) economic and mechanical feasibility of going after it."

These concerns range from the limited (or total lack of) data provided by foreign business publications to common translation problems to what has been called "a lack of sophisticated markets (abroad)." Clearly, the jump from the U.S. market and its abundance of market information is proving to be a monumental challenge for many industrial marketers. Similarly, the availability of highly specialized foreign trade publications, as well as accompanying readership detail, is of considerable concern.

Initially, the above questions were raised to complete the picture of how extensively industrial marketers are employing business press advertising research. (Glenn Ostle and I explored a number of these issues regarding domestic industrial advertising in an article in *Industrial Marketing*, August 1980.) Little or no information has been available regarding the extent to which research is used to prepare or evaluate foreign business publication advertising.

The need for such information was highlighted in discussions with industrial advertising managers at International Advertising Management programs presented at the World Trade Institute (New York) and recent B/PAA International Marketing Communications Seminars in Pittsburg and Chicago. At these sessions, I found much interest, but little information on the advertising research/effectiveness measure questions.

Therefore, I decided to conduct a mail survey to find out just "what is happening" in international industrial publication advertising. Samples were selected from three major industries (heavy equipment, medical laboratory equipment, and telecommunications), providing a total mailing of 200 questionnaires to international industrial advertising managers.

The results were quite surprising. First, the rate of response to the questionnaire itself was quite low (27, or roughly 13.5 percent). However, another 15 advertising managers wrote to indicate that they were just beginning to advertise overseas and were not in a position to provide information. (These responses in effect increased the overall response rate to slightly more than 20 percent.) Virtually all, however, wanted the study results and a few even asked for any other information that might be available on the topic.

Thus, the answers to the initial questions that were raised seem to have come almost as much from what was not said, than from what was said by respondents. For example, it is clear that many firms are just about to embark on international industrial marketing/advertising activities ... some with little idea where to begin. Further, the low response rate can be partially attributed to the fact that other potential respondents also simply had nothing to offer.

Results

Few U.S.-based industrial marketers conduct research on their international business publication advertising (or other media advertising).

This coupled with the fact that foreign business publications tend to offer much less readership information means that the international advertising executive must rely on inquiries, sales data, or "experience" in his or her advertising decisions.

At the same time, the industrial advertising effort is made more difficult because of cultural, language, media availability, and distribution problems. Often, heavy reliance for effectiveness measures is given to the views of the overseas sales force or others on the distribution side. Similarly, their views on trade publications advertising vs. trade shows or other promotional approaches are significant. In other words, the international industrial advertising manager's task of preparing and evaluating is often a difficult one and more decisions seem to be based on intuition than is true for their domestic counterparts.

Profiling the Respondents

The bulk of the responses (two-thirds) came from firms in the heavy equipment field. These were generally very experienced advertising executives—four to twenty-seven years in advertising—although their experience was *not* with their present company. The fewest responses (two) and the bulk of the letters came from advertising managers in the telecommunications field.

Many firms in this industry seem to be on the threshold of overseas activity, including all phases of marketing and advertising efforts.

From the survey responses and other comments from industrial marketers, the following profile seems to characterize the bulk of today's international industrial advertisers. These advertisers generally:

- sell their product in 10 or more foreign markets
- employ a single U.S.-based advertising agency
- have a rather limited current foreign advertising budget, but see increases in the future
- use their overseas local management or home office personnel to judge their advertising's effectiveness
- employ sales data and inquiries as their primary effectiveness measures
- use trade publications (foreign or U.S. international editions) as their primary medium
- do little, if any, formal advertising research (awareness studies are most popular)
- are unhappy with the amount and quality of research furnished by foreign business publications
- feel somewhat uncertain about the quality of their overall foreign advertising program

I should add that the latter is not due to any particular feeling of ineptness on their own part, but rather their frustrations with everything from media quality/availability to inadequate feedback methods.

As one respondent put it, we "are about to the point of dropping all international trade publication advertising due to our suspicions that we are not getting return on invested dollars." Clearly, the international advertising manager has had to rely more heavily on his or her "feel for the market" than on reliable information.

Standardized Advertising

An area where generalizations were impossible concerned the advertising manager's views on the use of standardized promotion themes. The survey respondents were almost equally divided on the question of whether they used the same advertising *themes* in each of their foreign markets. Twelve advertising managers favor following the "same theme" approach and as one advocate of this approach stated, we select "a universal theme which is not only understandable and meaningful, but (is) literally translatable in foreign languages." In contrast, those favoring multiple themes often cited differences in cultures and/or levels of economic development as their reasons. However, some took a perhaps more market-oriented view, e.g., the "appeal in (the) ad is based on the idiosyncrasy of (the) market as far as type of equipment (product) that is featured."

This international advertising standardization question has been the topic of debate in consumer advertising for many years—since Exxon's worldwide "Tiger in the Tank" campaign. Therefore, it is perhaps not surprising that there is some disagreement on this issue among industrial advertising managers as well.

While it is possible to profile the international industrial advertiser in terms of the points used earlier, many differences are apparent. Experience overseas, size of budgets, and the nature of the products/markets themselves obviously produce differences. In fact, it is perhaps the problems and frustrations they face that offer the primary similarities.

Domestic industrial advertisers employ much less use of advertising research than do their consumer goods counterparts. There are many reasons for this, including the role of advertising in the industrial marketer's mix, as compared with the consumer goods firm. However, this is not our concern here. Rather, what is important to note is that there is less use of industrial advertising research by firms in their international advertising than with their domestic advertising. This fact, coupled with the lack of foreign publications readership studies, means that there is less "effectiveness" information available to the international advertising manager.

As mentioned previously, the international advertising manager must rely more heavily on inquiries and sales data to evaluate campaigns. As one manager bluntly stated, "Although there is much merit in buying various kinds of research, the need to utilize every dollar we have for advertising per se precludes buying research." But he also saw this more than in dollar terms, adding that time constraints, lack of quality industrial research firms in many foreign markets, etc., made the question to some extent rhetorical.

What do these international advertising executives see as the biggest problems in trying to conduct some form of advertising effectiveness studies other than merely using inquiries or sales figures? Let us see from direct quotes what they said were problems:

- "Uniqueness of individual countries.
- "Bad mail lists, language problems, poor mail service, difficulty of identifying markets.
- "The ability to get a customer directly. It is almost impossible."
- "coordinating with subsidiaries, lack of sophistication in advertising research.

- "Cost; very costly to do on a country-by-country basis.
- "Lack of a singular source with which we feel comfortable."

These were representative of the bulk of the survey responses and comments and demonstrate a high level of frustration with employing any advertising research.

A few international industrial marketers are, of course, conducting one or more forms of formal research. For example, one reported using "qualitative surveys via focus groups and/or personal interviews and some quantitative surveys via mail," while another indicated the use of customer and distributor surveys to judge his firm's overseas advertising. These, however, were exceptions.

The above article is reprinted from the December 1981 issue of *Industrial Marketing*. The authors wish to thank Bob Donath, editor of *IM*, for permission to reprint it. (Note: *Industrial Marketing* has recently been renamed *Business Marketing*.)

Mr. Ryans acknowledges the assistance of Glenn V. Ostle, Mary Hotz, and Connie Mansfield.

——— 10 KEY POINTS ———

1. The international industrial advertiser is generally in a stronger position to maintain a centralized approach—and even standardized advertising—than is the consumer goods advertiser.
2. Culture is typically of limited concern to the international industrial advertiser, whose problems relate more to budget size (too limited) and differences in the environment in which the product is used.
3. The international industrial marketer needs to focus on market-to-market similarities rather than on differences; this is a key attitudinal concern regarding the approach to *any* industrial market.
4. Foreign editions of U.S. technical/professional publications are often important to the international industrial advertiser.
5. The international industrial marketer needs to carefully prioritize his or her overseas target audiences . . . the problem of too many possible groups ranging from sales reps to the general public can lead to ineffective communications.
6. Media such as direct mail and trade fairs have special significance for many international industrial advertisers; they provide the most effective means of reaching certain overseas target markets.

7. There is a trend toward major multinational U.S. advertising agencies' acquiring smaller industrial agencies or establishing their own international industrial departments in order to serve their clients' industrial needs.

8. The international industrial advertiser should select an advertising agency (or agencies) that considers the account to be *important*.

9. Many international industrial advertisers maintain their own in-house advertising department and, in addition, use specialists in such areas as media selection/scheduling.

10. The use of vertical-horizontal analysis is recommended as an aid to campaign strategy planning and media analysis.

12

The International
Advertiser's Responsibility
to a Host Country—
to the Corporate Future

— INTRODUCTION —

The first eleven chapters were addressed to the aggressive use of advertising by the multinational marketer. It has even been suggested that military precision tactics be assembled to fight for growth in an ever increasing competitive world market, that market growth opportunities were flattening out, and that energy shortage/cost-inspired inflation would be a long-term dampener to market expansion.

Product innovation leadership and brand image dominance have been described as the key to growth—if not, in some cases, the only prescription for survival. We have warned the multinational marketer from several different perspectives that the corporate/brand name image *is*, or *will be*, the most valuable asset to all corporations emerging successfully into the 1990s.

The valuable, positive corporate image will be a consolidated (all national markets) image that was given definition and direction . . . that was nurtured to development with skilled single-mindedness and that emerged as the consumer's symbol of confidence (quality—value—dependability —performance—trust). The corporate headquarters that abdicates this responsibility is creating an international fragmented image and designing diffusion into its future.

However, we cannot abandon this subject on a note of aggressive action to battle the tougher competition, and of headquarters generalship, without a caution regarding possible unpleasant side effects that are inherent in applying too much *muscle* to one's local management and not enough *ear, eye*, and *heart* to the publics that buy one's products. It is the people that make up those publics who have the final vote on the future corporate image.

The advertiser's responsibility will be discussed in the context of the following topics:

- how local nationals perceive the MNC
- counterproductive headquarters enthusiasm
- long-term objectives giving way to short-term goals
- multinational social responsibility in advertising
- putting the proper perspective on culture
- traditional factors
- cultural considerations
- a cultural checklist

- case history: "Is It Too Soon to Put a Tiger in Every Tank?"

Cultural, social, political, religious, and traditional differences do exist between countries, sometimes between sections of the same country. They are as real to the advertiser as are the literacy, income, and geographic differences, which cannot be dismissed through ignorance or apathy.
Mistakes can be costly!
Recognition of such differences on their own terms should make them, not obstacles, but rather workable variables. Most often it is not that different peoples perceive the same things differently; it is that they perceive different things in different environments.

Enthusiasm is essential to the success of any marketing activity. In advertising and sales promotion it is indispensable. The best of programs will fail without it . . . and even a mediocre program can achieve some success if high enthusiasm is maintained throughout the entire organization.

At the same time, enthusiasm needs to be well directed. The advertiser's enthusiasm for a successful result must not obscure his or her responsibility to the social culture of a host country.

Preceding chapters have discussed ways to maximize a return on advertising investment—how a multinational marketer can use its worldwide resources (its size) to every advantage, and exchange intelligence between markets to anticipate and neutralize probable competitive action; at the same time, it is often necessary to be "low key" regarding its identification as a multinational corporation.

The emergent and expanding efforts of social, cultural, political, and religious activist groups are putting new definitions into the vocabulary. Today, in many parts of the world, words like "industrialist," "capitalist," and "multinational" are being used as synonyms for negative labeling that connotes an exploiter or a force for local anticulture. International companies that anticipate such negative labeling before entering a market will often attempt to disguise their identity by maintaining the original name of a locally acquired firm, or they will introduce new product brand names that appear to be of local origin. Such measures often are not effective for very long, and disclosure can be counterproductive.

There exist social attitudes in some of the developing countries that present a paradox to multinational marketers. A general public will maintain an attitude that products from local manufacturers are inferior to imported products or to products produced locally by foreign companies—and this provides a reason to promote a company as one that enjoys worldwide consumer confidence. On the other hand, there can exist in these same countries activists who are effectively agitating against buying products made by foreign interests.

Of course, most marketers believe that the best course of action is to improve their image (e.g., by presenting their companies as contributing to the local economy and the local social welfare). Overseas offices of the U.S. Chamber of Commerce have made efforts to guide/recommend that U.S. companies improve their image in foreign markets. The MNC's public relations efforts often document the added employment, local career training, expanded local export that improves balance of payments, contribution to local education and other social services, new technology introduced, and improved standard of living that foreign companies bring to the host country. (Or they augment this message through a corporate advertising campaign.) All these actions can have a positive effect for such a marketer if the marketer does not destroy the effect with overzealous promotions.

Cultural differences between markets are usually acknowledged by international marketers as a caution and as an obstacle to international advertising. There are often-quoted classical "boo-boos" where foreign words were translated into local language obscenities. There are religious taboos and nationalist considerations. All these are workable and manageable obstacles that can be handled through local transliteration for local execution of an advertising campaign. There is a deeper obstacle that can have far greater consequences than errors in translation.

Counterproductive Headquarters Enthusiasm

The MNC Executive Career Development Program. Such a program can in itself be a force that works against the development of a positive corporate image in developing societies. Career paths are often clearly marked for the ambitious person. Upward movement is achieved by reaching sales volume goals, reducing sales cost, reducing production costs, and increasing market share. Upward movement is accelerated for those who set records as superachievers.

No one in business can deny that profit improvement and market growth is, and should be, the objective of any corporation. However, almost by definition, in the case of multinational corporations, each normal business problem, obstacle, and opportunity is magnified times the number of foreign operating subsidiaries.

It is quite natural for the parent headquarters of a large multinational corporation to view each subsidiary (a foreign operating company) in almost the same way that a large national corporation would consider sales districts — and analytically, overseas managing directors would compare to district or regional managers — but they are not. They are not in the eyes of the local national industrial fraternity — nor to a local government. To a local society of consumers, these "career path achievers" are the chief executives of their corporation. Their actions represent the image of the brands and the company that makes and sells those brands.

A family of foreign subsidiaries will naturally be ranked in priority of importance to the parent headquarters. As a progressing young executive works his or her way up the ladder to becoming a managing director (or its equivalent), the young executive's first post will usually be in a lower-priority national subsidiary — and the goal will be to move as quickly as possible to progressively larger, more important markets. But, is this objective totally in the best interest of the corporation . . . without also giving these people targets to achieve that have to do with building a measurable record of achievement for improvement of the corporate image, the product reputation with consumers, dealer relations, and recognizable community service achievements?

No one in industry will deny the importance of a corporation's having a social responsibility to its host country, or the wisdom of creating a strong, positive corporate image; however, such items have no entry on the balance sheet.

A headquarters can be separated from operating subsidiaries by long distances. Occasional visits by corporate officials can, at best, view only the veneer of its local corporate personality. Measurements of achievement are made in terms of financial performance, and goals are assigned in the same terms.

Regardless of any long-term objectives established for each market by a parent headquarters, if the resident manager is overwhelmed by his obligation to improve short-term profits (submerging the manager's ability to establish a sound growth for the future), the manager is forced to set short-term goals for himself or herself to: (a) keep his or her job and (b) assure his or her continued personal growth. This can lead to:

- selling every product he or she makes, or receives, without quality consideration
- disrupting the price structure of a local national industry
- stopping (or greatly reducing) all advertising investment to become an "expense reduction hero"

- demoralizing local nationals in management
- poor distributor (retailer) relations because of pressure and inconsistent policy
- poor labor relations
- weak government relations
- loss of creditable acceptance by a consumer public—*the most serious of all advertising problems.*

—— Multinational Social Responsibility in Advertising ——

It is not unusual for overenthusiasm (or desperation) of a local management to be most obvious to a public through a company's advertising. Headlines can become more challenging; quality gets a bit exaggerated; promises and claims start reaching a bit beyond safe ground; illustrations may resort to questionable taste; and, of course, in some cases prices can deteriorate—*the short-term goal problem.* Such actions can create public suspicion and defenses against certain brands. Such advertisers attract consumer protectionist and other activist groups inclined to look at multinationals for reasons to reinforce their nationalistic attitudes.

The local advertising agencies, whether part of an international network or indigenous firms, enjoy public anonymity. They can improve their relationship with the client by aiding in a short-term success, or they can jeopardize a relationship by advising against such action. The largest agencies are known only within the marketing fraternity. Their low-key awareness keeps their actions away from public notice.

With all good intentions from both advertiser and advertising agency, the drive for success can often be rationalized with complete justification, and further encouraged by head office executives, based on acceptable strategies proven in the home market. To some marketers, restraints on such action might appear to be overly conservative . . . it depends upon how many years a company plans to operate in each market. Good taste and social responsibility in advertising are defined differently with respect to different cultural backgrounds.

The consumer protection groups and government-sponsored agencies are focusing sharply on advertising that misleads, misrepresents, takes advantage of consumers' lack of knowledge, degrades local competition, or that is in poor taste according to cultural standards—and they are looking even more closely at the multinationals that "invade" their markets. It might be added that local, national competitors are often given "license" to aid protectionist groups in determining what is in violation and to provide incriminating details.

"Double guilt" is now being added to many of the laws and regulations governing advertising practices. In several countries (and the number is growing), an advertising agency shares guilt for any violation of advertising practices. Both parties are fined, or otherwise penalized, equally. To further cause agencies to take greater responsibility, France now removes anonymity by requiring the agency name to appear on its client's advertising. Other countries are considering taking similar actions, plus causing agency violaters to lose certain rights to participate in negotiations for advertising time or space in government-controlled media.

There are obviously many long-term profitable advantages for the multinational corporation that can create, in each overseas subsidiary company, an image of complete local integration, local social contribution, as well as the progressive image of providing "better things for better living." This is one of many reasons that several MNC companies are deemphasizing the idea of rotating executive managements and instituting serious career training programs to produce effective top management from the local national ranks. This does not, however, reduce the necessity for headquarters involvement.

A successful company will never design a policy of local integration that will cause it to lose momentum. It may be necessary to organize for more constructive long-range growth, but to keep the spirit alive and in perspective, headquarters will need to be firmly involved. A local management, whether expatriate or indigenous, will require the input necessary to make advertising work dedicatedly on a constant market-building goal; keep a planned, long-range product mix on track; and continue to introduce new techniques.

All actions, of course, are framed in terms of the local dynamics—which requires a level of international awareness. An awareness of the local problems that should receive attention and those that are merely transitional or may even be "contrived" is necessary for effective communications management. (It is not unusual for locals to overstress some relatively insignificant . . . insignificant in terms of the company's products/advertising . . . cultural differences.)

—— PUTTING THE PROPER PERSPECTIVE ——
ON CULTURE

Just how much attention should the firm give to cultural considerations? Are cultural differences throughout the world so great that they preclude using an effective worldwide approach to advertising? Which cultural factors should the advertiser recognize, and which should he or she ignore?

These and similar questions touch at the heart of the controversy regarding the importance of culture to the MNC's marketing and advertising strategies.

First, let us accept the fact that there are many differences between cultures. Edward T. Hall, whose book *The Silent Language* was a classic treatise on cross-cultural nonverbal communication, has identified a host of differences based merely on "time," "space," and similar "languages." For example, a North American's preoccupation with time and "deadlines" often works to a disadvantage in negotiating in Eastern Europe or South America.

More recently, Hall has suggested that we simply do not understand the Arabs.[1] He says that we view them as underdeveloped Americans who "wear sheets." Regardless of whether Hall's view is correct, it points to the main concern that we should have regarding culture. We must be sensitive to the fact that there are *differences between peoples*. But we need to go a step beyond this recognition and sensitivity. Once we identify differences, we need to ask which, if any, of them are significant in the marketing of our product or service and in our promotional effort.

In some instances, these differences can be turned to the MNC's advantage. Let us illustrate this by looking at *nationalism*. Nationalism is an important factor to a greater or lesser extent in every country throughout the world. However, "Made in America" or "Produced in the USA" may not always be negative. If the United States is seen in Liberia as having a "high level of technological knowhow or expertise," then the fact that an MNC has its home base in the United States is a *plus*.

Second, in a 1969 article entitled "Is It Too Soon to Put a Tiger in Every Tank?" one of the coauthors (Ryans) discussed the factors that help to decide to what extent culture should be important to the marketing and advertising efforts of a particular MNC. (This article is included in the appendix to this chapter.) The primary factors indicated are the firm's *product* and its *target market*. For an industrial product manufacturer whose promotion is targeted to engineers and chemists, the differences between cultures may have little or no importance. A U.S. chemical multinational in Geneva, for example, has a mailing list for certain of its chemical products that numbers only several hundred but that includes *every* purchaser or potential purchaser of these products in Western Europe. These buyers are all skilled technicians, and the promotional message must be highly technical . . . and . . . specification-oriented. Except for ensuring high standards in its translations, this company need have little concern for cultural differences.

Similarly, if the needs of the consumer and the uses of the product are the *same* in every market, a consumer goods producer may be able to *minimize* some of the cultural differences. This may be especially true if our target market is a highly urbane, upper-income consumer; this is especially true for the so-called international sophisticate described in the "Tiger in the Tank" article.

However, there are a few *caveats* to be noted here, and it is easy to go overboard too quickly in disregarding cultural differences even if you are producing something as ordinary as soft drinks or tires. Illustration 12–1 presents the findings of a study conducted among international advertisers and agencies. From the responses to statements 1 and 6, it seems that even today a few individuals may need to exercise some caution in their cross-market advertising. We perhaps need to remind them that even a product such as Coca-Cola is concerned about the appropriateness of background, as well as language,

---

[1] Edward T. Hall (interviewed by Kenneth Friedman), "Learning the Arabs' Silent Language," *Psychology Today* (August 1979), pp. 45–54.

— ILLUSTRATION 12-1 —

Comparison of U.S. International Agency Executives' and U.S. Advertising Managers' Opinions on Culturally Oriented Advertising Statements

	Respondents	Disagree		Agree		N	Total
		−5, −4	−3 to −1	+1 to +3	+4, +5		
		%	%	%	%		
Basic human nature is the same everywhere; therefore, traditional advertising appeals of economy, company advancement, and social approval are applicable to all markets.	Agency executives	29.3	4.8	43.9	22.0	41	100.0
	Advertising managers	16.0	17.4	43.5	23.1	69	100.0
In practical marketing situations, an individual approach in each country or region is entirely unnecessary.	Agency executives	24.4	56.1	14.6	4.9	41	100.0
	Advertising managers	31.8	29.0	24.7	14.5	69	100.0
Standardized ads can now be readily applied throughout the world because cultural lag between most nations is minimal.	Agency executives	38.5	35.8	25.7	0.0	39	100.0
	Advertising managers	31.8	36.3	27.5	4.4	69	100.0
An international agency preparing the ad in the U.S. can serve its clients as effectively as a local agency in any particular country.	Agency executives	22.5	20.0	45.0	12.5	40	100.0
	Advertising managers	24.7	43.5	24.7	7.1	69	100.0

In most cases, the only major difference between foreign markets will be that of language and idiom.	Agency executives	31.7	36.6	29.3	2.4	41	100.0
	Advertising managers	26.1	42.0	24.7	7.2	69	100.0
Girls in Tokyo and Berlin are "sisters under the skin"—on their lips, fingernails and in their hair styles. Therefore, ads using basic appeals can successfully reach all of them.	Agency executives	23.1	23.0	36.0	17.9	39	100.0
	Advertising managers	13.1	27.5	42.0	17.4	69	100.0

Source: John K. Ryans, Jr., and James H. Donnelly, Jr., "Selected Practices and Problems of United States 'International' Advertising Agencies," *University of Washington Business Review*, Vol. XXX, No. 1 (Autumn 1970), p. 53. Reprinted by permission of the Graduate School of Business Administration, University of Washington.

as it develops television commercials that will be seen in multiple markets; the famous "I'd like to give the world a Coke" commercial featuring children from many nations dressed in their national costumes is a case in point. Therefore, let us look at the cultural considerations that may be especially important to the international advertising manager.

Fred Bastl has stated that markets "are *some* people, the people with purchasing power—not *all* people."[2] In correctly assessing nondomestic markets and improving marketing and advertising decision making, it is necessary to develop those understandings about markets that are *relevant* to marketing and advertising, rather than just information for information's sake. What is relevant to marketing is *both* the traditional demographic/socioeconomic/political factors and an insight regarding the culture of an area or country.

Traditional Factors.   Naturally, one can gain a *first* impression of a potential market by examining such statistics as its balance of payments, disposable personal income, per capita income, gross national product, demographic data, and literacy rate. These must be coupled with considerations regarding language(s) spoken, political system, class system, education levels, and the like in order to obtain a broad overview of the country and its people. In fact, one would also want geographic and resource information, since topography, climate, availability of ports, and a sound resource base have their influence as well. For example, Bolivia is not only landlocked but is a mountainous country whose people and markets have been separated from normal international trade flows. These factors have influenced the nature and development of this market. An analysis of these concerns alone, however, is not adequate for a viable market assessment or for marketing and advertising decision making.

Cultural Considerations.   A decade or so ago, Maneck Wadia said that there "was a time, not so very long ago, when an anthropologist would not be caught dead among marketing men and marketing men would not lend an ear to anthropologists."[3] While exaggerating to make his point, Wadia was reflecting on the emphasis now being given to consumer behavior by international marketers and indicating the recognition now given to *cultural considerations,* predicting adaptability for the acceptance of change among certain cultures.

Cross-culture emphasis have produced innovative marketing successes which far outweigh most historical "horror stories" about unintentional cultural insults.

Certainly, nothing depicts culture more than eating and clothing habits. To this, witness the fast foods explosion in Japan—McDonald's unprecedented success in Tokyo—and in the gourmet capital of the world, Paris. Similarly, young men and women of the world are wearing jeans because Levi Strauss

---

[2] Fred J. Bastl, "Determination of the Export Potential," *Akron Business and Economic Review* (Summer 1971), p. 5.

[3] Maneck Wadia, "The Concepts of Culture in the Analysis of Consumers," reprinted in James C. Baker and John K. Ryans, Jr., *Multinational Marketing* (Columbus, Ohio: Grid, Inc.), p. 13.

has found it possible to change cultural habits. Innovative creativity, carefully managed, can produce extraordinary successes from facts that others have considered *negative* cultural obstacles.[4]

The concern here, however, is with attempting to better understand all principals in an overseas market, including the firm's potential consumers, retail channel members, company and advertising agency, as well as business associates, that may affect the MNC's success. These nationals' attitudes and beliefs are largely attributable to their cultural environment, so an understanding of the cultural environment is essential in improving advertising and marketing decision making. But what cultural factors are important to the international advertising managers?

Fayerweather has indicated that we must be particularly concerned with the influences of the *religious, family, educational*, and *social relationships* of a society on marketing efforts.[5] To these four cultural considerations, a fifth— the rigidity of its organizational system—needs to be added for emphasis, since we are concerned not only with the ultimate consumer but with industrial buyers and our own (and the agency's) employees as well.

One can easily see how the predominant *religion* of an area may influence attitudes toward hard work, honesty, and luxury goods, while the importance given to different *family* members can influence purchasing patterns in the household. Regarding the latter, one need only note the *contrast* between the way the elder is revered in the Chinese family hierarchy in Hong Kong and the way the senior citizen is treated with detachment in the U.S. family structure. Similarly, *education*—that is, who should be educated and how— will influence the qualifications of sales people, the size of the middle-income group, and even our own personnel problems. The *social relationship* factor considers the importance assigned to reference groups and status symbols as well as the influence of social pressures in general. It is another dimension that should be explored.

Finally, the perceived need for bureaucracy or a rigid structuring of all *organizational systems* is an important dimension, especially in determining the structure of the advertising and marketing organization and channel needs. It has been said that while the British may have invented bureaucracy, it is the Indian who has perfected it. In Japan, as in India, a firm needs to be able to demonstrate several levels of bureaucracy to be viewed as important.

Each society has its own unique cultural features, and thus it is difficult to generalize across markets. However, these five cultural considerations should be analyzed when attempting to better understand individual attitudes in any market. Naturally, other cultural concerns, such as a people's sensitivity to the arts, may be a factor for certain firms in individual countries, and in such instances it is necessary to examine the cultural aspects of a market in much greater detail than has been implied here.

By assessing both the traditional factors and the cultural dimensions, how-

---

[4] Dean Peebles and John Ryans, "One International Cultural Philosophy (Part II)," *International Advertiser*, January–February 1983, p. 16.

[5] John Fayerweather, *International Marketing* (Englewood Cliffs, N.J.: Prentice-Hall, 1965).

ever, the international advertising manager gains a better overall picture of the nature of the market than he or she would gain from assessing the traditional factors alone. This sort of analysis also provides the first stage in identifying the potential of an area or a country as a marketplace for the firm's product(s), as well as the special importance to attach to culture.

——— A Cultural Checklist ———

Given this discussion of cultural factors and the possible concerns, what sorts of specific questions might the international advertising manager wish to ask as he or she decides about the importance of cross-cultural differences to promotion decisions? Here are a few to consider:

Regarding the product and target market:
1. How is the product used in each market?
2. Is there a single, basic need to which it appeals everywhere?
3. Does the *price* of the product account for about the same proportion of the buyer's income (consumer product) in every market?
4. Is the same level of product knowledge/sophistication appropriate everywhere?
5. Is the competitive environment for the product about the same in each market?

Regarding the various cultures themselves:
1. Are there religious differences between various markets that could affect my product and its promotion?
2. Are there differences in the roles that respective family members have in various markets that could affect my product? (This is important even for industrial products, i.e., should the engineer shown with the product be young or old, etc.?)
3. Are there differences in status symbols, reference groups, or even classes that could affect my product's promotional theme?
4. Are there differences in educational background that could affect the message, the medium, or even the appeal that might be employed?

Because of the wide variation among products (industrial and consumer) and the markets in question, these are obviously only representative questions. What is apparent is that problems often arise because of the educational, family and religious, and economic/social/political differences frequently found between countries (or even within some countries). (An example of the latter is the French- and Dutch-oriented areas of Belgium.) Recognizing this, it is necessary for the international advertiser to determine which, if any, of the above questions/concerns should be considered as he or she approaches the target markets.

—— To Sum Up ——

There are indeed significant cultural differences from one market to another for which marketing and advertising people must stay constantly aware . . . to accommodate in the planning process and in the implementation of multi-national programs. Such differences are rarely insurmountable obstacles. They must be considered only as workable variables; and to deal with them, one must bring them into focus in the context of the society where they exist. Doing this requires patience, persistence, and understanding, as opposed to attempting to "force-fit" one's own culture over another, or using "sleight-of-hand" tactics as a means to circumvent the issue.

There are two primary reasons that many social and cultural errors occur in foreign market advertising, neither of which is excusable. *One:* "I didn't know" . . . ignorance of important facts throughout an entire international marketing organization (head office, line and staff management, or a local management group) is a poor reflection on an entire corporation. If one is advertising in a country where there is no corporate representation, it should be stopped until a reliable local contact can be established to look after the advertiser's best interests. *Two:* "I don't care" . . . an apathetic attitude sometimes, and inadvertently, is perpetuated by an aggressive executive career plan that encourages short-term gains.

To borrow from the Preface of this book, "We approach the subject of international advertising management with a sober respect for just how fragile a corporate image can be when transplanted into many different national environments, left unattended, or manipulated by careless hands."

—— APPENDIX ——

—— IS IT TOO SOON TO PUT ——
A TIGER IN EVERY TANK?
by
John K. Ryans, Jr.

Foreign tourists motoring across France are surprised to see a sign with a familiar theme: "Mettez un Tigre dans Votre Moteur." Tourists in other parts of Europe and around the world may expect to see the same theme in other languages. Esso carried its "Put a Tiger in Your Tank" campaign to a vast marketplace in the appropriate languages of the various countries.

What these travelers are seeing is a classic example of the use of the common approach to international advertising; an approach that is the source of considerable current debate in international marketing circles. Briefly stated, this controversy centers around whether common advertising themes or even advertisements themselves—with proper translations—are as effective as separate messages and advertisements developed specifically for individual national markets.

Although the common advertising approach has been a subject of discussion for some time, the apparent success of various firms, including Esso with its worldwide "Tiger" campaign, has focused attention upon its use. Traditionally it has been more or less accepted that nationalistic differences prevented the use of similar copy and advertising themes on a multinational basis. The impact of the "Tiger" campaign, however, along with the advantages of using a common approach, are leading other firms to examine the feasibility of universal advertising themes.

When they do so, they run into any number of barriers which must be overcome. In addition to the obvious language barriers between countries or regions, there are cultural, taste, and environmental differences, media availability differences, and developmental differences —standard of living, discretionary income, and other economic considerations.[1]

Most experienced international advertisers and advertising agency executives—even the outspoken proponents of the common approach—recognize these barriers to varying degrees. Yet the potential cost savings from a universal approach and the opportunity to maintain a common global image or theme are most attractive. Two strongly divergent points of view have created controversial dialogue among respected experts in the field. An executive for a large U.S. agency without overseas affiliations, for example, may claim that adapting campaigns along national lines is unnecessary and that a universal approach developed by a single centralized agency is best, while an executive in a small national agency located abroad and unaffiliated with a U.S. agency may say that advertisers should use domestic agencies in each area and direct their advertising specifically to that area.

One Theme

A number of writers and practitioners have for years been particularly outspoken in favoring the common advertising theme approach. Among them are Arthur C. Fatt, chairman of the board of Grey Advertising, who has stated that despite obvious language and cultural differences, peoples of the world have the same basic wants and needs. He says that most "people everywhere, from Argentina to Zanzibar, want a better way of life for themselves and their families," that the desire to be beautiful, to be free of pain, to be healthy, etc., is universal. He suggests that a successful campaign in one area of the world—utilizing a theme that would appeal to the basic wants or needs of the individual— could reasonably be expected to produce similar results in other areas of the world if the language is translated into the local idiom.

Fatt points out that today's rapid international communications, particularly television, increased international travel, and the growth of the truly international brand name have given even greater impetus to the trend toward a common advertising approach.[2]

Another advocate, Erik Elinder, though agreeing with the concept of a universal approach, has been principally concerned with its development at an all-European rather than at a worldwide level. Speaking from his years of experience as a Swedish advertising executive and as the chairman of the board of the Swedish Sales Institute, he says that many of the problems often associated with the common approach, such as language differences, are actually "lightweight."

Elinder cites the success that the international editions of *The Reader's Digest* have shown in varied markets, as well as the worldwide popularity of best sellers, films, etc., to support his view that similarity in sales appeals can also be successful. Further, he points out that a large percentage of Europeans now travel extensively on the Continent and that television, magazine, and newspaper coverage extends beyond national borders—two factors important to firms seeking to reach markets in several countries and to maintain advertising continuity.[3]

There are others, of course, who favor the universal approach, such as Nicholas E. Keller, managing director of McCann-Erickson Europe. Keller uses the Esso "Tiger" campaign to demonstrate how the same basic idea with very few modifications can be used in multimarkets.[4]

Advertisers supporting the common approach fully emphasize the advantages of presenting the same trademarks, brand names, and logotypes in many and varied markets. Such a universal approach permits the advertiser to maintain the same "image" in every country and prevents confusing the "border-crossing tourist" as he seeks the firm's product in a different market. Perhaps even more important to some advertisers, however, is the potential cost saving of the universal approach. The extra costs of using separate artists, separate copywriters, and the higher mechanical costs involved in preparing entirely different campaigns and individual advertisements for each country where their advertising is to appear are an important incentive to the advertiser for using the univeral approach.[5]

Probably the most active opponent of the universal approach is John M. Lenormand, a Paris advertising agency executive. Lenormand has stated that to achieve a universal approach a common denominator would have to be found that would have the same impact "for South Americans, Swedes, Germans, and Spaniards, not to mention Flemings and Sudeten Germans." According to Lenormand, such a common denominator has not been found.

Like other critics of the universal approach, Lenormand cites many additional obstacles to achieving successful common advertising. He points out that problems arise due to differences in mentalities, customs, religious beliefs, living standards, laws, media, etc.[6] These problem areas, along with language barriers, literacy rates, varying distribution channel structures, and the lack of truly international advertising agencies, are the ones most frequently mentioned by those either opposed to the common advertising approach or dubious about its present applicability.

Generally, opponents of the common advertising approach point to dissimilarities between countries and even between regions in the same country to support their opinion. Most of these differences are cultural or environmental. For example, the status of women in several tropical African countries where they are considered chattel differs from their status in Western countries. In such an environment, advertisements appealing solely to women, as are frequently found in Western societies, would mean ignoring the fact that it is the man who makes the final approval of the purchase. Basic differences between Far Eastern cultures and European cultures have also been noted. Others refer to cultural variations between Latin Americans and Spaniards or French Canadians and French Swiss who speak the same basic languages. German villagers from Schleswig-Holstein and Barvaria have difficulties in communicating with one another.

Cultural differences, however, are not the only obstacles to the use of common advertising. Areas vary widely in terms of availability of media and media capabilities. There are some regions where magazines and newspapers are "available," but where their facilities are so inadequate that illustrative matter is not satisfactorily reproduced. Similar criticisms can be made regarding other media in specific world areas. Differences in the amount of discretionary income and the standard of living among countries and regions are still another argument against the technique.

A recognition of the obstacles does not necessarily make one an opponent of the common approach. In fact, proponents and opponents alike recognize these problems to varying degrees. Rather, the question seems to be whether these differences are considered insurmountable at one extreme or to be of minimal importance at the other. There is some agreement that a universal or at least a "European" style of advertising is coming, but many of those who have adopted this point of view also see the need for further research and experimentation before such an approach is widely adopted by advertisers.[7]

One Theme—With Differences

Between these polarized views is a broad middle ground of opinion: principally those who believe that some degree of uniformity of advertising theme is needed, but agree that individual area differences must also be recognized. An often used approach by such companies is to let an international advertising agency—an agency with branches in key locations around the world—handle both their domestic and nondomestic advertising. This permits the advertiser to have as much uniformity as he desires, while at the same time the local nationals employed by the international agency in each of its branches can indicate those characteristics of the advertising theme, campaign, or individual advertisements that are not appropriate in their particular area. Others prefer to employ separate advertising agencies in each country or region in which they operate but furnish

these agencies with a theme, trademark, and/or campaign developed by the company's home office or its domestic agency. This is done to insure that some similarity in advertising will be maintained and local differences recognized.

Much of the success of using an international agency to handle varying degrees of uniformity depends upon the abilities of the nationals it employs in various areas, the degree of centralization in the agency, and consequently the freedom the nationals may have or feel they have to question or change themes, etc. Some agencies have wholly owned branches, while others have only partial ownership or perhaps just an exchange arrangement with their "branches," which are really independent foreign agencies. Also, since the development of uniform themes, trademarks, and even individual advertisements involves creativity, many criticisms from the branches may simply reflect disagreement with some creative aspects of the theme or campaign and not with its suitability in the nationals' markets.

The use of separate agencies in each area increases the problems of maintaining some degree of uniformity in advertising. The tendency for the local agency to want to develop its own original approach tailored to its market and its unwillingness to accept a theme developed elsewhere are problems that again have to be recognized.

Another approach some advertisers employ is to seek the advice of nationals in their own overseas branches or their representatives in various countries or regions in attempting to develop a uniform theme that can successfully be used multinationally. These branch officials or representatives may be asked to submit suggestions or ideas, examine advertising proofs, coordinate efforts, or work closely with a local agency in their area.

Obviously, companies have devised a

variety of ways to obtain the advantages of the common advertising approach and still take into consideration the cultural, economic, and other differences among global areas. In some instances, recognition of the differences has been more or less token, while in other instances considerable efforts have been made to adapt the uniform themes to particular local differences.

The Product and the Market

In most of the dialogue regarding the common advertising approach, two key considerations are generally either ignored or only briefly noted. These considerations are the product to be marketed and its place in the market.

The nature of the product may be the single most important factor in determining whether or not it is feasible for a firm to employ a common or universal approach in its multinational advertising. Certainly, there are low-priced, nondurable goods fulfilling basic needs that have broad potential markets. Firms selling such products may not be too concerned about many of the differences among global areas. Coca-Cola, for example, has successfully appealed to a broad market and become a byword among consumers around the world. However, Coca-Cola is so low-priced and appeals to such a basic biological need—thirst—that its potential market includes a large number of consumers wherever it is introduced.

Virtually all durable goods producers and most nondurable goods producers are not blessed with such a broad potential market for their products. Questions relating to the product and its market need to be considered to determine whether or not the common approach is desirable. One would have to assume that all consumers either within a single country or region or worldwide were basically the same to give a simple yes or no answer to the question of using the common advertising approach to reach a mass market.

There is a school of thought that states that people everywhere are basically the same and that a truly universal appeal will be successful in any market. One needs only to compare the literacy differences between Somaliland and Sweden, or familiarize oneself with cultural differences between countries or within countries to realize that consumers are not all alike. Even the strongest proponents of the common advertising approach would agree that there are national or regional differences between peoples.

Perhaps more realistically, some writers, such as Elinder, see the advent of the all-European consumer (or an all-Western European consumer). They point to increased inter-European tourism and the growth of television—particularly Eurovision—as leading toward such a consumer. Yet, if one is familiar with rural France or Portugal, for example, he will find a degree of provincialism that raises doubt about the early arrival of the all-European consumer.

Consumer Categories

Rather than a single all-European consumer or worldwide consumer for the mass marketer, one can suggest at least three broad categories of consumers based solely on their potential receptivity to the common advertising approach:

- International sophisticate
- Semisophisticate
- Provincial

Though not exhaustive, this grouping identifies some of the consumer characteristics that separate those who might be somewhat responsive to a good universal approach from those who would find such an approach meaningless or might even be repelled by it—regardless of the product.

International Sophisticate. Although the term "jet set" has perhaps been overstressed by gossip columnists and the press in general, there are at least a few people that might be termed "world citizens" in most countries and particularly in the Western world. These people would be equally comfortable in St. Moritz and Acapulco and are frequently multilingual. Such individuals, regardless of home base, would probably be as responsive to a universal campaign as would anyone with their same economic background and interests in the advertiser's own country.

This is a relatively small group of world citizens, but the growth of another, larger group that might be called the "international sophisticate" has more relevance to most advertisers considering using the common advertising approach. This group of middle- or high-income consumers includes those who have a genuine interest and awareness for products, fashions and cultural activities in countries other than their own. This may be reflected by their having traveled extensively in various countries; by their familiarity with the international editions of publications or such international publications as *Paris Match, Der Stern,* etc., or perhaps even by their being in an area where television programming from other countries is available. Regardless of the ways this multinational interest has been obtained or is expressed, the most important characteristic of this group is their appreciation and "feel" not only for the cultures but also for their peers in other countries.

The growth of the international sophisticate has generally occurred in Europe, the United States, Canada, and Japan. travel between various European countries, as well as between Europe and the United States, has increased dramatically in the last decade. However, this is more a reflection of the effect, rather than the cause, of the growth of the international sophisticate, who is apparently a product of greater disposable personal income, better education, and an environment that offers the greatest promise for the advertiser seeking to be truly universal in his advertising approach. Such consumers would be expected to be highly responsive to a good campaign theme, whether it originated in the United States or Switzerland or Japan.

Educable

Semisophisticate. In addition to the "sophisticate," there is a much larger group of people found in varying numbers around the world that might be called the "semisophisticates." This group includes many of the burgeoning number of middle- and high-income individuals found in the United States, Western Europe, Japan, Canada, and South America. In this group are found the people with an increasing discretionary income and a growing but as yet unmotivated awareness of the world around them. Through limited travel, television, or documentary programs, reading, or a variety of other ways, these people have begun to become interested in other lands and cultures.

This increased interest may manifest itself in the curiosity to sample a few inexpensive products from "abroad" or to own Danish furniture actually produced in Denmark or a Toyota from Japan. Often this willingness to try such products may be due only to the desire for the status such unique products may afford. On the other hand, it may be due to a growing appreciation of other cultures and a willingness to sample goods from those areas. It is important to the advertiser, however, that such semisophisticates have no hesitancy to purchase at least certain types of items produced outside of their own country.

Consumers of the semisophisticate type are found in both urban or rural areas. They are more apt to be located near metropolitan cities because of their wider range of varied interests.

In terms of advertising, they can be made receptive to an international approach. However, they probably would be even more receptive to advertising demonstrating the use of this "foreign" product in their own environs and indirect references to the advantages (mainly status) of having something unique. Further, they might well miss any subtleties included in the universal advertisement, and care would need to be taken to insure that no such subtleties are included in advertisements.

Antiforeign

Provincial. Whether city or rural dwellers, the "provincials" have one characteristic in common: a lack of interest, appreciation, or "feel" for the nondomestic. For some, this may be due to a strong spirit of nationalism that affects the way they perceive anything from the outside. Others may simply be unaware of things outside their sphere of interest and may be too involved to develop a new sense of awareness. Still others may lack the opportunity to become involved with things outside their locale, region, or country.

Provincials range the full continuum in terms of wealth and education. This group includes a range from those who are wealthy and well educated, who abhor anything from beyond their political boundaries or area of interest, to an illiterate peasant too involved in the battle for survival to notice the world. Even more important for some geographic areas, however, this group includes many middle-income individuals who feel their own country to be self-sufficient in all its aspects and simply have no interest in other nations.

Because of their introverted attitude, some consumers of this type may purchase imported products without realizing that these products are nondomestic. For this reason, many firms have initiated programs, such as changing their brand name if it indicates or implies the country of origin, to prevent their products from being clearly identified as nondomestic products in areas outside their home country.

This is a large group. Most obviously it would not be responsive to the universal advertising approach. For some, the subtleties would be too great or the message too foreign for their frame of reference. For others, they would simply have no interest in any product unless it was tied closely to their own habitual needs and wants. Finally, some would be antagonized by any product from the outside and their nationalistic feelings would build an impenetrable perception barrier to the advertiser's message.

There are undoubtedly other categories and many subcategories of world consumers in terms of their receptivity to the universal advertising approach. They all add up to the conclusion that a simple one-world consumer does not exist at this time. Firms must exercise caution in adopting the same or similar advertising in multiple markets, especially if they are seeking a mass market. For the firm seeking clearly distinguishable market segments in terms of sociocultural, socioeconomic, and demographic qualities, a thorough job of identifying the characteristics within various markets might lead to a central theme that would be appropriate. Even this may be difficult if their desired segment includes consumers of the provincial type. Yet, nationalistic tendencies may be overcome to some extent if the problem is recognized.

Few, if any, would disagree with the view that advances in communications, education, etc., will ultimately create an atmosphere where the common advertising approach will be the rule rather than the exception. However, adoption of such an approach today is premature and advertisers should make use of it with caution.

Notes

1. Norton B. Leo, "Creative Strategy for International Advertising," in S. Watson Dunn, *International Handbook of Advertising* (New York: McGraw-Hill, 1964).
2. Arthur C. Fatt, "A Multi-National Approach to International Advertising," *The International Advertiser* (September 1964), and Arthur C. Fatt, "The Danger of 'Local' International Advertising," *Journal of Marketing* (January 1967).
3. Erik Elinder, "How International Can European Advertising Be?" *Journal of Marketing* (April 1965), and Erik Elinder, "How International Can Advertising Be?" in S. Watson Dunn, *International Handbook of Advertising* (New York: McGraw-Hill, 1964).
4. Carol Kurtis, "Ads Need a Different Touch in Each Country of Europe," *Herald Tribune International*, June 9, 1967.
5. Dean Peebles, "Goodyear's Worldwide Advertising," *The International Advertiser* (January 1967).
6. J.M. Lenormand, "Is Europe Ripe for the Integration of Advertising?" *The International Advertiser* (March 1964).
7. Ilmar Roostal, "Standardization of Advertising for Western Europe," *Journal of Marketing* (October 1963).

The above article is reprinted from the March–April 1969 issue of the *Columbia Journal of World Business*. The authors wish to thank the editors of the *CJWB* for permission to reprint it.

——— 10 KEY POINTS ———

1. The MNC label is difficult to handle in the corporate image process. It can be an advantage in attracting consumers and a disadvantage in avoiding the attention of nationalistic activists.
2. Executive career path programs can be counterproductive to long-term corporate image objectives.
3. Overenthusiasm for corporate growth can produce advertising

with the flavor of desperation. Consumers can become suspicious of the advertiser's sincerity.

4. A strong dynamic image can be successfully achieved if it carries with it the strong projection of concern for local public welfare.

5. A multinational advertiser can appear to be awkward to absurd in attempting to recognize cultural differences in its advertising. Any basic sales stimulus is acceptable when presented in the accepted life-style of the local environment.

6. The most critical situation where "cultural," or any psychographic, differences between peoples requires serious attention in advertising is when a given product has different end uses among different peoples. This most often occurs for food and personal care products.

7. The first criterion of advertising is to communicate. Peoples' differences aside, it is done best when relating to the consumer's environmental experience.

8. Cross-cultural emphasis can be effective advertising. McDonald's hamburgers and Kentucky Fried Chicken did not succeed in the Orient because they were illustrated as being eaten with chopsticks. Levi Strauss took young ladies out of every traditional costume in the world and put them in jeans.

9. Too often the term "cultural differences" is used as a scare phrase and as a rationale for concluding that all advertising must be conceived and developed locally. Not only is this very expensive to the multinational marketer; it will almost assuredly fractionate the marketer's world image.

10. If we can say that almost any well-conceived corporate world advertising strategy can be adapted to the social/demographic environments of all world markets, we must also say: *Do not place advertising in any foreign market without expert counsel.*

Index